Migrating borders and moving times

MANCHESTER
1824

Manchester University Press

RETHINKING BORDERS

SERIES EDITORS: SARAH GREEN AND HASTINGS DONNAN

Rethinking Borders focuses on what gives borders their qualities across time and space, as well as on how such borders are experienced, built, managed, imagined and changed. This involves detailed and often richly ethnographic studies of all aspects of borders: finance and money, bureaucracy, trade, law, new technologies, materiality, infrastructure, gender and sexuality, even the philosophy of what counts as being 'borderly,' as well as the more familiar topics of migration, nationalism, politics, conflicts and security.

Migrating borders and moving times

Temporality and the crossing of borders in Europe

EDITED BY HASTINGS DONNAN,
MADELEINE HURD AND
CAROLIN LEUTLOFF-GRANDITS

Manchester University Press

Published by Manchester University Press
Altrincham Street, Manchester M1 7JA, UK
www.manchesteruniversitypress.co.uk

British Library Cataloguing-in-Publication Data is available

ISBN 978 1 5261 1538 6 *hardback*
ISBN 978 1 5261 1642 0 *paperback*

First published by Manchester University Press in hardback 2017

This edition first published 2019

Contents

List of figures and tables

Figures

Table

List of contributors

Kathryn Cassidy is a Senior Lecturer in Human Geography at Northumbria University, UK and an Associate Member of the Centre for Research on Migration, Refugees and Belonging (CMRB) at the University of East London, where she worked as a Senior Research Fellow on the EUBORDERSCAPES project. Kathryn is a feminist human geographer with research interests in bordering and everyday carceralities in contemporary Europe. She recently completed the co-authored *Bordering* (Polity, 2017), with Nira Yuval-Davis and Georgie Wemyss, with whom she has also recently co-edited two special journal issues: 'Racialised Bordering Discourses and European Roma' in *Ethnic and Racial Studies* and 'Intersectional Borders' in *Political Geography*.

Hastings Donnan is Director of the Senator George J. Mitchell Institute for Global Peace, Security and Justice and Co-Director of the Centre for International Borders Research at Queen's University Belfast, Northern Ireland. He is a Fellow of the British Academy, a Member of the Royal Irish Academy and Fellow of the UK's Academy of Social Sciences. He has published over twenty books and numerous journal articles, including, with T. M. Wilson, *A Companion to Border Studies* (Wiley-Blackwell, 2012); *Borderlands: Ethnographic Approaches to Security, Power and Identity* (University Press of America, 2010); *Culture and Power at the Edges of the State: National Support and Subversion in European Borderlands* (LIT, 2005); *Borders: Frontiers of Identity, Nation and State* (Berg, 1999) and *Border Identities: Nation and State at International Frontiers* (Cambridge University Press, 1998).

Nataša Gregorič Bon is a Research Fellow at the Institute of Anthropological and Spatial Studies in the Research Centre of the Slovenian Academy of Sciences and Arts and an Assistant Professor at the Postgraduate School ZRC (Research Centre of the Slovenian Academy of Sciences and Arts), Ljubljana, Slovenia. She is author of *The Spaces of Discordance* (ZRC Publishing), which has been translated into Albanian; co-editor of the Moving Places series (Berghahn Books), and author of numerous peer-reviewed articles and book chapters on spatial anthropology and movement in Albania. She is also Book Review Editor for *Anthropological Notebooks* and co-editor of the Space, Place, Time Series (ZRC Publishing).

Robin A. Harper is an Associate Professor of Political Science at York College, City University of New York, USA. Her research focuses on migrant public policy in comparative context in Germany, Israel and the United States. Research questions explore the meaning(s) of citizenship, belonging, inclusion/exclusion, borders and temporary labour migration.

Madeleine Hurd is an Associate Professor in the School of Historical and Contemporary Studies at the University of Södertörn, Stockholm, Sweden. Among her many publications are *Public Spheres, Public Mores, and Democracy: Hamburg and Stockholm, 1875–1914* (University of Michigan Press, 2000) and a number of anthologies on borders and territory in Scandinavia. Her current research focuses on environmentalist discourses and eco-nationalism in the Baltic Sea region.

Iosif Kovras is a Senior Lecturer in comparative politics at City University, London, UK. His research interests include comparative politics, post-conflict transitional justice and human rights. His work has been published or is forthcoming in *Comparative Political Studies*, *West European Politics*, *Comparative Politics*, *Nations and Nationalism*, *Political Geography* and *Cooperation and Conflict*, among others. His research has been funded by the Economic and Social Research Council (ESRC), the British Academy and other funding bodies, while in 2012 he received the Basil Chubb Prize for the best dissertation in Political Science, awarded by the Political Studies Association of Ireland.

Olivier Thomas Kramsch is Senior Lecturer in the Department of Human Geography at Radboud Universiteit, Nijmegen, the Netherlands, where he is also a leading member of the Nijmegen Centre for Border Research (NCBR). He has written extensively on the power geometries associated with transboundary regional governance within the European Union, while training attention on Europe's governmentalising practices on its external frontiers (i.e. the Mediterranean, North Africa and South America), viewed through a postcolonial lens. He is himself a *Grenzgaenger*, fully inhabiting the Dutch/German borderland he has chosen to make his home.

Carolin Leutloff-Grandits is a social anthropologist who specialises on topics of family and social security, migration, transnationalism and ethnic conflict. She has carried out long-term fieldwork in Croatia, Serbia and Kosovo. She is the author of *Claiming Ownership in Post-war Croatia: The Dynamics of Property Relations and Ethnic Conflict in the Knin Region* (LIT, 2006) and editor of *Social Security in Religious Networks: Anthropological Perspectives on New Risks and Ambivalences* (with Anja Peleikis and Tatjana Thelen, Berghahn, 2009). Based at the University of Graz, Austria, she is currently finishing her monograph 'Families and Solidarity in a Translocal Space: The Case of Kosovo Albanians from Opoja'.

Zaira T. Lofranco is Lecturer in Social Anthropology at the University of Bergamo, Italy. Her research focuses on place-making in contemporary Sarajevo, social relations, microeconomic transactions and debt in the everyday life of households. As a research fellow in the EU-funded ANTICORRP project, she completed an ethnography of corruption in Bosnia and Herzegovina. Among her most recent publications are 'Refurnishing the house in post-war neoliberalism: consumption strategies in the Sarajevan household economy', *Human Affairs*, 25(1): 81–92 (2015) and 'Displaced in the native city: movement and locality in post-war Sarajevo', in Nataša Gregorič Bon and Jaka Repič (eds), *Moving Places: Relations, Return and Belonging* (Berghahn Books, forthcoming 2016).

Simon Robins is a humanitarian practitioner and researcher with an interest in transitional justice, humanitarian protection and human rights. His work is driven by a desire to put the needs of victims of violations at the heart of efforts to address their legacies, and this has driven a victim-centred and therapeutic approach to histories of violence. The issue of persons disappeared and missing in armed conflict remains a focus of his work: he recently published *Families of the Missing: A Test for Contemporary Approaches to Transitional Justice* (Routledge, 2015). He is a Senior Research Fellow at the Centre for Applied Human Rights at the University of York, UK and consults for a range of international agencies.

Jelena Tošić is a Research Fellow and Lecturer at the Department of Social and Cultural Anthropology (Vienna, Austria) and the Institute of Social Anthropology (Berne, Switzerland). Her research interests include (forced) migration and border studies, political anthropology, anthropology and history, south-eastern Europe and the Middle East. Her recent publications include 'Localizing moralities: power and temporality in SEE' (special issue, *Southeastern Europe and Black Sea Studies* 2015/3, co-edited with Sabine Strasser) and *Memories on the Move: Experiencing Mobility, Rethinking the Past* (co-edited with Monika Palmberger (Palgrave Macmillan, forthcoming 2016).

Hani Zubida is an Associate Professor and the acting Chair of the Department of Political Science at the Max Stern Yezreel Valley College, Israel. His main research areas are immigration, labour migration, remittances, identities and identity formation, football and politics, Israeli elections and Israeli society in general. Hani is also a socio-political activist.

Series foreword

Rethinking Borders

Crossing to the other side has many meanings, depending on what is crossing, where, when and why. Yet it always involves borders: there can be no other side without a dividing line, something that gives the sense of a difference between here and that other place. Equally, refusing to cross, or refusing to accept the crossers, requires such a marker.

Rethinking Borders focuses on what gives borders their qualities across time and space, as well as on how such borders are experienced, built, managed, imagined and changed. This involves detailed and often richly ethnographic studies of all aspects of borders: finance and money, bureaucracy, trade, law, new technologies, materiality, infrastructure, gender and sexuality, even the philosophy of what counts as being 'borderly,' as well as the more familiar topics of migration, nationalism, politics, conflicts and security.

While there has been much discussion about globalisation, transnationalism, networks and digital technologies, and how these have radically changed relations between people and places, the world is still full of efforts to cut through the flow, to create stops somewhere. This is both so as to control movement (not only of people, but also of goods, animals, plants, money, ideas, diseases) and so as to define somewhere as being different from somewhere else. The *Rethinking Borders* series is dedicated to scholarship which provides fresh ways to think about these continuing efforts to mark differences spatially, and to understand both the major and more localised ways in which that has been changing.

The series originated with the work of a COST research network, EastBordNet (www.eastbordnet.org). EastBordNet was dedicated to rethinking the concept of border in the eastern peripheries of Europe. In the first decade of the twenty-first century, it was clear that something radical was happening with borders in that region, but more collaborative work across multiple borders was needed to understand and rethink the process. The first few volumes of *Rethinking Borders* reflect the regional origins of the series, but we welcome manuscripts from any part of the world.

Preface

It is ironic that the focus of this book is time, given how long the collection has been in development, as our long-suffering contributors know only too well. Its origins lie in an extended series of conversations over many years stimulated initially by a network of researchers whose focus was principally on Europe's eastern borders but which also included scholars with a conceptual and theoretical emphasis. EastBordNet, as the network was known, was richly stimulating and productive and, under the leadership of Sarah Green, then at the University of Manchester and now at the University of Helsinki, secured EU funding (COST Action IS0803) for 'Remaking eastern borders in Europe: a network exploring social, moral and material relocations of Europe's eastern peripheries', which enabled EastBordNet researchers to take their work further. Three years of intense and frequent workshops and two international conferences followed, for which we gratefully acknowledge this EU support. It was from this concentrated and sustained engagement that a series of themes emerged, of which the focus of this volume on border temporalities is one.

Given this long period of gestation, it will be no surprise that many colleagues have contributed along the way. Sarah Green is clearly foremost amongst them and we wish to thank her for her enormous energy, insight and leadership not only in driving the programme forward from the outset but in negotiating a book series with Manchester University Press to ensure its legacy. To our contributors we record our heartfelt thanks both for their inspiring contributions and for their faith that the team of apparently leisurely editors would ultimately deliver. And to our many EastBordNet and COST network friends and colleagues we offer our thanks for stimulating suggestions and critique as well as for their warmth, passionate scholarship and camaraderie. We are especially grateful to Emilio Cocco for his help in shaping the focus of this volume at a very early stage. The Imre Kertész Kolleg at the University of Jena provided Carolin Leutloff-Grandits with a highly appreciated advanced study scholarship and a stimulating intellectual environment as the volume entered its final stages. Tom Dark and Rob Byron at Manchester University

Press were a pleasure to work with, always prompt and clear-headed about what was required. Juanita Bullough and Sally Phillips, copy-editor and indexer respectively, did an outstanding job. We believe our text has been substantially improved with the input from our referees and we also thank them in the hope that they too will recognise where we have benefited from their suggestions.

Finally, we should be clear that this book and its introduction are the result of equal authorship, regardless of the order in which our names appear.

Hastings Donnan, Madeleine Hurd and Carolin Leutloff-Grandits
May 2016

Introduction:
crossing borders, changing times

Madeleine Hurd, Hastings Donnan and Carolin Leutloff-Grandits

This book explores how crossing borders entails shifting time as well as geographical location. Spaces may be bordered by both territory and time: in spatial practices,
memories and narratives, and in the hopes and fears that anchor an imagined community's history to a given (imagined) territory. Those who cross borders must,
therefore, negotiate not only the borders themselves, but the practices, memories
and narratives that differentiate and define the time-spaces they enclose. Border-
crossers – and those who find that old borders have moved – must come to terms
with the novel intersections of the temporal and the spatial they encounter. In this
volume, we focus on the perspectives of those whose borders have shifted, as well as
on those who themselves cross borders – exploring their subjectivities in the context of spaces that are not just physically separated but also zoned in time (Giddens
1991: 148).

Migrating borders and moving times examines how people interpret life after
moving across a political border, as well as their reactions to their 're-placement'
when a national border has itself been moved around. Our contributors seek to
grasp how such changes are understood – emotionally, in terms of (new) futures
and pasts; as part of trans-border community or network formation; and in terms
of the time-space materiality of border-crossing bodies and things. The 'moving' in
the title of our book thus indexes both mobility and affect, since when something
'moves' us, it stirs an emotional response. How do different groups – contract workers, labour migrants and smugglers – conceptualise the borders they have crossed
or those recently imposed upon them? How are those who have crossed defined
by 'host' populations; and with what new eyes do they view themselves in time and
place, reworking their relationships to the times and spaces of both their 'own' and
the 'other side'?

In order to answer these questions, we focus on borders that are embedded in
specific political contexts, which we refer to throughout as 'polity' borders. These
enclose and define areas controlled by national or supranational state authorities.
They often appear as lines on a map, claiming a physical presence. On the ground,

however, they are constituted first and foremost by regimes of practice, established, over time, by a territory's administrative, political and economic authorities (Simmel 1992: 697; Schwell 2010: 93). These practices interact with, reflect and reinforce those of local populations, as well as of actual and potential border crossers. However, they are also anchored in something more intangible: the validation of different communities' shared narratives of history and the future.

Such narratives show the extent to which borders, like national communities, are also imagined into being. As Houtum et al. (2005: 3) put it, 'a border is not so much an object or a material artefact as a belief, an imagination that creates and shapes the world, a social reality'. Borders might thus be better seen in terms of bordering, as more verb than noun. In this regard, we address borders less as lines of territorial demarcation than 'as countless points of interaction, or myriad places of divergence and convergence' (Donnan and Wilson 2010: 7). As we shall see, crossing borders results in variously bordered combinations of time as well as space, superimposed on, challenging and reinforcing one another in shifting patterns of spatio-temporal overlap and disjunction.

Three interrelated themes connected by a focus on the relationship between borders and time run throughout this book. First we consider how polity borders that delimit imagined communities are narrated as separating time-spaces between 'Us' and 'Them' to generate a hierarchy between 'East' and 'West'. Such spatial–temporal representations and hierarchies change with time as borders are redrawn. Our second theme explores how time features in the cross-border networks of migrants, emphasising in particular the affective networks that link, fragment or rupture ties between spouses, neighbours, friends and families. Here the challenges posed by temporal synchrony and disjuncture both within and beyond the borders across which these migrants move shape not only the practical but also the moral and emotional contexts in which they live their daily lives. Our third theme explores time in relation to the body itself as borders are shaped, felt, experienced and embodied according to prevailing constellations of power and opportunities for individual agency.

Time and b/order

While since the early 2000s there has been an enormous proliferation of books about borders, few focus specifically and systematically on the intersections of time and space, although this is a topic of emerging interest (see Andersson 2014a). Space has long dominated the field of border studies, and the 'spatial turn' across the social sciences has amplified this focus. Thus the many books on borders emphasise the 'where' and 'placed-ness' (or 'for whom?') of borders and largely focus on the 'when' only to sketch historical context or emphasise change. In this book, however, the focus on time is not just on historical transformations of borders but on the way 'border time' is shaped by, shapes and constitutes the borders themselves.

This emphasis on borders and time is innovative and fruitful. It both complements the classic analytical pre-eminence of 'space' in the study of borders (itself a consequence of border studies' beginnings in the study of geography); and highlights borders as layers of political history inscribed in space, from which can be read with varying degrees of visibility the historic cross-border shifts in population as well as the shifting nature of the borders themselves. It is not so much that time has been ignored in border studies, it is rather that, where it does feature, it is less privileged analytically or is assimilated to 'history'.

For instance, time is integral to developmental taxonomies that treat borders in terms of evolutionary stages. Baud and Schendel (1997), for example, stress the usefulness of the 'life course' as a framework for the comparative analysis of borders which emerge, develop, mature and disappear. Other scholars establish developmental sequences in accordance with borders' changing spatial organisation and integration, or with their shifts in political and economic functionalities (see Reitel 2013). While yet others advocate a typology that classifies border interactions as alienated, coexistent, interdependent and integrated in a way that implies a developmental temporal analysis even if it does not explicitly pursue it (Martinez 1994: 6–10). This introduces one type of time: linear and abstract, moving forward, so to speak, irrespective of the institutional and personal temporalities of local and border-crossing practices. But there are other types of time, as well – as this volume seeks to show.

One way of rethinking the relationship between time and borders is captured in the metaphor of *tidemark*. This concept does not postulate a border line being located 'somewhere in particular – at the edges of a territory, or at crossing points; tidemarks can appear anywhere, and can be imagined as much as seen or drawn' (Green 2009: 17). The concept of the tidemark implicitly informs several of our chapters, not surprising perhaps, given that Sarah Green coordinated and inspired the COST-funded research network from which this collection arose. The concept of tidemark stresses how borders can be seen not as static givens, but as emergent from practices, flows and processes. Like tides, changing borders might leave material traces; they pattern the landscape's contours; and leave behind layers of embodied memories of movement and emotion.

The lingering legacy of borders, both new and old, can also be captured by the concept of 'phantom borders' (Grandits et al. 2015). Even after border regimes are gone and their political and administrative aspects have vanished, the memories and practices of the borders can still exercise cultural, social and legal power. They shape both events and identities, continuing to embrace, albeit as ghosts, specific social spaces.

Several chapters in this collection build on the usefulness of thinking of time and borders in terms that echo the notion of tidemark and phantom, in their interest in the ephemeral and enduring traces of border movement (Green 2012: 585). In Chapter 1, Kramsch explores a tidemark-like layering of time and space along the border between Germany and the Netherlands. At one time heavily patrolled, the Dutch/German border has been reduced to near-insignificance by recent European Union (EU) decisions; but borderland signifiers encourage observers to remember and challenge both past and present meanings. The border can, therefore, be seen as a montage which gives time a spatial representation for those who pass through it. It invites a flâneur-like gaze on memory and mobility; a variety of signs present a palimpsest of meanings and historical referents, revealing the strangeness of a 'blocked temporal passage' between different types of border regimes. The flâneur recounts the spatial experience of relics of the past, whose afterlives awaken the observer to new conceptual constellations. Indeed, the juxtaposition of arbitrary relics, randomly witnessed, denaturalises assumed truths about the present and about borders, including the spatial power relations of conflicting border regimes. Arguably, borders are therefore better seen as process than as product – in terms of 'becoming' rather than in terms of 'dwelling' (Radu 2010). As we shall see, however, the implication of a repetitive, cyclical ebb and flow associated with the tidemark can struggle to accommodate the many unruly, arrhythmic and disjunctive temporalities reported in this volume.

In this book we try to shift attention towards what we refer to as everyday forms of border temporality – the ways in which people through their temporal practices manage, shape, represent and constitute the borders across which they move or at which they are made to halt. When we refer to border temporalities, what we have in mind, then, are the subjective, interpretative experiences and discursive representations of time by groups and individual agents rather than objective, measurable forms of time that may be taken as characteristic of particular historical periods. Certain things follow from this approach to temporality that are worth spelling out briefly in general terms. First, there is no presumption amongst our contributors that time is linear, progressive and orderly. It may be concurrent, parallel and synchronic; past, present and future may *coexist* in experience and imagination and/or *follow* one another, as a number of our chapters show. Second, in so far as the chapters emphasise the possibilities of anticipated futures and how these shape the border mobilities of the present, they are prospective and forward-looking rather than retrospective and focused principally on identifying defining phases of the past. Imagined futures coexist with lived presents, as our contributors explore, with people navigating different temporal regimes across the course of the day in a bordered space of parallel and multiple temporalities. Third, and closely related to this future orientation, our contributors emphasise the simultaneity of competing temporalities which may at times diverge, converge, overlap or collide, raising questions about the political implications of the presence or absence of temporal 'synchronicity' (Little 2015: 432).

In this volume, then, we explore time as an element in imagining and managing territorial, personal and communal identities, focusing particularly on how the temporal is recalibrated when a border has been crossed or when a border itself has been moved. Some contributors distinguish between different types of time – familial, national and transnational – and consider how these shape and are shaped by borders and border crossings. Others argue that such time dimensions, which are tied to a social collective, are both situational and emplaced. They can also be both cyclical and linear, and coexist alongside the 'clock time' that provides a universal measure of the passage of time worldwide.

Clock time, the time that obtains no matter who or where you are, can be defined as the empty, universal time that enables what Giddens (1991) terms global 'entrainment' through which complex international mobility and communications become possible. Clock time was globalised by the Enlightenment West; like the maps similarly produced, this global time allows the world to be viewed as a standardised unit (and thus, post-colonial theorists argue, open it more easily to imperialist gaze and control). Clock time supersedes local or personal time (measured by sunrise and sunset, local tasks, the people one meets and one's daily routines). It provides us with a non-personal, non-local time measured in hours so scientifically uniform that all can relate to it, no matter who or where one is.

Most of us, of course, also relate to national times – the clocks by which national politics are set, the shared times of a given nation's newspaper-readers. National time is inseparably linked to nation-states and their polity borders, which legitimate themselves by establishing national histories – stories of heroic people performing historic acts at historic places. Authoritarian sub-national time-spaces exist in state institutions (schools, nurseries, prisons, hospitals, factories, offices), and therewith structure our everyday life and worldview from early childhood, often unconsciously.

Massey (1991) finds great exclusionary potential in the combination of time and space. With advancing globalisation and the use of new communication technologies, the compression of space and time leads not only to an elision of spatial and temporal distances (Harvey 1989), but also to places becoming romanticised and idealised – sites of remembered childhood, of specific, characteristic practices. This idealisation is often accompanied by a defensive and reactionary response to the seemingly chaotic world 'outside'. The result is also, often, exclusionary. If we believe that places have a single, essentialised identity, based on a single history of past practices, we must keep out those who would disrupt time-spaces by imposing alien histories. We must impose border regimes – gated communities, patrolled barriers, 'locals-only' parks, neighbourhood watchdog committees, zoning and taxation laws (see, for instance, Atkinson and Flint 2004). All are products of fierce place-claiming, ranging from movements to exclude from our own backyards those deemed undesirable to nationalist xenophobia, a disposition that can extend to more generally imagined regions (the Arab world, Europe, the West, North America).

The great importance of national time and clock time has not, however, eradicated local and personal times, like the linear narratives of personal lives, the alternative, often 'cyclical' times of families (Hareven 1991) and neighbourhoods, or of play and illness. Such times exist parallel to clock time and national time, as people owe allegiance to multiple, layered time-spaces, as already noted. They overlap, and are variously invoked and prioritised, depending on the context. While such personal time-spaces may fit into national narratives, they may also challenge national time-spaces, especially when related to border-crossers' experiences, as we outline later. First, however, we consider how time constitutes a central element in defining Self and Other across bordered regional geographical imaginaries.

As often pointed out, bordering draws a line not just between the spatial 'here' and 'there' but also between the temporal 'now' and 'then'. Such divisions can come to define the content of the relationship between one side and the other, separating the ordered progress within a region or nation-state from the underdeveloped and timeless 'primitive' disorder that exists in the world beyond (Fabian 1983; Walker 1993). Nowhere has this been more prominent than in the distinction between Europe's 'West' and 'East' – an important sub-theme of this book – which was brought into being by what Fabian (1983: 32–33) would see as an 'allochronic' political cosmology that differentiates 'the Self-here-and-now' from 'the Other-there-and-then'.

This spatial–temporal ordering of Europe's 'East' and 'West' is a phenomenon that is many centuries old. It arose long before the foundation of nation-states, in the era of the great multinational and multi-religious states of the Ottoman and Hapsburg Empires which ruled central and south-eastern Europe and Asia Minor from the sixteenth to the early twentieth centuries. With the changing political order of Europe, these discourses also changed in content, yet without ever losing their general moral tone in which 'the West' considered 'the East' as its dangerous, Muslim-dominated antagonist. This notion fostered the establishment of a territorial border region within the neighbouring, mainly Christian-dominated Hapsburg Empire, which acted as a buffer zone towards Islam and the Ottoman state while simultaneously emerging as a frontier of cultural contact and tolerance, migration and conversion. Such themes still resonate today and deepen the significance and meaningfulness, for instance, of the transborder family networks described for the Albanian and Montenegrin borderlands by Tošić in Chapter 4.

With the dissolution of the multi-national empires and the foundation of nation-states which began in the nineteenth century, the new visions of Europe's East and West that were gradually created often drew on these long-standing images of backwardness and modernity to characterise the present, particularly in south-eastern Europe. They thus continue not only to influence political entities and polity borders that have been moved, reshaped or newly created in a geographical sense, but also to re-establish and redefine the discursive and cultural boundaries amongst the diverse populations of the region, as we shall see in several chapters in this book.

The imagined collectivities and geographies of the 'West', like those of nation-states, are tied to a particular history, one that claims a special pre-eminence: the linear time-space of exemplary progress. This particular time-space underpins many other narratives, including the differentiation between East and West Europe, as well as the hierarchical ranking of individual actors and nation-states which 'East' and 'West' 'contain'. This hierarchical relationship and its recent transformations are themes that preoccupy a number of our contributors whose 'Eastern' case material shares the wider historical and political temporal borderings and reborderings outlined below.

With the Enlightenment, local, cyclical and biblical ideas of Western time gave way to linear and progressive time. According to Nisbet (1980), this involved tenets that are naturalised today. First, there is the assumption that knowledge of the (linear) past will function as a means of understanding the present and predicting the future. Second, allied to this, is the faith in the cumulative march of reason and scientific knowledge which together enabled the economic and technological growth that preconditioned the nobility of Western civilisation. This definition is, of course, derived in contradistinction to other imagined regions, such as the South and the East. As Said (1978) suggests, the concept of linear, progressive time allowed Western countries to rank the rest of the world according to a progressive axis. Other regions lagged behind. If the West was modern, East Europe was romantically backwards, the Middle East regressive, the Far East 'timeless'.

The recent history of West–East relations shows what such differentiation might entail. The Cold War denoted, first, dichotomised spaces. But the border between East and West also functioned as a boundary between time zones. The Soviet-oriented, socialist 'Eastern Bloc' and US-oriented, 'Western' capitalist zone were divided not only by the Iron Curtain, but by competing time-bound systems. Although Soviet East Europe traced its founding myths to the Communist Revolution of 1917, many countries of the Eastern Bloc became socialist only after the Second World War, which was presented as a liberation from fascist powers. The West, home to individualist capitalist parliamentarianism, went further back, to the French and American revolutions. These two time-spaces (contemporaries believed) were engaged in a battle for the future.

Of course, there were regional and national time-space hierarchies within the West and East, as well. In the West, it was the United States and northern, Protestant Europe that led the way. In the East, meanwhile, socialist time fragmented when Albania and the Federal Republic of Yugoslavia broke with Stalin in the 1950s. They each then went their own time-space ways. Borders played a part in defining their relative position vis-à-vis the universal story of linear progress. The issue of which borders were permeable, in what direction, came to symbolise progress through time. Albania's hermetically sealed border symbolised its lost-in-time isolation. Yugoslavia's border was relatively open; Yugoslavs could, if they liked, travel to neighbouring countries to shop or for holidays. In both East and West, popular time-space conceptions placed Albania towards the bottom of the ladder of progress, and Yugoslavia rather higher up. Yugoslavia had moved 'forward': as a 'block-free' country, it was courted by and sometimes collaborated with Western countries. The relative status of Albania and Yugoslavia – one supposedly 'medieval', the other approaching modernity – became, thus, discursively linked to the stringency of their Western borders.

The border thus contributed to the delegitimisation of the socialist regime and to a downgrading of all countries bent on stopping outward border movement. Because the socialist world needed to seal itself off, the West presented it as a pre-modern, even regressive system, its occupants hostages in a time-space warp from which the only escape involved life-threatening defiance of inhuman border regimes.

By the 1980s, the West insisted, and the population of the East increasingly agreed, that the Communist path towards the future, deceptively successful at first, was fatally lagging behind (Brandtstädter 2007). Westerners returned to narratives – as old as the Enlightenment – that had labelled eastern Europe as an eternally backward periphery (see Wolff 1996; Todorova 1997). In eastern Europe, popular disillusionment contributed to the fall of the Communist systems (and with them, the Communist versions of past and present). Now the future belongs to the capitalist West.

The collapse of the Soviet system led to a major (re-)creation of polity borders. In the East, nationalism was immediately introduced as an alternative to communist collectivity: post-Soviet states claimed borders according to national criteria with all that this entailed, including a separate, ethnically based history, a shared and special future and a particular, nationally bounded time-space. These reconstructions often resulted in forced migrations and wars along ethno-national lines. 'Old' Europeans – those in the West – used it as 'proof' of the pre-modern barbarity of the would-be 'New' Europeans – thereby 'forgetting' their own history of genocidal blood-letting, which had peaked in the Second World War.

The phantom tidemarks of older time-space hierarchies persist, of course, and continue to affect this future, as our contributors show. In her contribution on postwar Sarajevo, Lofranco (Chapter 2) concentrates on the imposition of the new 'inter-ethnic boundary line' that divides 'Serbian' Sarajevo from the rest of the city. This imposition changed many neighbourhoods, as people were either forced to leave, or found themselves living with strange, albeit ethnically 'correct' neighbours. The new, mono-ethnic neighbourhoods have, in fact, drastically disrupted the everyday associations and relationships that make for local belonging. The supposed ties of shared ethnicity cannot overcome other barriers to sociability: different socio-economic groups' disparate ways of being sociable; the seemingly incommensurate practices of long-term city dwellers and recently immigrated country cousins. The result, Lofranco argues, has been a reformulation of neighbourhood time-space. First, there is a shift in communal memory. Older neighbours contrast tales of recent ethnic violence, the intolerant, primitive, unneighbourly present, with their nostalgic memories of a more progressive, civilised, good-neighbour past.

Their attachment to the socialist past, however, may render them marginal, even orientalised. After all, those who remain loyal to the 'old' values espoused under socialism, such as urban cosmopolitanism, are now officially behind the times – even as they complain, in their turn, of a city made primitive, backward and rural by village refugees and settlers. The result (they maintain) of the dismantling and dispersal of the old multi-national and multi-religious neighbourhoods is, in fact, a forced return to a more primitive past.

The deterioration of shared neighbourhood space, another post-socialist change, has accelerated this trend. As a result, neighbours find new spaces; neighbourhood practices, so difficult to maintain on site, have escaped, somewhat, into virtual and commercial space. Former neighbours meet, now, in cafés and restaurants, and communicate through phones and computers. Exchange and communication makes possible such a multiplication of coexisting time-spaces (Castells 1996). As Appadurai (2004) suggests, the ability of social imagination to inhabit various localities simultaneously via cross-border social media can even strengthen the local; the local can be projected across borders, creating an arena in which people acquire greater 'capacity to aspire'. This virtual mobility, a radical disruption of the colonial division of space, allows for new forms of cross-border mobilisation. The power of imagination empowers subaltern groups, helping them to reinterpret the borders imposed by the time-spaces of polity regimes. Such is the complex reaction when borders move according to nation-state agendas, redefining time-spaces even for those who have never left their homes, as Lofranco shows in the case of Sarajevo (cf. Demetriou 2013).

Neither ethnic homogeneity nor the abandonment of Soviet for Western history automatically put so-called Eastern countries on the road to (what is still presented as) the West's progressive, modernising time-space. To be sure, significant borders changed; the EU was extended to include many east European countries. As Buchowski (2006) points out, this EU enlargement is presented as generously assisting certain Eastern countries to catch up with the West. Of course, it will take time for even the most progressive of these to make proper progress – old time-space distinctions linger (Brandtstädter 2007; Kaschuba 2008). Old (western) Europe is, after all, more European than the New (Eastern) Europe. West Europeans claim greater rootedness in the manifold virtues of truly European history, and have thus a firmer step on the road to the future. East Europe's past makes many wonder if it will manage to stay the modernising course. Thus do collective memories of former time-spaces, combined with the powerful imagery of linear progress, reimagine old borders and resist the imposition of new.

Disappointed by their continued separation from the West's modernity, successor states of the USSR also rank each other according to their perceived progress towards wealth, ease and welfare. Some find, to their disgust, their own status diminished since (what might seem increasingly to be) the good old days. Kathryn Cassidy (Chapter 3) describes how citizens of Ukraine, when part of the

Soviet Union, might lord it over their less wealthy Romanian neighbours – those who, after the rift with Stalin, had followed a different, less effective path towards communism. Today, however, Romania is a member of the EU; Ukraine is not. Ukrainian citizens in the borderland with Romania suddenly feel disadvantaged. Their reversal into an impoverished and unmodern time-space is symbolised by a local way of making money: smuggling goods from Ukraine to Romania. The smugglers' changed and changing views of the relative positions of the time-spaces on either side of the border they traverse – that is, their respective pasts and futures – give an added dimension to their conflicted relationship to the polity border.

On-the-ground reactions to re-bordering can, in the Ukrainian as well as the Sarajevo case, be complex and creative. Changed border regimes can stimulate the creation of new pasts; these, in turn, may open up opportunities and thus brighten the future. In Chapter 4, Tošić shows how another 'moving' post-socialist border – that dividing Albania and Montenegro – inspired new ways of narrating a family's border-crossing past. In this case, as mentioned above, this past may reach back not only to the pre-socialist period, but to the multi-national rule of the Ottoman Empire, within which Montenegro was a relatively autonomous organisational unit, albeit one with shifting borders.

With the fall of socialism, the Montenegrin–Albanian border, sealed for fifty years, was suddenly penetrable. Today, goods and people can travel across; families can be reunited. Indeed, substantial energy has been invested in rediscovering and acknowledging old family ties. Tošić describes how locals are busy mapping – often *ex post facto* – elaborate family genealogies, extending far into the past, in which forefathers who migrated across borders are enthusiastically embraced. This reworking of ancestral memory creates a (new) multi-layered past which facilitates concrete future strategies. The kinship ties thus discovered (or invented) are invested with affect; all kin are welcome. This provides an excellent tool in the maintenance and extension of cross-border contact and patronage networks, an essential step towards future welfare.

In the process, unsurprisingly, many Montenegrin/Albanian, Muslim/Christian oppositions (the legacy of Ottoman-era migrations and conversions) are now retold as unimportant. National as well as religious divides are downplayed. Of far greater relevance are cross-border patrilineal ties. In this way, recently elaborated genealogies of border-crossing kin use ancestral male bodies (following a gender division typical of family trees) to create a living time-space of kinship memory that transcends ethnic, religious and national divides, giving space to ethnic, religious and cultural diversity.

However, the fall of socialism and the shifting and opening up of some borders within south-eastern Europe, as well as the integration of various central and eastern European states into the EU, do not necessarily lead to the strengthening of cosmopolitan ideals within these regions, or to a readiness to sacrifice national interests for what are perceived as European values. In fact, the recent refugee crisis suggests that the opposite may be the case. Instead of being loyal to the EU and showing solidarity with its member states and compassion to the refugees in their search for sanctuary, eastern European governments have developed an anti-refugee response. They were the first to close their doors by fencing in their borders, thus challenging the EU's model of an open society within the Union. Rather than trying to be good Europeans – as many states did in the first decade after the fall of socialism – and searching for a pan-European solution to the massive influx of refugees, eastern European states have flouted the EU authorities in favour of returning to ideals of ethnic homogeneity and a culturally based nation-state. As a result, the refugees, many of whom have already endured precarious crossings of the Mediterranean to reach European shores and ultimately the destinations in Germany, Sweden or Britain that seem to promise them a future, are trapped at borders in Macedonia, Hungary, Croatia and Slovenia where newly constructed fences impede their progress. The fact that citizens of states like Kosovo, Albania, Macedonia and Serbia may themselves be among those who strive to leave, given the difficult conditions they face at home, does not seem to have tempered these new border-crossing policies of foreclosure.

Migrant networks and temporal be/longings

So far we have emphasised how bordered time may underpin discursive regional hierarchies between East and West and have touched only briefly on the transformations that occur with the passage from one to the other. When people and things cross borders they become subject to new regimes of value and meaning which may take temporal as well as political and economic form. Disparities of economic and political value between each side of a border may encourage traders and others to move in pursuit of a better life. But for those whose lives are lived across borders, managing multiple temporal regimes can be just as critical an element of their daily practice as securing income or political voice. Yet time is seldom mentioned in analyses of their experience. In one recent and compelling account of how people deal with the hierarchies and asymmetries of cross-border encounters, for example, time scarcely features at all (Lauth Bacas and Kavanagh 2013).

   In this section, then, we emphasise the time-spaces that connect or disconnect groups across borders, focusing in particular on cross-border migrants and exploring the extent to which they feel they 'belong to' or 'long for' the place they moved to or from, respectively. Tensions between belonging and longing frequently characterise the migrant narrative analysed by our contributors below. And what they show is how it is possible simultaneously to invest emotionally in the history of both the 'here' and the 'there' while living in a time-space that is complex, situated and multiple. Our focus on this simultaneity, fragmentation and dispersal of space and time has a somewhat different emphasis from discussions of time-space compression which explore the relationships between capitalism and time. While related in a general way to the themes of this book, such analyses do not share its emphasis on the emotional and experiential temporalities that characterise cross-border mobility. It is these experiences that we seek to understand here through a bottom-up analysis of bordered time that reflects on the corporeal and emotional alongside identities such as ethnicity, gender and class. Nevertheless, it is important to remember in the present context that spatial and temporal practices are significant sites of social struggle framed by the relations between money, space and time 'as interlocking sources of social power' (Harvey 1989: 227). It is the 'differential powers of geographical mobility for capital and labour' (Harvey 1989: 234), after all, that provide the political economic context within which migrant temporalities are formed; and which in the last few years have encouraged many thousands to embark on precarious and uncertain crossings in the hope of a safer and perhaps more prosperous life.

Our objective is thus primarily to emphasise the subjective apprehension of time and its phenomenological manifestations in these bordered migratory crossings. Such experiences have led some commentators to characterise the migrant passage from one bordered time-space to another as liminal – a journey that is never complete, but is repeatedly caught between the moments of departure and arrival (see Donnan and Wilson 1999: 110). Liminality is generally considered to reflect particularly the experience of the undocumented, irregular migrant who is compelled to live a life of bureaucratic and social invisibility lest the state's pursuit of legibility result in imprisonment and deportation. Many such migrants fear leaving, for it may prove impossible to return; for them, exit can be just as risky (or riskier) as entry. They are, further, not only trapped in space but also stuck in time, unable to visit elderly and infirm relatives, or children who grow up in their absence, leaving the migrant fixed in an 'eternal present' of things-as-they-had-been when they left (Anderson et al. 2011: 77). In this sense, the bordered temporality of the irregular migrant is suspended, 'freezing … life opportunities through the enduring temporariness that precarious status affords' (Nyers 2013: 43). Irregular migrants might thus be said to experience a chronic liminality, a pathological state from which for many there is no exit phase of reincorporation or resolution. The insecurities and unpredictabilities of this experience of time stood still, of 'dead time' and 'non-existence', are eloquently evoked in Khosravi's (2010: 91) account of his long illegal flight to Europe from Iran. The future cannot be predicted or foreseen since the capriciousness of the present renders it unknowable; a make-believe future denied in all but fantasy.

Liminality can also be experienced by crossers who, despite appropriate documentation, feel that they have never arrived. This includes migrants who are socially and culturally excluded, denied access to opportunities and future prospects that others take for granted. As Newman (2006: 179) puts it: 'one border (the physical) has been crossed while the new one (cultural) presents itself, which may never be crossed successfully in their lifetime'. Even when the geographical crossing of a border is a momentary bureaucratic formality – for migrants with the requisite documentation – its social and cultural crossing may be a never-ending process which even a lifetime offers insufficient time to complete. As we see from the lives of the migrant labour outlined in the chapters here, migrants may find work, and even buy a home, but they remain liminal outsiders isolated from the rest of society, separated by boundaries that are not just spatial but temporal as well. Long hours, demands for constant availability and shift work combine with fixed-term contracts to set temporal parameters that differentiate this section of the population from the rest, ensuring that the time-space they inhabit is one in the interstices of a normalised, hegemonic temporal regime.

While this is the case in the EU, it is especially evident in Israel, a country that offers insights into the European neighbourhood policy at the eastern shore of the Mediterranean Sea which has long been a zone of shared cultural exchange between Europe, the Near East and North Africa. Israel, with its exclusive concept of citizenship, makes it difficult for migrants with non-Jewish beliefs to integrate and to enter the same time-space as its citizens.

Harper and Zubida (Chapter 5) explore precisely these relationships between labour migrants in Israel and their subjective apprehension and organisation of time. They build on the idea of a border as defining a given time-space and of border crossing as generating new concepts of time. Migrants, they argue, do not always march to the same clock as citizens (even as the atomisation of individuals associated with neoliberalism politically disempowers both migrant *and* citizen; Feldman 2015). There is national time; but there is also the time of non-nationals, two parallel and sometimes divergent temporalities. Migrant experiences of time are conditioned by their legal status, their distance from home and family, and their relative power or powerlessness. This is particularly true of the increasingly large migrant labour population in Israel. The authors introduce the concept of 'rupture time' and 'freedom time' as two opposing time frames particularly associated with temporary labour migrants. These, in turn, either enable or hinder immigrant incorporation into national, institutional Israeli time-space. For these migrants, then, time is the metaphor through which they represent and experience their precarity; it variously slows down or accelerates in contexts of uncertainty, a process Harper and Zubida compellingly describe in the immediacy of their account of the 'frenzied time' of deportation (cf. Griffiths 2014: 1992). The result is a vivid illustration of how migrant border crossings are composed of diverse temporalities between which migrants must navigate both in their everyday lives and as a past–future migrant trajectory.

Many migrants respond to this challenge by continuing to invest in multistranded relations with family and friends left behind, a practice that can create a time-space field that transcends both polity borders and social and cultural boundaries (Glick Schiller et al. 1995). The use by migrants of long-distance communication, exchanges and visits to reinforce a sense of common history, common value system and emotional investment in a sense of a shared future is now well documented. However, attempts to sustain these ties to others left behind are often diverse and varied and can be directly affected by the time-space inequalities and asymmetries encapsulated by and lending potency to polity borders. These may create disjunctures and ruptures between working life and domestic life that many migrants struggle to reconcile, as they deal with discrimination in one setting and accusations of loss of tradition in the other. Individuals who want to maintain their personal, network relations are often forced to think of them in different ways – to find them new spaces and times. The result is reflected in deeply individual processes of enacting and transcending borders. This can reflect a rich medley of layers of additional time-spaces – the no-time of asylum seeking, the cyclical times of family, the sacred times of rituals, the hierarchies of linear, national times – all of which implicate a series of complex, overlapping and situational identification processes.

Leutloff-Grandits (Chapter 6) analyses the shifting and layered temporalities within Kosovo Albanians' transnational family networks, illustrating both changing border regimes and divergent experiences and representations of border crossing. Since the mid-1980s, in particular, there have been significant changes in Kosovo Albanians' past–future spatialities. Before 1989, many Kosovo Albanians viewed migration to west Europe – male, labour-contract – as unpleasant and temporary. Europe might be more 'modern', but the migrant could bring this modernity back to home and family; the future was at home.

After 1989, Kosovo's ethnicised conflicts problematised the migrant's 'home time'. Despite patriotic faith in their nation's heroic future, many migrants now decided to have family members join them abroad. Here, however, tighter border regimes could force them back into other, less modern times like the 'passive waiting time' of asylum seekers (though see Hage 2009). Today, many migrants dismiss home time as stagnant. They plan a future within the EU for their children. Yet many also hope that their children will marry someone from home, in order to retain links with a static, idealised home, a time-space to which, indeed, they themselves often hope to retire. Many villagers share at least part of this dream; they hope to flee stagnation and build a future abroad, a dream which, due to increasingly stringent entry regulations, is realised primarily through marriage migration. But marriage, in turn, is pre-eminently a village and family affair. Thus are the different time-space experiences of migrant and non-migrant resynchronised through the strategies of transborder family networks. These times are brought into alignment, not least by the cyclical temporalities of family festivals (such as marriages) that draw migrants home.

Visits home, in fact, allow migrants to recalibrate disjunctive temporalities through the 'social glue' of transnational connections. Email, Skype and home visits (Vertovec 2004) create the 'worm holes' that Sheppard (2002) suggests connect territorial spaces to each other through variously structured relationships and flows.

Clusters of migrants create parallel time-spaces through marriage patterns, remittances, gifts, life-cycle rituals and visions of the family past. These constitute critical temporally connective networks. Such transborder exchanges can be (and often are) routine, repetitive and predictable, based on daily, weekly or monthly contact at specified times, and consequently are experienced as an integral and natural part of everyday life. Time and space may thereby be compressed to generate complex feelings of anchorage in a home community, one which migrants support, visit, and, often, plan to retire to. In this way, home time and away time can be synchronised, assuming a 'planar (as well as linear) character, making it possible to move not only from past to future but also from one present to another' (Coutin 2005: 200).

For families spanning two sides of a polity border, the ritualisation of community plays an important role in constituting and maintaining a common time-space. This can range from holidays at home, during which migrants' children can experience the time-space of their parental past, to participation in religious and life-cycle festivals marking the seasons, births and deaths. Communal ritual celebrations often look to the future; they may provide migrants with markers of passing time, in contrast to the stagnant or liminal temporality discussed earlier. These markers, moreover, follow community traditions. However much these are reinvented, traditions root participants in the community's imagined past, mapping time in terms of (what can be seen as) the community's own life stages. Participation in such festivals allows even border-crossers to feel part of a higher collective, in emotional and sacralising performances, uniting them in imagined, semi-sacred time (e.g. Jasper 1997: 197). Rituals thus confirm migrants' belonging in community time-spaces, irrespective of the individual migrants' place on different sides of polity borders or their everyday negotiations with opposing, majority time-spaces.

This shared sense of collective commitment to a common temporality established through mutual participation in family festivals and rituals of reproduction is vividly evoked for Kosovar migrants by Leutloff-Grandits. However, as she points out, it is ironically through these very same migrant return visits that time-space disjunction can be strengthened and reinscribed, as some migrants experience home as static and conservative; a sense of alienation mirrored by stay-at-home villagers who dream of a better future abroad, while still experiencing returned migrants as cultureless and philistine. These divergent temporalities, Leutloff-Grandits argues, deeply affect the solidarity of transnational family networks.

So while migrant time-spaces periodically realign with those at home, disjunctions may remain or even intensify, exacerbated by a lingering sense that the border crossed follows the modern–backward axis of national hierarchies and is marked by the rich–poor gap that prompted migration in the first place. Kosovar migrant tensions when at home echo those experienced by migrants elsewhere and reflect the differences entailed by the status they enjoy when abroad. For example, migrants with residency or citizenship rights maintain that higher status vis-à-vis other network members and are able to sustain more intensive ties to home than those whose status is irregular (Carling 2008; Al-Ali et al. 2001); while those with better-paid employment can use their superior resources to enhance their ability to cross the border and even to plan a future, triumphant return (Portes 2001). The fact that borders are variously permeable by different migrants thus establishes hierarchies within the cross-border networks themselves, shaping their temporal compatibilities and incompatibilities with home.

The same lopsided relations also affect network exchange, in so far as the flow of remittances and gifts are generally asymmetrical from the migrant to the home community. Successful migrants are expected to help those who stayed behind, not just by sending cash but also by assisting others to travel abroad and by providing care for the elderly and young who remain. Migrants often feel compelled to repay what could be termed 'the gift of communality' with remittances and /or emotional care in the form of presents, phone calls and letters (Baldassar 2007). This may generate a sense of absent-presence when migrants who are not physically there to care for their children or elderly parents are regularly in touch with them in a way that functions as a surrogate form of support (Izuhara and Shibata 2002: 159, 167).

In Chapter 7, Gregorič Bon examines the processes and ramifications of migrants' proxy presence in her analysis of Albanian–Greek border crossing. The opening of this border in 1989 encouraged massive labour migration from Albania to Greece, while the subsequent financial crisis in 2008 shifted the balance of migrants in favour of women. Where couples had originally migrated together, it was often the wives who remained abroad, while their husbands returned home, following redundancy or retirement. Gregorič Bon explores this phenomenon, focusing on the transnational time-spaces such couples establish. These time-spaces usually depend on material flows, with wives remitting money, food, furniture and other goods. This gives a concrete dimension to the couple's relationship, dynamically materialising the female migrants' presence despite their physical absence. It also affects temporality. First, the rhythmic circulation of things sent and received complements electronic communication in creating a common, cross-border time-space between absent wives and at-home husbands. Second, the woman's remittances should be understood as inalienable, in the sense that they are simultaneously both investment and insurance. Managed by the husband, remittances underwrite house-building, which when completed provides tangible testimony both to his wife's role as caregiver and to the couple's anticipated future together.

Gregorič Bon's material demonstrates how space, time and gender intersect in this Albanian case with the temporality of the gendered life cycle shaping male and female status in shifting ways as they move through time, crossing and recrossing space between home and abroad. According to Gregorič Bon, male migrants are more likely to dream of returning home than migrant women, who are inclined to feel that return will compromise the status they enjoyed when they could send remittances from somewhere seen as 'progressive' and 'modern' relative to Albania. Male migrants, by contrast, gain more by return (see Čapo Žmegač 2003), and despite its empowerment of migrant women, the new, transnational time-space hardly challenges traditional female–male power relations 'at home', in the village. As women age and return, they find that the local gender relations which momentarily their migrant experience seemed to subvert have not substantially altered. In short, seen in context of their life cycle, the liminality of their sojourn abroad is underscored by their reincorporation into local patriarchal structures that, paradoxically, their remittances helped to sustain.

As we saw earlier for Sarajevo, border temporalities may be altered not only by movements of people but also as borders themselves are shifted and redrawn, when those who remain sedentary may find that they too must navigate novel bordered time-space topographies. It is a sign of the semi-colonial nature of EU expansion that individuals who experienced the collapse of the Soviet Union are also seen as encased in alien time-space – in this case, unmodern Soviet time. In Poland, as Buchowski (2006) shows, those harmed by the new, neoliberal system are 'orientalised' – that is, accused of being lazy, backward or foolish, the irredeemable victims of communist socialisation. As in the case of migrants, here also social differences are culturalised and individualised, with the unsuccessful trapped in a backward, nowhere time-space. Carried by bodies, then, the Orient can be located within European societies, a time-space endemic to the unmodern – in former Soviet countries, survivors of a dead regime; in the West, as lost-in-time migrants. And it is migrants, of course, who are impeded at polity borders, particularly now at the height of the refugee crisis as they seek to cross Europe's external borders as well as its borders within. For them, border crossing can become a very bodily experience, one which renders the body vulnerable or which is even deadly.

Embodied borders and bordered bodies

As the discussion above suggests, the body may become the site on which far-flung temporalities condense, a simultaneity of the 'now' and 'then' that the body's distinctive relationship to space can bring about (Lefebvre 2004). A resonant example of this situated condensation is the East German driver who automatically decelerates when approaching the site of a former Soviet checkpoint, a deeply internalised, habitual and embodied reaction that collapses the present and the past (Berdahl 1999: 45). It is this relationship between borders, time and bodies that constitutes the third theme running through our contributions.

Most obviously, borders slow, impede or advance the traffic of bodies. Bodily movement is constrained, accelerated, delayed or halted altogether, not just at the moment of crossing the borderline itself but subsequently, as we have emphasised above. Thus events at port of entry may now reverberate far away at successive border pressure points where movement is cumulatively impeded; and where waiting, ironically, becomes the migrants' way of life. At one end of the continuum is speed, the gold card of elite travel with its fast-track processing of the body and at the other end the uncertain waiting of undocumented labour and those who claim asylum. Time itself here becomes another 'weapon' of migration management with its stops and starts and moments of transit and waiting that generate an 'endless, anxious present' in which mobility is regulated through time not space (Tsianos et al. 2009: 8; Andersson 2014a: 796, 2014b: 237). Speed of transit maximises sense of comfort and minimises visibility of controls while missing documentation triggers setback and delay (Bigo 2011: 67; Nyers 2013: 42–43). This creates a bordered time-space punctuation that imposes differentiated limits on mobility whereby the 'wrong bodies' are subject to friction and prevention, regulating flows rather than preventing them completely (Smart and Smart 2008).

Bodily experiences of border crossing are often shaped by forces of power and domination. According to Donnan and Wilson (1999: 129): 'those forces that demarcate geographical and political space as lines on a map simultaneously inscribe the body's topography, and from each can be read the history of the struggle to define and delimit personal identities, both on the part of the state and of those who oppose it'. This is often most visibly played out in the asymmetrical intimacy of border encounters (Lauth Bacas and Kavanagh 2013) when, alongside the rise of biometrics and sophisticated surveillance technologies, bodies may be physically searched for external or internal evidence of irregularity. This public penetration of the personal and exposure of the intimate by strangers once again recalls the concept of liminality where usual conventions of time, space and person do not apply and ordinary rights are suspended. They are liminal spaces over which state power is absolute, imposed on that most personal of our possessions, our body, whose experience of the border on such occasions is felt, sensed and visceral.

At the same time, the body provides a locus of concealment and resistance, offering cavities to hide contraband or to dissimulate. Small-scale smugglers, for example, may use condoms to swallow compact parcels of drugs in order to import proscribed goods or to take advantage of economic differentials across borders. Others use performative strategies that deploy the body in ways to amuse, distract and preoccupy those whose responsibility it is to intercept. Such tactics take control of border time by introducing novel elements to the repetitive, impersonalised bureaucratic interventions that generally characterise the actions of border guards at the moment of crossing. They reclaim agency over how time is structured at the border by disrupting the conventional, routine flow of monitoring and inspection. For the guards, who are similarly susceptible to border boredom generated by routinisation and repetitiveness, this can be a very enticing diversion (Konopinski 2014).

These themes are developed by Cassidy (Chapter 3) in the context of how female bodies and sexualised performances characterise the smuggling of contraband from Ukraine to Romania. Female traders regularly facilitated their passage with prohibited goods by flirting with the border guards. Such flirtatious behaviour was often successful and the Romanian guards easily diverted from their routines, enabling movement of smuggled goods. One guard, locally nicknamed King Kong because of his size, so enjoyed such encounters that he would let female smugglers pass, force them back, and have them apply to cross again and again; a moment in which time was paused so that he could savour a replay of the border crossing. Although villagers engage in these border flirtations and joke about them afterwards, they do so in ways that reveal feelings of humiliation and shame. This is most obviously the shame associated with having to behave in a sexualised way. However, as we noted earlier, it also entails a broader shame: that of having to make trips to Romania, 'the poorer neighbour', in order to make ends meet. Here again border temporalities are a factor, this time in relation to the time-space hierarchies we considered above, which rank nations according to their modernity or backwardness. In this schema, Ukrainians feel humiliated at having to smuggle goods into neighbouring Romania, which in the socialist era they saw as peripheral and impoverished, a position that through time now appears to have been reversed. Romania has been an EU member state since the 1990s, while Ukraine is still knocking at the door, a poor and war-torn periphery of Europe whose hopes of entry seem increasingly to recede. In short, the border now separates 'idealised past' from 'problematic present' (Zhurzhenko 2013: 206). For Cassidy, these transtemporal processes are best understood in terms of how the integral entailment of shame within both the body and the body politic shape Ukrainian narratives of their presents, pasts and futures.

But it is in context of large-scale irregular mobility that the impact of the asymmetry of border encounters on bodies is most strikingly and tragically played out. 'People' may or may not carry documents but 'bodies' themselves are often held to betray other signs, particularly 'alien bodies' (Luibhéid 2002; Donnan and Magowan 2010: 99–104). The EU's Eastern enlargement was accompanied by the heavy securitisation of its external borders, a task given in 2010 to the military-like agency Frontex. Its regimes have changed the EU border, where practices now enact complex sets of categorisations – sorting people into officials, citizens, commuters or tourists, regular and irregular migrants, those from European countries and from 'third' countries, some with inferior rights and others with no rights at all. For some, border crossing is simple, even routine; for others, it is time-consuming, expensive, risk-filled and deadly.

Irregular migrants are most directly affected by the latent violence of the border's well-patrolled fences, closed doors and exclusion zones, its checkpoints, cameras, computers, weapons and watchtowers. These have extended borders into international waters; the Mediterranean, in particular, is increasingly militarised and monitored by Frontex patrol boats. Migrants respond with new, desperate strategies, paying huge sums to smugglers who often send them out to sea in overcrowded, fragile and underfuelled boats. These boats are part of a dangerous gamble. Migrants hope that patrolling Frontex boats will rescue their foundering vessels and bring them to land. Once there, they hope to be given the deportation papers that will allow them either to go underground or seek asylum. But for many it is a gamble that ends in death.

The dead migrant body undergoes a cruel translation. In their study of the treatment of the corpses of migrants who tried to cross the Aegean Sea, Kovras and Robins (Chapter 8) describe how dead or missing migrants are constituted as a singular legal, political and moral category. While alive, the migrant body is indissolubly tied to its original territory, and carries with it its distinctive national identity, its belonging and its illicit practices. Living, the undocumented migrant is abjected – without the right to have rights (Agamben 1998). At the same time, however, they must be managed, processed and decisions taken on their status. By contrast, European securitisation regimes are indifferent to the dead bodies of migrants and deny any legal responsibility for such deaths, including the responsibility to identify and/or repatriate their remains. As a result, the Aegean has become one of the EU's most deadly borders, an 'empty zone' into which lives can simply disappear.

Time drags for irregular migrants, especially those awaiting decisions on asylum claims, but for those washed up on the beaches of Lampedusa and Lesbos, time has stopped altogether. Denied a future, the absence of documents and identifying kin now also acts to erase their past. Interred in unmarked graves, their 'very identities are vacated' in a moment of maximum social exclusion; dead, they literally 'go underground' (Coutin 2005: 199). Marginal to the concerns of the biopolitical, as Kovras and Robins show, the migrant corpse is an absent-presence that occupies an indeterminate space ignored by the legal and political order and the border regimes responsible.

On Lesbos, however, this empty space has been filled by civil society. Local people grant both recognition and status to migrant corpses washed ashore. In a subaltern subversion of the sovereign assertion of European border power, they bury them, providing the bodies with graves and memorials that assign them a place in space and memory. The migrants are dead but receive post-mortem acknowledgment by political and moral communities other than the state, their corpses transformed into the stage on which belonging and exclusion are enacted (Stepputat 2014; Trans 2014: 77).

Conclusion

We have suggested here that divergent experiences and interpretations of time characterise the lives of those whose lives are divided by borders. Our book, then, complements the analytical emphasis on the spatial that continues to underpin much of the study of borders and border crossing by locating crossing within a more extended temporal and geographical context than the immediate passage across the borderline itself.

In this sense Ingold's (2007) metaphor of 'meshwork' might serve better than 'line' or 'network' to encapsulate the multidirectional entanglements and intersections that we have been trying to capture here. Ingold sees 'meshwork' as lines that 'wander' and cross-cut in ever-shifting configurations: similar to the 'countless points of interaction, or myriad places of divergence and convergence' that we mentioned earlier. Integral to these multiple entanglements is passing time (see Green 2009: 10). Pred (1984) stresses the need to look at temporally and spatially specific actions, knowledge build-up, and 'biographies' or 'individual paths' in order to understand the creation and experience of what he refers to as 'time geographies'. Individual narratives, memories and experiences – 'life path–daily path' (Pred 1984) – make up spaces and, by implication, challenge, modify, ignore or confirm polity borders.

As the chapters show, border crossers' time-spaces embody, challenge or modify national and institutional spatial and temporal orders, promoting deep divides and opportunities for time-space negotiation between border crossers and those who stay home, citizens and irregular immigrants, far-off spouses and nearby neighbours. They emphasise the different means by which new time-spaces are negotiated, ranging from trans-border material exchanges through family networks, genealogies and cyclical festivals, to memorials to the migrant dead; and the associations between these processes and cross-border networks. And they draw attention to the tensions and contradictions between the speed of ever-faster connectivities and the disjointed decelerations of the migrant border crosser's life. It is these synchronies and divergences of border temporalities that is our focus here.

References

Agamben, G. (1998) *Homo Sacer: Sovereign Power and Bare Life*. Stanford, CA: Stanford University Press.

Al-Ali, N., R. Black and K. Koser (2001) 'The limits to "transnationalism": Bosnian and Eritrean refugees in Europe as emerging transnational communities', *Ethnic and Racial Studies* 24(4): 578–600.

Anderson, B., N. Sharma and C. Wright (2011) '"We are all foreigners:" no borders as a practical political project', in P. Nyers and K. Rygiel (eds), *Citizenship, Migrant Activism and the Politics of Movement*. New York: Routledge, pp. 73–91.

Andersson, R. (2014a) 'Time and the migrant other: European border controls and the temporal economics of illegality', *American Anthropologist*, 116(4): 795–809.

Andersson, R. (2014b) *Illegality, Inc.: Clandestine Migration and the Business of Bordering Europe*. Oakland: University of California Press.

Appadurai, A. (2004) 'The capacity to aspire: culture and the terms of recognition', in V. Rao and M. Walton (eds), *Culture and Public Action*. Stanford, CA: Stanford University Press, pp. 59–84.

Atkinson, R. and J. Flint (2004) 'Fortress UK? Gated communities, the spatial revolt of the elites and time-space trajectories of segregation', *Housing Studies*, special issue, 'Community, Neighbourhood, Reponsibility', 19(6).

Baldassar, L. (2007) 'Transnational families and the provision of moral and emotional support: the relationship between truth and distance', *Identities: Global Studies in Culture and Power*, 14(4): 385–409.

Baud, M. and W. van Schendel (1997) 'Toward a comparative history of borderlands', *Journal of World History*, 8(2): 211–242.

Berdahl, D. (1999) *Where the World Ended: Re-Unification and Identity in the German Borderland*. Berkeley: University of California Press.

Bigo, D. (2011) 'Freedom and speed in enlarged borderzones', in V. Squire (ed.), *The Contested Politics of Mobility: Borderzones and Irregularity*. London: Routledge, pp. 31–50.

Brandtstädter, S. (2007) 'Transitional spaces: postsocialism as a cultural process', *Critique of Anthropology*, 27: 131–145.

Buchowski, M. (2006) 'The specter of Orientalism in Europe: from exotic Other to stigmatized brother', *Anthropological Quarterly*, 79(3): 463–482.

Čapo Žmegač, J. (2003) 'Transnationalität, Lokalität, Geschlecht: kroatische Transmigranten in München', in C. Köck, A. Moosmüller and K. Roth (eds), *Zuwanderung und Integration: Kulturwissenschaftliche Zugänge und soziale Praxis*. Münster: Waxmann, pp. 125–140.

Carling, J. (2008) 'The human dynamics of migrant transnationalism', *Ethnic and Racial Studies*, 31(8): 1452–1477.

Castells, M. (1996) *The Rise of the Network Society: The Information Age: Economy, Society and Culture*, Vol. 1. Oxford: Blackwell.

Coutin, S.B. (2005) 'Being en route', *American Anthropologist*, 107(2): 195–206.

Demetriou, O. (2013) *Capricious Borders: Minority, Population, and Counter-conduct between Greece and Turkey*. Oxford: Berghahn.

Donnan, H. and F. Magowan (2010) *The Anthropology of Sex*. Oxford: Berg.

Donnan, H. and T.M. Wilson (2010) 'Ethnography, security and the "frontier effect" in borderlands', in H. Donnan and T.M. Wilson (eds), *Borderlands: Ethnographic Approaches to Security, Power, and Identity*. Lanham, MD: University Press of America, pp. 1–20.

Donnan, H. and T.M. Wilson (1999) *Borders: Frontiers of Identity, Nation and State*. Oxford, New York: Berg.

Fabian, J. (1983) *Time and the Other: How Anthropology Makes its Object*. New York: Columbia University Press.

Feldman, G. (2015) *We Are All Migrants: Political Action and the Ubiquitous Condition of Migrant-hood*. Stanford, CA: Stanford University Press.

Giddens, A. (1991) *Modernity and Self-Identity: Self and Society in the Late Modern Age*. Cambridge: Polity Press.

Glick Schiller, N., L. Basch and C. Blanc-Szanton (1995) 'From immigrant to transmigrant: theorizing transnational migration', *Anthropological Quarterly*, 68(1): 48–63.

Grandits, H., B. von Hirschhausen, C. Kraft, D. Müller and T. Serrier (2015) 'Phantomgrenzen im Östlichen Europa. Eine wissenschaftliche Positionierung', in B. von Hirschhausen et al. (eds), *Phantomgrenzen: Räume und Akteure in der Zeit neu denken*. Göttingen: Wallstein, pp. 13–56.

Green, S. (2012) 'A sense of border', in T.M. Wilson and H. Donnan (eds), *A Companion to Border Studies*. Oxford: Wiley-Blackwell, pp. 573–92.

Green, S. (2009) 'Lines, traces and tidemarks: reflections on forms of borderli-ness', EastBordNet Working Paper WG 1:1. www.eastbordnet.org/working_papers/open/documents/Green_Lines_Traces_and_Tidemarks_090414.pdf. Accessed 3 August 2016.

Griffiths, M.3.E. (2014) 'Out of time: the temporal uncertainties of refused asylum seekers and immigration detainees', *Journal of Ethnic and Migration Studies*, 40(12): 1991–2009.

Hage, G. (2009) 'Introduction', in G. Hage (ed.), *Waiting*. Melbourne: Melbourne University Press, pp. 1–11.

Hareven, T. K. (1991) 'Synchronizing individual time, family time, and historical time', in J. B. Bender and D. E. Wellbery (eds), *Chronotypes: The Construction of Time*. Stanford, CA: Stanford University Press, pp. 167–182.

Harvey, D. (1989) *The Condition of Postmodernity: An Enquiry into the Origins of Cultural Change*. Oxford: Basil Blackwell.

Houtum, H. van, O.T. Kramsch and W. Zierhofer (2005) *B/ordering Space*. Aldershot: Ashgate.

Ingold, T. (2007) *Lines: A Brief History*. London: Routledge.

Izuhara, M. and H. Shibata (2002). 'Breaking the generational: Japanese migration and old-age care in Britain', in D. Bryceson and U. Vuorela (eds). *The Transnational Family: New European Frontiers and Global Networks*. Oxford: Berg, pp. 155–169.

Jasper, J. (1997) *The Art of Moral Protest: Culture, Biography, and Creativity in Social Movements*. Chicago, IL: University of Chicago Press.

Kaschuba, W. (2008) 'Europäisierung als kulturalistisches Projekt? Ethnologische Betrachtungen', in H. Joas and F. Jaeger (eds), *Europa im Spiegel der Kulturwissenschaften*. Badenp-Baden: Nomos, pp. 204–225.

Khosravi, S. (2010) *'Illegal' Traveller: An Auto-Ethnography of Borders*. Basingstoke, Palgrave Macmillan.

Konopinski, N. (2014) 'Borderline temporalities and security anticipations: standing guard in Tel Aviv', *Etnofoor*, 26(1): 59–80.

Lauth Bacas, J. and W. Kavanagh (2013) *Border Encounters: Asymmetry and Proximity at Europe's Frontiers*. New York, Oxford: Berghahn.

Lefebvre, H. (2004) *Rhythmanalysis: Space, Time and Everyday Life*, trans. S. Elden and G. Moore. London: Continuum.

Little, A. (2015) 'The complex temporality of borders: contingency and normativity', *European Journal of Political Theory*, 14(4): 429–447.

Luibhéid, E. (2002) *Entry Denied: Controlling Sexuality at the Border*. Minneapolis: University of Minnesota Press.

Martinez, O.J. (1994) *Border People: Life and Society in the US-Mexico Borderlands*. Tucson: University of Arizona Press.

Massey, D.B. (1991) 'A global sense of place', *Marxism Today*, 38: 24–29.

Newman, D. (2006) 'Borders and bordering: towards an interdisciplinary dialogue', *European Journal of Social Theory*, 9(2): 171–186.

Nisbet, R. (1980) *History of the Idea of Progress*. New York: Basic Books.

Nyers, P. (2013) 'Liberating irregularity: no borders, temporality, citizenship', in X. Guillaume and J. Huysmans (eds), *Citizenship and Security: The Constitution of Political Being*. London: Routledge, pp. 37–52.

Portes, A. (2001) 'The debates and significance of immigrant transnationalism', *Global Networks*, 1(3): 181–193.

Pred, A. (1984) 'Places as historically contingent process: structuration and the time-geography of becoming places', *Annals of the Association of American Geographers*, 74(2): 279–297.

Radu, C. (2010) 'Beyond border-"dwelling": temporalizing the border-space through events', *Anthropological Theory*, 10(4): 409–433.

Reitel, B. (2013) 'Border temporality and space integration in the European transborder agglomeration of Basel', *Journal of Borderlands Studies*, 28(2): 239–256.

Said, E. W. (1978) *Orientalism*. Harmondsworth: Penguin.

Schwell, A. (2010) 'Grenzen mit und ohne Kontrollen: Der Mythos vom "sicheren" Nationalstaat', in N. Langreiter, J. Rolshoven et al. (eds), *Bricolage: Innsbrucker Zeitschrift für Europäische Ethnologie*, Vol. 6, pp. 90–110.

Sheppard, E. (2002) 'The spaces and times of globalization: place, scale, networks and positionality', *Economic Geography*, 78(3): 307–330.

Simmel, Georg (1992) *Soziologie: Untersuchungen über die Formen der Vergesellschaftung*, Gesamtausgabe Georg Simmel, Vol. 11. Frankfurt am Main: Suhrkamp.

Smart, A. and J. Smart (2008) 'Time-space punctuation: Hong Kong's border regime and limits on mobility', *Pacific Affairs* 81 (2): 175–193.

Stepputat, F. (2014) 'Governing the dead? Theoretical approaches', in F. Stepputat (ed.), *Governing the Dead: Sovereignty and the Politics of Dead Bodies*. Manchester: Manchester University Press, pp. 11–32.

Todorova, M. (1997) *Imagining the Balkans*. New York: Oxford University Press.

Trans, L. O. (2014) 'Travelling corpses: negotiating sovereign claims in Oaxacan post-mortem repatriation', in F. Stepputat (ed.), *Governing the Dead: Sovereignty and the Politics of Dead Bodies*. Manchester: Manchester University Press, pp. 75–94.

Tsianos, V., S. Hess and S. Karakayali (2009) 'Transnational migration: theory and method of an ethnographic analysis of border regimes', Working Paper No. 55. University of Sussex: Sussex Centre for Migration Research.

Vertovec, S. (2004) 'Cheap calls: the social glue of migrant transnationalism', *Global Networks*, 4(2): 219–224.

Walker, R.B.J. (1993) *Inside/Outside: International Relations as Political Theory*. Cambridge: Cambridge University Press.

Wolff, L. (1996) *Inventing Eastern Europe: The Map of Civilization on the Mind of the Enlightenment*. Stanford, CA: Stanford University Press.

Zhurzhenko, T. (2013) '"We used to be one country": rural transformations, economic asymmetries and national identities in the Ukrainian–Russian borderlands', in J. Lauth Bacas and W. Kavanagh (eds), *Border Encounters: Asymmetry and Proximity at Europe's Frontiers*. New York, Oxford: Berghahn, pp. 193–212.

EU cross-border *Passagenwerk*

Olivier Thomas Kramsch

For us, the solution was in the direction of the horizon. We were those who scruti-
nised the horizon. We looked forward, not back. To the question, 'What is thinking?'
we didn't respond, 'Being' [like Heidegger] but with 'the possible'. (Henri Lefebvre,
cited in Hess 1988: 54)

Thoughts from a deckchair in Wyler, Germany

Walking through the village of Wyler, the last German settlement before the border
crossing into the Netherlands, one drifts past cavernous, odoriferous farmhouses,
fleeting images of green fields tucked between stolidly built single-family homes,
thick, tall shrubbery, and then, on the left: the hulking grey carapace of a defunct
border truck stop (Figure 1.1), and passing that again: a small sandy beach pocked
with two flimsy canvas deckchairs flanked by an awkward attempt at a fountain in a
low-lying pool spraying mistily into the thin sunshine (see Figure 1.2). The 'beach'
is attached to a newly expanded travel agency which caters largely to a Dutch clien-
tele and forms part of its 'exotica'-inducing public relations strategy. Experiencing
the juxtaposition of the ruins of border infrastructure with the travel agency's
'beach', at the forward edge of two major European states, invites the bordercrosser
to *dream* ...

References to 'walking', 'drifting' and 'dreaming' are of course intimately associated with the practices of early twentieth-century artistic movements such as
Dadaism and Surrealism, whose advocates attempted to counter the rationalising
and instrumentalising impulses of modern capitalism with an artistic sensibility
capable of foregrounding the still potent realms of memory, the unconscious and
the irrational in modern social life (Bigsby 1972; Henning 1979; Bradley 1997).
Such a sensibility would find expression not only in poetry, literature, painting
and sculpture, but would find further inspiration in the vast, teeming spaces of
the modern metropolis, whose chaotic flows, unpredictable sequences of events
and opaque and shadowy interstices provided the ideal sensorium for the classical

1.1 Ruins of border truck stop, Wyler, Germany

1.2 'Beach' in front of Hagemann's travel agency, Wyler, Germany

flâneur (or *flâneuse*) (Aragon 1926). This chapter seeks to draw on the unruly energies spawned by these earlier, urban-based political and artistic *avant-gardes* in order to explore questions of time, memory and mobility within a contemporary internal European borderland, located between Germany and the Netherlands. The 'method' of modern *flânerie* will specifically allow me to connect the temporal dimension of this borderland to a recent and growing interest in the fields of social and cultural geography with practices of 'walking'.

Current attention to ambulatory practices within human geography can be productively understood as emerging within the context of a widely heralded 'affective turn' in the field (Thrift 2008). As a result of this development, the emotional, experiential and embodied dimensions of space are foregrounded not only as a new frontier for empirical analysis but as useful in setting ambitious social-theoretical agendas aiming beyond the perceived limitations associated with traditional political-economy perspectives (Pile 2010; Jones and Evans 2012; Navaro-Yashin 2012; Sparke 2012). A lively interest in the 'geographies of walking' is further informed by concerns with the politico-aesthetic conditions for negotiating and resisting scopic regimes of modern state power, largely within the urban realm (Crary 1990; Jay 1993; Pinder 2011); as a tactic capable of rendering visible a historical, relational and 'affective geopolitics' of state sovereignty (Sidaway 2009), and as a potentially productive pathway for charting the normative valences associated with heightened 'mobilities' across the social sciences (Urry 2007; Cresswell and Merriman 2011). This chapter builds on the foregoing literature, but argues that the shadowy figure of the border *flâneur* can reveal tensions and contradictions in the workings of modern state power that cannot be captured simply by urban- or state-centric narratives of space walking. At the fringes of state territoriality, the *flâneur* becomes a bordering body, literally in-corporealising a border-crossing experience within himself. The experiential force of such a 'limit event' opens the body not only 'against' a singular border but channels it to an affective transnationalism connecting it to myriad border sites not contained by the state line proper (Kramsch and Dimitrovova 2008; Kramsch 2016). It is here, in effect, that the act of border walking invokes a critical comparative lens that refuses to be subsumed under a monolingual regime of state power purportedly enforced at the border. And it is here that such an embodied border perspective could add something new to urban-centred debates, particularly as they relate to current anxieties relating to the properly *political* dimension of ambulatory mobility across time and space (Pinder 2001; Cresswell 2006).

In short, this chapter argues that by bringing the past and present into a dynamic 'constellation' while crossing the national border, the border *flâneur* actively produces the border as an emotionally charged, future-oriented *horizon*. Understood in this way, the horizon invites us to rethink our notion of political borders as merely a geographic endpoint between states, as the expression of the limits of state sovereignty or as the interface between mutually ignorant 'homogenous empty' times, as the temporality of the nation has so eloquently been described by Benedict Anderson (1983). Parrying the notion of borders defined primarily as sites for the articulation of hostile and mutually ignorant socio-spatial differences (i.e. 'Us vs. Them'), the notion of horizon mobilised in this chapter suggests a space-time of the 'possible' in the sense expressed by Henri Lefebvre in the epigraph opening this chapter: a space articulating a set of diverse and heterogeneous relations in space and time, relations which in their intricate scalarity open up the space of the state border to deeply affective connections with 'other border temporalities', as well as to 'other borders' located far from the dividing line being traversed by the individual border crosser. Importantly for our argument, the concept of horizon works within and across the grain of different regimes of state-centric visibility, and is rooted in the premise that both within the internal borders of the European Union (EU) as well as at its outer edges the panoptic visual power of state governmentality is always partial, never fully effective in classifying and ordering the myriad elements of borderland life within its totalising gaze. This intuition, I argue, is what makes possible a politics 'of' the border, stretching the borderline into an affective-political 'constellation' suturing the past and present into a future-oriented time-space capable of revealing 'hidden' connections and affinities between a multiplicity of borderland contexts in ways not permitted by two-dimensional cartography.

But now it is time to get up from our Wyler deckchairs, stretch our legs, go for a stroll, and in the process pick up some real and imagined fellow-travellers.

Re-*cognising* the time-space(s) of modernity with Walter Benjamin

To accompany our *flânerie* of the Wyler borderland I turn not to a Dadaist or Surrealist, however, but to the mid-twentieth-century persona of Walter Benjamin, an iconic figure of the Frankfurt School of social theory. Benjamin's work crystallises a preoccupation with time, memory, movement and space that inevitably prefigures contemporary social-theoretical debates, and indeed often serves as their inspirational wellspring (Pred 1995; Pile 2000). For Benjamin, two tendencies characterised nineteenth- and twentieth-century modernity: an acceleration of the 'ever new', coupled with its complement and shadow, the 'eternal return of the same'. The dialectical tension between these two developments produced 'phantasmagoria' (or myths), which for Benjamin were most visibly expressed through attempts to negotiate 'what has been' and the social inadequacies of the present. The production of such myths in turn set the stage for what he called 'dreamworlds', real and imagined spaces produced while society still found itself 'sleepwalking' through the transition phase between pre-modern and fully modern forms of socio-spatial organisation (Pile 2000). In the realm of architecture and aesthetics, a powerful example of such a world is *Jugendstil*, that design form often made out of modern industrial materials – steel, glass, cement – moulded to reveal pre-modern, organic shapes (Benjamin 1999b). The master example of such a dreamworld was constituted for Benjamin by the Paris Arcades, those giant, *fin-de-siècle* enclosed shopping 'streets' framed by *Jugendstil*-influenced materials: 'glass houses of the future' (Benjamin 1999a: 213).

Sites such as the nineteenth-century Paris Arcades, which by Benjamin's time had lost their functionality ('aura'), according to an older set of use values, represented key locations for modern phantasmagoria, pointing to an unfulfilled future 'outside' and beyond capitalism:

> [The Surrealists were] the first to perceive the revolutionary energies that appear in the 'outmoded', in the first iron constructions, the first factory buildings, the earliest photos, the objects that begin to be extinct, grand pianos in the salon, the dresses of

five years ago, fashionable restaurants when the vogue has begun to ebb from them. (Benjamin 1996: 234)

The political-aesthetic task for Benjamin consisted not in showing how the past of the Arcades influenced the present, nor how the present shed its light on the past, but to reveal in the ruins of the Arcades a historical 'truth' whose 'afterlives' were capable of producing an 'awakening' into what Benjamin called the 'now of recognisability'. Crucial for Benjamin's way of conceptualising history, this *Jetztzeit*, which in a 'lightning flash' produced by a moment of 'danger' created a 'new constellation', had a fundamentally spatial character, rather than a temporal one. Like the Arcades of Benjamin's time, the extant infrastructure of border guardhouses and customs buildings that dot the landscape of Europe's internal borders constitute the 'ruins' of *our* previous century, the traces of a pre-Schengen[1] time when movement across Europe's internal member state borders was tightly controlled. And as in the case of the Parisian shopping streets that so fascinated Benjamin, I argue that the remains of today's border infrastructure exude an 'aura' and an 'afterlife' to the degree that, though they have lost their original function as points of direct observance and control, they remain sites charged with meaning and emotional-affective power for those who live nearby, as well as for those who cross the border in carrying out their everyday lives. We thus do not necessarily need to subscribe to Benjamin's larger redemptive and 'weak messianic' project (Pile 2000) to retrieve from his work the idea that the 'ruins' of the Dutch/German border, as is similarly the case within innumerable borderland contexts across the width and breadth of the EU, are infused with just such an 'aura', caught as they are between a time of fixed border controls that is no more and a future borderless horizon yet to come.

Benjamin employed several stratagems in spatialising the temporal dimension of the modern arcade. Drawing explicitly on the politico-aesthetic traditions of Surrealism, he drew on the artistic practice of 'montage': the juxtaposition of images (preferably photographs) so as to reveal, in the very spatial adjacency of their arrangement, 'surprising' lines of force and telluric pull that could resist the violent amalgamation of linear, historical narrative. Mobilised in this way by Benjamin, montage would produce a particular 'dialectic of seeing', one which could 'freeze' history's ceaseless production of castaway rubbish while enabling the emergence of an ethical tableau in which the losers and winners of capitalist development could exist, at a 'standstill', in a relation of tenuous equality (Buck-Morss 1989). Benjamin located another spatial strategy in the practice of the dandy, or *flâneur*, who, as exemplified in Louis Aragon's *Paris Peasant*, strolled haphazardly through the capital's streets, letting the city 'happen to him' (Aragon 1926). Benjamin's *flâneur* has no goal, no objective, no purpose: he is a 'collector' of useless debris, a pure 'witness' to the world around him, and, as such, its most ethically cogent critic. From his 'isolated' perch, footloose on the street, the *flâneur* is able to witness and report firsthand on the ravages and depredations of capitalist urbanisation, as was the case for Aragon during the 1920s 'Hausmannisation' of Paris, whereby large boulevards brutally cut up the dense, largely working-class Marais district. In this respect, the practice of Surrealist or Dadaist *flânerie* can be associated with one of the first critiques of capitalist urban modernity, albeit involving a 'poetics of space' that some subsequently conceived as being too individualist, voluntarist and quietist for the mass political mobilisation required to confront this kind of urbanisation (see especially Lefebvre 1991). As I forge a path on foot across the ruins of the Dutch/German border, I am aware of the perceived limitations projected onto the lone figure of the *flâneur*, but choose to retain his company nevertheless as a useful guide for a kind of emotionally attentive *praxis* in reading the affective topographies of this border-as-horizon. As with contemporary attempts to read, understand and remap geographies of the city by excavating its 'hidden histories and geographies', thus revealing some of 'the other cities that exist inside the city' (Ackroyd 1985; Sinclair 1997; Pinder 2001: 8), I undertake in the same spirit an exploration of 'the other borders that exist inside the border' that is Wyler.

'Wyler peasant': re-*cognising* the ruin

The ruin of the former German border truck stop in Wyler sits like a rotting carcass alongside a road which, not coincidentally for this walker, was formerly the *Via Romana* linking marching columns of Rome's finest to the cold, north-west barbarian peripheries (Figure 1.3).[2] The truck stop's mottled grey cement awning juts out over a row of barred windows whose dark interior casts foreboding shadows on rusty ramps facing the street. The entire area surrounding the truck stop is dotted with weeds and overgrown grass. An air of dereliction reigns over the whole surface of the structure, made all the more acute by being juxtaposed with the prim row of single-family detached houses situated just opposite. As I circle the building on foot, it feels like walking around a wartime ruin. And, in a flash, I am transported to the images of wartime destruction which fell upon this Dutch/German borderland during the Second World War in September 1944, when the Allies unsuccessfully attempted to force an entry from France into Germany over the Rhine by seizing bridges across the Maas, the Waal and the Lower Rhine (Korthals Altes and Zuidgeest-Perquin 1984). In subsequent months, as the war drew to a close, the nearby German city of Kleve would be flattened by Allied aerial bombardment, causing hundreds of deaths, as occurred with many German cities in the final stages of the war (see Figure 1.4) (Michels and Sliepenbeek 1964; Sebald 2003).

The Dutch city of Nijmegen would not be spared, either. As it was located so near the border, it would be mistaken for a German town by an American bomber pilot, who proceeded to destroy much of its historic centre on 22 February 1944 (Brinkhuis 1984). Hundreds died in the ensuing fire. As part of discussions over the immediate territorial post-war settlement between the Netherlands and Germany, a Dutch proposal sardonically named 'Black Tulip' proposed moving

1.3 Ruins of border truck stop, Wyler, Germany

1.4 Ruins of Kleve, Germany, 11 February 1945

the Netherlands border into Germany by several hundred kilometres, creating an ethnically cleansed buffer zone between the two countries. Despite the failure of this proposal, confusion over the exact location of the border between the two countries reigned for several months, causing its position to move erratically in the village of Wyler. The owner of the travel agency, whose business now sits on the site of the house where he grew up as a child, exclaims: 'Before the war, the border ran through [the neighbouring villages of] Beek, Berg en Dal, Groesbeek; after the war, it moved over [our village]. Overnight, my grandmother became "Dutch", then later "German" again.'[3]

The memory of wartime destruction and the aftermath thrown up by walking round the Wyler 'border ruin' tells another story of the border than that represented on the existing map of north-west Europe, where 'The Netherlands' and 'Germany' are shown as clearly delineated cartographical entities. It speaks to a 'hidden' dimension of the border, one defined by a shared experience of massive Allied aerial bombardment and the subsequent imposition of geopolitical manoeuvrings staged from distant state capitals – The Hague and Berlin – in which the actual lived space of borderlanders was rendered invisible. The Second World War *Raumgeist* of this borderland also brings to mind repressed memories revealing how this urbanised border was enmeshed within wider, imperial geographies of colonial power; for centuries Nijmegen served as a training ground for the Dutch colonial infantry (*KNIL*), who would depart for the global colonial theatres of Surinam and Indonesia from the banks of Nijmegen's River Waal (Hooghoff 2000; Kramsch 2006). When this Dutch/German borderland was bombed, Nijmegen continued to carry out this function, as it was still actively involved in the colonial administration of Indonesia. Like all haunted houses, the physical persistence of the Wyler truck stop thus speaks to and serves as a testament to a blocked passage between moments of wartime ruin, declining imperial power, strict national border controls and a contemporary European horizon trapped in the uncertainties, contradictions and ambiguities flowing from the unmastered colonial past. As if anticipating the emotional response to such an anxiety-producing condition, graffiti on the side of the truck stop, featuring a rose surrounded by barbed wire, screams, '*HADER ZEIT!*' ('TIME OF DOUBT!'; see Figure 1.5).

The effect of 'strangeness' produced by the difficulties of this blocked temporal passage is exemplified in the way the truck stop, some twenty years after the formal removal of internal European border controls, has developed a number of 'afterlives' for both the Dutch and German communities surrounding it. One such effect strikes me as I round the far corner of the building: a stack of freshly cut wood lines the lower part of a loading embankment at the rear of the structure (see Figure 1.6). Across the street, a *Bratwurst* vendor plies her trade. When I ask her opinion of the truck stop, she answers: 'The owner has tried to sell it twice, but can't find any buyers … The neighbours [largely comprising Dutch transmigrants] want it to stay as it is, rather than be converted into a car dealership or hotel.' When I note the

1.5 Ruins of border truck stop, Wyler, Germany, showing graffiti

1.6 Ruins of border truck stop, Wyler, Germany

1.7 Former Dutch/German border guard hut, now Lotto shop. The bicycle path shows approximately where the actual border guard hut once stood

stack of freshly cut wood at the corner of the building, she adds: 'I once saw a wedding party take photographs over there ... historic, you know.'[4]

The truck stop ruin, in short, has developed a life of its own, and takes on an almost visibly anthropomorphic shape as it 'stares' out melancholically westward, towards the site of the former Dutch/German border guardhouse, which, since the removal of border controls in 1990, has been converted into a Lotto shop (Figure 1.7). Drifting in the direction of the truck stop's gaze, I continue my walk past a series of farmhouses, passing a sign set back from the street announcing the border with the word '*Nederland*', surrounded by a sea of blue and yellow stars. I slouch onwards to the German Lotto shop, popular among Dutch visitors. From this vantage point, standing exactly on the spot where the old Dutch/German border-guard hut used to stand, I can look back and appreciate an advertising billboard attached to the rear wall of Hagemann's travel agency, displaying a sunny beachside tourist destination, with what appear to be cacti filling up the foreground (see Figure 1.8). Palm trees against an azure sky explode from the boundary of the advertising frame, and fill up the entire wall of the building. Here, on the very spot where Germany and the Netherlands once controlled the movement of each other's citizens, this gestures to a potentially happier 'elsewhere' beyond the Dutch/German borderland proper.

This tropical island tourist paradise pictured on the outside wall of Hagemann's travel agency evokes a contrapuntal horizon at the Levantine edges of Europe. In June 2004, Belgian-born and Mexico City-based performance artist Francis Alÿs walked 24 km along Jerusalem's 'Green Line', originally drawn as a ceasefire line by

1.8 Advertising mural to the rear of Hagemann's travel agency (English translation: 'Holiday like in a picture book! Holiday, as I like it')

General Moshe Dayan in 1948 to mark out the separate zones of the city after the Arab–Israeli war. A publicly available video accompanying Alys's exhibit identifies him ambling across streets and markets, negotiating paths between houses and trees, across fields and stubbly hills while dribbling a thin line of green paint from an open can. Exhibition patrons can choose between 11 soundtracks, each revealing a different Palestinian, Israeli or European commentator reflecting on the walk and its wider geopolitical significance. The broader meaning of the walk, made at a time when Ariel Sharon was constructing a new eight-metre-high cement 'separation wall', were further contextualised and made public by Alys in his 2007 New York exhibition, entitled 'Sometimes Doing Something Poetic Can Become Political and Sometimes Doing Something Political Can Become Poetic'. According to cultural geographer David Pinder, the green trail of paint, quickly smudged by daily traffic and eventually rendered invisible, 'evokes both the memory and the arbitrariness of the original line, reawakening a demarcation that was erased following Israeli expansion after the 1967 war' (2011: 686). Pinder remarks that 'as an artist and outsider', Alys's walk raises the question of how bodies are able to move with different degrees of freedom around this borderland, depending on their gender, ethnicity, age, class and place of origin (2011: 687). Assessing the tenor of critical reactions to Alys's performance from Arab and Jewish Israelis, one may conclude that 'The Green Line' triggered an important discussion in the region addressing the need to re-evaluate the issue of power as it conditions differential mobilities in and around the line.

Seen through a critical comparativist lens, the intertwined problematics of ambulatory mobility, memory and power at the Levantine edges of Europe speak just as eloquently to the Dutch/German border context of Wyler, where, despite the formal abolition of border controls and the supposedly 'free' movement of goods and people across internal European state boundaries, national capitals manoeuvre to reinforce their ability to scrutinise and filter movement into and out of national territory. Such a move is exemplified through recent attempts by the Dutch border police, or *Koeniglichke Marechaussee*, to erect sophisticated 'camera bridges' along 15 different cross-border passage points between the Netherlands and Germany and the Netherlands and Belgium (Koch 2012). The new border-monitoring system, codenamed '@migoboras', shorthand for 'mobile intervention for better data-gathering and security', is meant to photograph each car entering the territorial space of the Netherlands. The camera 'bridge', to be legal, needs to be situated just a few metres over the border in Dutch national territory; due to higher sensitivity over privacy and data protection in Germany, no such apparatus is allowed on the German side of the border. Data gathered via the '@migoboras' camera system is sent directly to a Dutch border-control centre, where a so-called 'producer' (*regisseur*) can, at a glance, identify the type of automobile in question, its country of origin and its licence-plate number, as well as the identity of the driver and its passengers. Although under European law sensitivity remains as to how and under what conditions data gathered under '@migoboras' can be saved, under a parallel programme sardonically labelled 'amigo-boras', the Dutch *Marechaussee* have instituted a system whereby border-crossing data can be saved indefinitely, to be shared with Interpol in the case of terrorist searches or other instances that might jeopardise national interests (Koch 2012). Dutch moves to tighten the surveillance of its borders have been matched by current German attempts to claim the right to close down temporarily its land borders in case of migration pressures from outside the EU, as was the case with France and Italy in the wake of the large-scale migration flows towards those lands triggered by the 2011 Arab Spring (*Rheinische Post* 2012).

'Walking on the moon', or hiding in plain sight?

Indeed, it is by connecting, in a novel 'constellation', the ambulatory flows – migrant as well as artistic – stemming from the border space of Francis Alys's *flânerie* to my own walk in Wyler that the reconverted Dutch/German border guardhouse and truck stop acquire the aura of a shared horizon. This horizon is manifested in the fact that in both contexts – Jerusalem and Wyler – what constitutes the state border is always shadowed by a largely invisible counterpoint to the mainstream construction of the modern state: in the case of Jerusalem, the many Arab Israelis who inhabit Israeli territory, thus making a silent mockery of the Green Line; in the Dutch/German context, the many Dutch residents who live around the Wyler 'ruin' in Germany, destabilising any notion of an 'Us' 'over here' and a 'Them' 'over

1.9 Bicycle track leading across the international border into the Netherlands

there'. The *horizon effect*, linking seemingly disparate border experiences through a novel critical comparative lens, has profound implications for how we traditionally perceive and conceive of Europe's borders, as is already being demonstrated in the work of scholars of the Global South who argue for 'new geographies of theory' in urban studies that seek to 'dislocate the center[s]' of Euro-American knowledge production on cities (Robinson 2002; Roy 2009). These concerns haunt me as I continue walking in the direction of the international border between Germany and the Netherlands. The sun is out; a soft breeze caresses the grass. As there is no pavement, I amble along a new *accessoire*, a cycle track, the first sign of Dutch urban planning (see Figure 1.9).

As I step onto the soft crimson shoulder of the Dutch cycle track, I feel I might be being watched, though no 'camera bridges' are in sight, no potential *amigos* in my line of vision. Just to be on the safe side, I give a friendly wave in the direction of the Netherlands (a few cows nod back in my direction). Who has freedom of mobility to cross this line, unperturbed? And how does walking allow for a different 'sense of the border' (Green 2012) from that of the automobile, one that might allow for a different kind of aesthetic experience of the border, a different politics of the border? Critics of Alys, falling in with a long line of detractors that could easily stretch back to attacks on Benjamin and Aragon, fault the politico-aesthetic strategy of the *flâneur* as one that is hopelessly 'indulgent' by being 'merely' descriptive, unable to address the large-scale structural dimensions of modern power nor capable of thinking strategically as to the nature of social movements that could rise to challenge that power. By drawing attention to the 'repressed' and 'hidden' tactics of the individual at street level navigating the absolute spaces of technocratic planning (see also de Certeau 1984), the philosopher–*flâneur* is charged with complicity in neoliberal individualisation (Kwon 2002; Scalway 2006) and, ultimately, political quiescence in the face of hegemonic power whose corruption and domination are enabled precisely by opacity and lack of transparency (Pinder 2011).

In partial response to these criticisms, and walking in Aragon's and Benjamin's footsteps through the Wyler borderland, I would like to close with a reflexive reading of the aesthetic as well as political promise of what we may productively call the 'space of hiddenness at/on the border-as-horizon' (see also Kramsch and Dimitrovova 2008; for a historicisation of this phenomenon, Kramsch 2012). In the wake of recent writing that attempts to reappropriate 'secrecy' as a strategy for the Left (Birchall 2011; Phillips 2011), I argue that a streetwise sense of the Wyler borderland teaches us that under the panoptic anxieties of state capitals there lie within the border-as-horizon hidden but interconnected 'worlds', surprising yet deeply related singularities that 'detonate' our understanding of the border as either completely deterritorialised 'flow' or all-seeing and controlling 'line'. Significantly, such a vision of the Wyler horizon is attained not by walking as if one was in the air or 'on the moon', but as a fully corporeal and emotionally sentient observer immersed in the very material geographies of the border. Nevertheless, the question is well posed to what extent the observations of the single *flâneur* can be mobilised to inform social-scientific theorising. Sharply put, how can the insights of the *flâneur* be 'framed' socially in such a way as to provide the kind of nomothetic insights allowing the field of border studies to develop categories that can 'travel' in the service of wider theory-building?

We may begin to address this question by stating simply that nomothetic enquiry has always depended on its obverse, 'idiographic' side: the hidden, subterranean perspective 'from below' (some have called this simply 'fieldwork'). To suggest a choice between (or even an accentuation of) one epistemic approach over the other does violence to both. But in this respect I suggest there is more to our *flâneur* than meets the proverbial eye. As I hope to have shown through my own *flânerie* of the Wyler border-as-horizon, the *flâneur* is not 'just' an idiographic monad, wandering detached through space. For it is precisely through his ability to connect seemingly disparate and uncoordinated fragments – temporal fragments of the past and spatial fragments of the present – that she is in a position to construct relational sympathies, aleatory geographies of the *Jetztzeit* that awaken us into 'worlds' of multiply bordered connections, then and here, there and now. This signifies perhaps the emergence of a new form of nomothetic enquiry, one that requires a comparative way of seeing altogether different from that which the traditional social sciences have long dictated: a 'decentred' social-scientific enterprise, at once centred and de-centred, localised and de-localised, isolated and worldly. This is the ambiguous space of the *flâneur par excellence*, whose time might just be coming into its own at the dawn of the twenty-first century. By way of the spatial practice of photographic montage and the 'botanising on the asphalt' of the *flâneur*, Benjamin (1999b: 19) hoped to produce a new 'angle of vision', one that would serve to draw a redemptive new border rescuing elements that have the capacity to 'fan the spark of hope in the past', to wrest historical tradition 'anew ... from a conformism that is about to overpower it' (Benjamin 1968: 255). From our 'hidden' vantage point on the Wyler border-as-horizon, out of view of those Dutch 'bridge cameras' and German pontificators of 'closure', we can only be inspired to do the same.

Acknowledgements

The author would like to thank the editors of this volume for incisive but sympathetic critiques of an earlier draft of this chapter, which went a long way to making it a better read. Gratitude is also due to Emilio Cocco, who generously provided two opportunities to air the ideas expressed here: ('Liquid Lands, Solid Seas: The Making of a Region of Mobility in the Adriatic–Ionian Sea' (COST WG2 Workshop, Istituto Luigi Sturzo, Rome, Italy, 27–28 April 2009) and 'Remaking Borders' (First EastBordNet Conference, Monasterio dei Benedettini, Catania, Sicily, 20–22 January, 2011). *Grazie* for both, Emilio. I gratefully acknowledge the Kleve municipal archive for permission to reproduce Figure 1.4.

Notes

1 'Schengen' refers to the agreement which led to the creation of Europe's borderless Schengen Area. The treaty was signed on 14 June 1985 between five of the then ten member states of the European Economic Community (EEC) near the town of Schengen in Luxembourg.
2 Further productive allusions to walking can be made. In June every year, hundreds of thousands of tourists flock to the next largest city on the Dutch side of the border, Nijmegen, to take part in a four-day walkathon known as the *Vierdaagse*. In recognition not only of Nijmegen's Roman past as a military garrison town, but also as tribute to the Allied forces who died in 'liberating' Nijmegen during the Second World War, many active-duty soldiers from all over the world participate in this event. As can be imagined, although they maintain an active presence in this border area, German soldiers do not take part.
3 The interview with Mr Hagemann took place on 24 April 2009.
4 The interview with the Wyler Bratwurst vendor took place on 24 April 2009.

References

Ackroyd, Peter (1985) *Hawksmoor*. London: Abacus.
Anderson, Benedict (1983) *Imagined Communities: Reflections on the Origin and Spread of Nationalism*. London: Verso/NLB.

Aragon, Louis (1926) *Le paysan de Paris.*

Benjamin, Walter (1968) *Illuminations.* New York: Schocken Books.

Benjamin, Walter (1996) *Selected Writings, vol. 2.* Cambridge, MA: Belknap Press of Harvard University Press.

Benjamin, Walter (1999a) *The Arcades Project,* trans Howard Eiland and Kevin McLaughlin. Cambridge, MA: Belknap Press of Harvard University Press.

Benjamin, Walter (1999b) 'The Paris of the Second Empire in Baudelaire', in *Selected Writings, vol. 4, 1938-1940.* Cambridge, MA: Belknap Press of Harvard University Press.

Bigsby, C.W.E. (1972) *Dada and Surrealism: The Critical Idiom.* London: Methuen.

Birchall, Clare (2011) 'Introduction to "secrecy and transparency": the politics of opacity and openness', *Theory, Culture & Society,* 28: 7–8, 7–25.

Bradley, Fiona (1997) *Surrealism.* Cambridge: Cambridge University Press.

Brinkhuis, Alfons E. (1984) *De fatale aanval, 22 februari 1944: de waarheid over de mysterieuze Amerikaanse bombardementen op Nijmegen, Arnhem, Enschede en Deventer.* Weesp: Gooise Uitgeverij.

Buck-Morss, Susan (1989) *The Dialectics of Seeing: Walter Benjamin and the Arcades Project.* Cambridge, MA: MIT Press.

Crary, Jonathan (1990) *Techniques of the Observer: On Vision and Modernity in the Nineteenth Century.* Cambridge, MA: MIT Press.

Cresswell, Tim (2006) *On the Move: Mobility in the Modern Western World.* New York: Routledge.

Cresswell, Tim and P. Merriman (eds) (2011) *Geographies of Mobilities: Practices, Spaces, Subjects.* Aldershot: Ashgate.

de Certeau, Michel (1984) *The Practice of Everyday Life.* Berkeley: University of California Press.

Green, Sarah (2012) 'A sense of border', in Thomas M. Wilson and Hastings Donnan (eds), *A Companion to Border Studies.* Oxford: Blackwell, pp. 573–592.

Henning, Edward B. (1979) *The Spirit of Surrealism.* Cleveland, OH: Cleveland Museum of Art in cooperation with Indiana University Press.

Hess, Rémi (1988) *Henri Lefebvre et l'aventure du siècle.* Paris: A.M. Métailié.

Hooghoff, Pieke M.A.V. (2000) *Bandoeng aan de Waal: Indische Nijmegenaren in het begin van de twintigste eeuw.* Nijmegen: Boekhandel Roelants.

Jay, Martin (1993) *Downcast Eyes: The Denigration of Vision in Twentieth-Century French Thought.* Berkeley: University of California Press.

Jones, Phil and James Evans (2012) 'Rescue geography: place making, affect and regeneration', *Urban Studies,* 49(11): 2315–2331.

Koch, Jennifer (2012) 'Holland fotografiert die Grenzgaenger', *Rheinische Post,* 25 August, A3.

Korthals Altes, Alexander and M.E. Zuidgeest-Perquin (1984) *September 1944: Operation Market Garden.* Weesp: Fibula-Van Dishoeck.

Kramsch, Olivier (2006) 'Postcolonial shadow plays in the Dutch/German borderlands', in Salvatore Engel-Di Mauro (ed.), *The European's Burden: Global Imperialism in EU Expansion.* Berlin: Peter Lang, pp. 29–51.

Kramsch, Olivier (2012) '"Swarming" at the frontiers of France, 1870–1885', in Thomas

Wilson and Hastings Donnan (eds), *The Blackwell Companion to Border Studies*. Oxford: Blackwell, pp. 230–248.

Kramsch, Olivier (2016) '"Spatial play" at the ends of Europe: Oyapock bridge, Amazonía', *Tijdschrift voor Economische en Sociale Geografie [TESG]*, 107(2): 209–213.

Kramsch, Olivier and Bohdana Dimitrovova (2008) 'T.H. Marshall at the limit: hiding out in Maas-Rhein *euregio*', *Space & Polity*, 12(1): 31–46.

Kwon, Miwon (2002) *One Place After Another: Site-Specific Art and Locational Identity*. Cambridge, MA: MIT Press.

Lefebvre, Henri (1991) *The Production of Space*. Oxford: Blackwell.

Michels, Wilhelm and Peter Sliepenbeek (1964) *Neiderrheinisches Land im Krieg: ein Beitrag zur Geschichte des Zweiten Weltkrieges im Landkreis Kleve*. Kleve: Boss.

Navaro-Yashin, Yael (2012) *The Make-Believe Space: Affective Geography in a Postwar Polity*. Duke, NC: Duke University Press.

Phillips, John W.P. (2011) 'Secrecy and transparency: an interview with Samuel Weber', *Theory, Culture & Society*, 28:7–8, 158–172.

Pile, Steve (2000) 'Sleepwalking the modern city: Walter Benjamin and Sigmund Freud in the world of dreams', in Gary Bridge and Sophie Watson (eds), *A Companion to the City*. Oxford: Blackwell, pp. 127–153.

Pile, Steve (2010) 'Emotions and affect in recent human geography', *Transactions of the Association of British Geographers*, 35(1): 5–21.

Pinder, David (2011) 'Errant paths: the poetics and politics of walking', *Environment and Planning D: Society and Space*, 29: 672–692.

Pinder, David (2001) 'Ghostly footsteps: voices, memories and walks in the city', *Ecumene*, 8(1): 1–19.

Pred, Allan (1995) *Re-cognizing European Modernities: A Montage of the Present*. London: Routledge.

Rheinische Post (2012) 'Grenzkontrollen – EU bremst Berlin und Paris', 27 April, A6.

Robinson, Jenny (2002) 'Global and world cities: a view from off the map', *International Journal of Urban and Regional Research*, 26: 531–554.

Roy, Ananya (2009) 'The 21st-century metropolis: new geographies of theory', *Regional Studies*, 43(6): 819–830.

Scalway, Helen (2006) 'The contemporary *flâneuse*', in Aruna D'Souza and Tom McDonough (eds), *The Invisible* Flâneuse: *Gender, Public Space, and Visual Culture in Nineteenth-Century Paris*. Manchester: Manchester University Press, pp. 168–171.

Sebald, Winfried Georg (2003) *Luftkrieg und Literatur*. New York: Random House.

Sidaway, James (2009) 'Shadows on the path: negotiating geopolitics on an urban section of Britain's South West Coast Path', *Environment and Planning D: Society and Space*, 27: 1091–1116.

Sinclair, Ian (1997) *Lights Out for the Territory: 9 Excursions in the Secret History of London*. London: Granta.

Sparke, Mathew (2012) 'Ethnography, affect, geography and unemployment', *Annals of the Association of American Geographers*, 102(2): 510–514.

Thrift, Nigel (2008) *Non-Representational Theory: Space, Politics, Affect*. London: Routledge.

Urry, John (2007) *Mobilities*. Cambridge: Polity.

⇥⇤ **2** *⇥⇤*

Negotiating 'neighbourliness' in Sarajevo apartment blocks

Zaira Lofranco

This chapter analyses the experiences of internally displaced Sarajevans, focusing on the destruction and reconstruction of their social networks and neighbourly ties as they have been compelled to move across borders and as borders have shifted and been redrawn around them. It emphasises that borders are shifting *places* and *moments* which variously connect and divide as territory and power are reconfigured. Borders are thus seen here as dynamic and relational, moving in both space and time (see Green 2009).

In Sarajevo, the capital of Bosnia–Herzegovina (BiH), the shifting urban frontline that united and separated the city's neighbourhoods was an expression of the violent dispute over borders in the former Yugoslavia. During the 1992–95 war, a process of ethnic displacement meant that the frontline functioned as an ethnic threshold across which Sarajevans experienced (forced) mobility or immobility. In the aftermath of the conflict, the Inter Entity Boundary Line (IEBL), with its administrative separation of Sarajevo and Serb Sarajevo, replaced the frontline, profoundly changed the configuration of urban space and encouraged the resettlement of people across it on the basis of ethno-nationalist loyalties.

During the Bosnian war, anthropological analysis was preoccupied by inter-ethnic neighbourly relations, while after the war attention shifted to studies of inter-ethnic reconciliation (Christie and Bringa 1993; Bringa 1995; Helms 2010; Stefansson 2010; Baškar 2012). Sorabji's (2008) critical 'revisiting' of the Bosnian neighbourhood challenged the mainstream interpretation of national issues that had monopolised wartime attention, while other anthropologists documented how shifting borders and border crossings had had unpredictable effects on inhabitants' production of identity, affiliations and moral maps in ways that often unsettled identity markers like religion, ethnicity and nationality and their political connotations (Ballinger 2003; Pelkmans 2006). As Pelkmans (2006: 73) notes for neighbourhoods caught up in the reconfiguration of the Turkish–Soviet border, 'discontent focused on more subtle differences that only became obvious in face-to-face communication, through values such as trust, hospitality, and reciprocity'.

Moreover, we should not dismiss the impact of global cultural processes on neighbourliness in a context like Sarajevo, even as we emphasise the consequences of wartime ethnic displacement. As Appadurai (1996: 189) points out, in a globalised society the cultural production of locality arises from the 'steady erosion, principally due to the force and form of electronic mediation, of the relationship between spatial and virtual neighbourhoods'.

This chapter follows such leads in moving away from a conflict or ethnic-centred analysis of neighbourhood relations. It is based on comparative ethnographic research carried out between 2006 and 2007 in two contiguous neighbourhoods, Grbavica (Sarajevo) and Lukavica (Eastern Sarajevo), which were part of the same city (Sarajevo) and municipality (Novo Sarajevo). With the outbreak of war in 1992, they fell under Serb military control but in 1996, immediately after the Dayton Peace Agreement, Grbavica was reintegrated into the predominantly Muslim-inhabited part of Sarajevo, while Lukavica remained part of the newly established city of Serb Sarajevo, which was renamed Eastern Sarajevo in 2005.[1]

Although the recent history of both neighbourhoods has been officially presented as a demographic mass movement across rapidly shifting borders based on a process of 'ethnic cleansing', inhabitants themselves point out that displacement did not end up in a reassuring ethnic 'realignment'. Rather, they described how they experienced a cultural disorientation caused by the disruption of the historically specific socio-cultural (space-time) order perceived as normal before the war. This had placed residents in relation to urban space and to each other, and helped them structure daily contexts of interaction as neighbourhoods. After the war, regardless of whether they moved or stayed put, everyone I interviewed in Sarajevo felt like newcomers in their own city.

In both Grbavica and Lukavica, this feeling of 'cultural displacement' was particularly acute among people who had been living in the socially owned apartment blocks before the war. These apartment blocks had been built by the socialist government to accommodate the newly urbanised working class and had been allocated to the employees of socially owned companies (*preduzeće*) on the basis of socio-economic criteria rather than national affiliation.[2] As a result, these apartment blocks were characterised by informal inter-ethnic mixing that contrasted with neighbourly relations in rural areas (Bringa 1995) or in the *mahale*, old neighbourhoods built in the Ottoman period to group together inhabitants of the same religion (Sorabji 1989). In the neighbourhoods of my fieldwork many inhabitants of the socially owned buildings thus had to face what for them was an unusual process of ethnic homogenisation; a post-socialist transformation that was swiftly followed by the privatisation of ownership of the blocks in which they had once lived.[3]

Furthermore, displacement across the shifting IEBL in Sarajevo challenged the urban and cosmopolitan spirit of the modernisation process that underpinned neighbourly relations in socially owned housing. The post-war transformation process of national homogenisation was perceived as a process of ruralisation by the pre-war inhabitants.

In Grbavica, the flight of Serbs was followed by the arrival of Muslims from different areas of BiH controlled by the Army of the Serb Republic (VRS).[4] The neighbourhood was thus settled by people from different areas of the country with (real or supposed) rural origins, who lived side by side with the pre-war urban inhabitants.[5] Lukavica, a peri-urban zone (*prigradska*) sparsely inhabited before the war, was marked by the arrival of a significant number of Serbs displaced from the Sarajevo urban area who had to interact with other Serbs and a few Muslims who had lived there before the conflict and who were unfamiliar with 'the culture of living in a flat' (*kultura stanovanja*).

Analysis of post-war neighbours displaced from formerly socially owned housing, living in Grbavica and Lukavica, invites us to explore asymmetries and cross-ethnic patterns of division between and within the two neighbourhoods.[6] These emerged as a consequence of physical as well as political mobility engendered by a wider reconfiguration of geopolitical borders that involved local neighbouring interaction in complex political and cultural processes.

The chapter analyses how borders are experienced and newly configured in daily contexts of formal and informal interaction in Sarajevan neighbourhoods. It focuses on the cultural elaboration of social distance and proximity, relations of trust, collaboration, reciprocity and affect amongst neighbourhood inhabitants. Ultimately, it aims to explore how borders are shaped and reshaped by the daily interaction of displaced neighbours during the modernisation process that was central to the socialist housing project and is now reformulated in the conjuncture of post-war recovery and transition to private property and to European and/or global society.

Displaced in-the-city blocks: decoupling ethnic and urban neighbourliness

Ethnic affiliation of neighbourhoods changed several times as the frontline in Sarajevo shifted. Even before the line was stabilised, it maximised the perception of social distance between the two sides it separated. In neighbourhoods – the context of daily interaction – people were separated by ethnic origin, creating ethnically homogeneous areas in which territory, power and ethnic belonging should have been isomorphic. In wartime in-group and out-group membership was based on ethnic identity and was embedded in a new way of thinking in quantitative terms about majority/security and minority/insecurity (Jansen 2005; Appadurai 1998, 2006) aimed to convey social interaction in circumscribed and ethnic homogeneous contexts. Knowledge of a neighbour's ethnic identity became crucial to personal safety. Fieldwork carried out after the war revealed that people had detailed knowledge of the ethnic identity of their new neighbours and everyone I asked about the national structure of their neighbourhood was able to quantify in percentage terms the presence of people belonging to the national majority and minority groups.

Fieldwork also revealed how the pre-war neighbours' residential choice and positioning on the opposite side of the line was often interpreted as their lining up with the hostile warring or political side. As a result, the IEBL dividing neighbourhoods like Grbavica and Lukavica was often represented by interlocutors as a line dividing good from evil, and mobility across it highlighted incompatibility between 'us' and 'them' (Barth 1969: 39). People who lived on the other side were seen as morally to blame, in part because violence is a barbaric act (inhumanity is often associated with backwardness), but above all because they had visibly betrayed an ideal model of a civilised, ethnically mixed and secularised urban community of neighbours (Maček 2001: 218). The inhabitants were increasingly aware after the war that, despite ethnic displacement, their neighbourhood had not become ethnically homogeneous. Sarajevans I spoke with in Grbavica and Lukavica pointed to their ethnically diverse neighbourhoods as evidence of the residents' loyalty to the model of a cosmopolitan community that under socialism had symbolised 'brotherhood and unity' (*bratstvo i jedinstvo*) as well as modernity. This former ethnically mixed model of interaction left its traces so that some Serbs were still living in Grbavica and some Muslims in Lukavica. As a consequence, Sarajevans on both sides did not really present the IEBL as a moral line dividing discrete national groups but rather as a line that cut across both groups.

In Sarajevo this widespread attitude recalls the 'authentic hybridity' rhetoric that Ballinger (2003: 261) argues was used in the Istrian context as a defensive strategy against newcomers. Ballinger maintains that in the former Yugoslavia, marked by transnational population movement and border crossings triggered by the ethnicisation of territory, discourses of hybridity are meant to support the rootedness of a pure 'mixed' community of autochthons and the exclusion of ethnically homogeneous newcomers (Ballinger 2003: 261). For this reason, though forced mobility was aimed at fostering spatial closeness and social interaction among co-ethnics and at naturalising monoethnic neighbourhoods, solidarity and intimate relations in the neighbourhoods did not immediately appear as ethnically oriented. On the contrary, the demographic turnover across the line and the lack of past interaction with the new neighbours of the same ethnic group transformed the post-war neighbourhood into an unfamiliar social context. In several cases, even the names and professions of new neighbours were unknown to other inhabitants. Yet when I asked my interlocutors about their pre-war neighbours who had left, they could still recall their first names and other personal details. Ethnically homogeneous neighbouring relations generated by displacement were often disapproved of because they introduced people of putative rural origin to neighbourhoods where multi-ethnicity was presented as a distinguishing feature of the local urban community.

As Stefansson (2007: 63) notes, a particularly common concern among Sarajevans was the so-called 'cultural contamination' of the urban lifestyle by rural habits that they barely tolerated even in the aftermath of the Second World War,

as well as after the recent Yugoslav war. After the Second World War, the socialist politics of modernisation, with its emphasis on urbanising peasants and their
transformation into an industrial working class, was accompanied by the cultural
construction of the 'rural Other' as a negative pole in neighbourly relations.

By contrast, after the Yugoslav war, the cultural construction of the 'rural
Other' by the urbanised Sarajevan working class is linked to displacement and
ethnic homogenisation experienced as a 'forced de-urbanisation', simultaneously
perceived as a de-modernisation. De-urbanisation was consequently expressed by
Sarajevans living in Grbavica and Lukavica as a broad cultural process triggered by
the shifting of urban boundaries and forced mobility across them. This process was
accompanied by the generalised impoverishment and downward socioeconomic
mobility of most urban inhabitants, who had not only suffered armed conflict
but also the collapse of the socialist project with its promise of 'endless economic
growth'.

In Grbavica, de-urbanisation resulted from the humanitarian emergency during
the war, when buildings and the plots on which they stood acquired a utilitarian
function and, like everything else, were valued only if they contributed to people's
sustenance and survival. Hence, given the scarcity of food, every available space
between buildings, including flower beds and balconies, was used to grow food,
giving a rural feel to urban life reminiscent of a farming lifestyle (Maček 2007).
Nevertheless, Sarajevans complain about how newcomers behave in the city,
because they introduce practices and smells considered inappropriate in an urban
context and especially inappropriate in buildings (Stefansson 2007). In Lukavica,
where displaced urban Sarajevan Serbs constitute the majority of the post-war
inhabitants, the lack of 'urban-style' residential buildings and the inadequacy
of urban infrastructures were given as reasons for frustration by many of my
interlocutors.

They also lamented that they were forced to live in buildings where the rural
practices that they used to consider backward were evident. Many Sarajevans
displaced to Lukavica had no hot water at home and were forced to boil water
in a pot. Others complained of a lack of facilities for socialising with neighbours,
like benches and gardens, something they had been used to in Sarajevo. Instead,
they found their apartment blocks located on construction sites, where footpaths
were gravel tracks that were the result of ongoing urbanisation of rural areas, and
which they said meant that their stairs and flats were always dirty. Their frustration
at these conditions was often manifested in ethnic hatred and animosity towards
pre-war neighbours living in Sarajevo who still enjoyed urban comforts. Blame was
also directed towards the former Serb inhabitants of Lukavica who, regardless of
the needs of the urban newcomers, still occupied the space between buildings with
their agricultural tools, poultry and goats.

More concretely, in both neighbourhoods, ethnic homogenisation coincided
with stigmatisation of the 'rural Other' whose presence increased Sarajevans'

self-awareness of the impoverishment and de-urbanisation of the Self. As Pelkmans (2006: 86) notes for the village of Sarpi on the Georgian–Turkish border, the movement of people across borders may disturb patterns of identification of Self and Other. In the particular case of Grbavica and Lukavica, the Other may begin to mirror a reversed image of the Self and to threaten the pre-war economic and cultural superiority of urbanites. According to Pelkmans, this condition often results in the need to reinforce social boundaries. In the Sarajevo context 'contamination' and 'authenticity' thus become the discursive tropes of a trans-boundary and trans-ethnic cultural attempt to delimit spatially and temporally the community of neighbours to urban Sarajevans.

The displacement which is experienced as de-urbanisation introduces a trans-ethnic element of nostalgia for a disrupted social order embodied by a shared idea of an idyllic urban neighbourhood that resembled that of the pre-war urban era. At the same time, the desire of Sarajevans to share in the technological progress and infrastructural development enjoyed by other contemporary Europeans defines the distinctive features of the urban and modern community to which they belong and to which they aspire. As a result, in both Grbavica and Lukavica ethnic differences amongst members of the pre-war community of neighbours were often downplayed compared to differences experienced in daily interaction with co-residents in the mono-ethnic post-war neighbourhoods.

Building management in displaced urban neighbourhoods

Conflict over the position of the frontline damaged residential buildings both materially and socially. In all war-damaged apartment blocks I visited, I was surprised by the destruction of the main doors and intercom systems that allowed residents to control entry to the building. As a result, the boundary between the inside and outside of the building was completely blurred and the effects of vandalism, trafficking, looting and plundering were still visible even after the war. In residential blocks in both Lukavica and Grbavica, the inhabitants complained of experiencing a sense of the unfamiliar and even danger, because of the ease with which strangers could enter. Two common concerns were the absence of lighting in the stairwells, and external doors that did not lock or close. With a continuous turnover of residents, the social bonds among neighbours were weakened and shared norms not always applied to the care of common spaces. In this situation, hallways and other common areas were perceived by some of the inhabitants as a no man's land from which they could take things for personal or family survival without regard to the collective good. During my stay in Grbavica, for example, we had no light in the stairwell for several days because someone had stolen the light bulb. This was widely criticised by the residents, who lamented the lack of protection against such actions and suspected one of their neighbours of stealing it for his own use.

Displacement across shifting (geo)political borders also affected formal relations among neighbours in their role as tenants. This was particularly evident in the immediate aftermath of the war, when they had to cope with the urgent need to agree rules for managing common areas that would ensure the building was cleaned inside and out on a regular basis and that electricity bills were paid so that there was lighting on the stairs and in the basement.

People in Grbavica and Lukavica tried to cope with the problems by restoring a model of management similar to that which had previously applied in socially owned apartment blocks. In both neighbourhoods the need to organise life in common spaces led to the organisation of a tenants' meeting with a building manager on the basis of the socialist concept of *kućni savjet*. Tenants' meetings were more frequent in Grbavica, which had been extensively damaged during the conflict, in order to liaise with the builders responsible for the reconstruction. Here the system of outsourced building maintenance implemented during socialism was restored in many skyscrapers (*neboderi*), where the large number of floors and the presence of a lift required particular attention and expertise for maintenance and, consequently, regular intervention by a specialist company. The substantial difference compared to the socialist period was that these companies were now privately owned while during socialism they were socially owned, as were the buildings. In smaller residential buildings in Grbavica and Lukavica, however, routine maintenance was financed by small sums regularly contributed to one of the residents, usually an elderly or unemployed woman, who regularly cleaned the common spaces in buildings. More rarely, routine maintenance was on a voluntary basis.

The implementation of these systems in a post-war and post-socialist context could not guarantee effective building maintenance and in many cases it challenged harmonious relations among tenants. Most Sarajevans living in Grbavica and Lukavica expressed their dissatisfaction with the hygiene standards of their building. They blamed this situation on the turnover of tenants who had been assigned temporary occupancy rights, which made it difficult to secure regular payments towards renovations and cleaning. In Lukavica, Janko explained:

> We take care of cleanliness of the main entrance and we pay a woman to do this but I live in a neighbourhood where people come from I don't know where and they are not so interested in paying someone to have the building cleaned. That's why we can't reach an agreement about the work this woman should do, and the reason is that we have to pay her! So in the end every family cleans the space near its door and we seldom clean communal spaces.

Similarly, for Grbavica, Džoko told me:

> I'm only partially satisfied with the cleanliness of my building. The less you pay, the less you get. Maybe tenants who have always lived here pay, but those who came from outside … they don't pay and say, 'I'll be here for a year and then I'll leave. Why should I pay?' So they don't pay for water, for cleaning, nothing!

The termination of temporary occupancy rights over flats and the acknowledgement of private property rights, processes almost complete by the mid-2000s, demonstrate clearly that daily tensions over the use and care of shared spaces were a consequence of the incompatibility between the different socioeconomic conditions of the tenants and their failure to agree on the principle of equal rights and duties that should govern their collective life in the building.

The privatisation of homes and the liberalisation of the property market signalled the end of the pre-war system in which employers assigned flats to their employees, a system that had ensured all tenants had a job and a standardised level of income. Furthermore, the privatisation of apartment blocks that were formerly owned collectively created differences in ownership status among tenants.[7] The frequent arguments over shared bills or cleaning services are thus the result of the newly emerging social and material differences among tenants in the post-war, post-socialist transformation.

In post-war Grbavica, tenants in blocks constructed during socialism who are experiencing economic difficulties are likely to avoid paying for utilities like water, since this is supplied centrally, and it is not easy to cut off one tenant in the building without also cutting off the supply to all the other residents. At the same time, a household in economic difficulties is not in the position to reduce consumption of water and, consequently, its costs. In these pre-war buildings, there is a general water meter for the block so it is impossible to calculate individual household bills. Tenants pay a fixed sum that approximates their household consumption, which is calculated by dividing the building's overall consumption by area in square metres. Daily conversations among neighbours revealed that fixed costs for other communal bills are also hard to afford for many current tenants with unstable incomes. Quarrels often arose because of the collective consequences of one individual refusing to pay for stair-cleaning services, building services or for upgrading sub-standard plumbing. Such subjects were more frequently the reason for conflict than ethnic issues and tenants avoided socialising with one another in order to prevent disputes like that mentioned by one resident, Katica, who accused her neighbours of fabricating a claim to humanitarian relief in order to evade paying communal bills.

The shift from socialism to a market economy provoked the collapse of a principle of self-management and collective responsibility for public space. Restriction of private space and commitment to public/common spaces were central to the production of the modern socialist self and the socialist state (Brandtstädter 2007: 139). For instance, during the socialist period building embellishment or renovations were often carried out on a voluntary basis, referred to as *akcije* by my informants.

Although in both neighbourhoods some tenants still invested money and time in enhancing shared spaces, in the post-war, post-socialist context, most households tend to take part in building management as individual units with different needs and economic assets. This more individualistic behaviour cannot simply be interpreted as a disregard for the common good brought about by the introduction of the private property system. The economic disadvantage that some households experienced after the war put some people (especially those who had experience of life under socialism) in the embarrassing position of having to disobey tenets under which they had previously lived. The most common response to this predicament was to accuse the 'Other' of disregarding rules as a way of justifying their own negligence. For example, Dženana, an inhabitant of Grbavica in her fifties, told me:

> I care about the green spaces around the building! I pick up waste. Especially when springtime comes, I organize some *radne akcije* with children who live in this building and we clean, but it's useless … couples who have little children throw anything out and we could clean endlessly, but as long as they behave like this these spaces will always be dirty.

Others justify their private use of resources by stressing that non-interference in someone else's property is required by the new modern post-war system. Opinions recorded in both neighbourhoods were similar to that expressed by Subuljka: 'I don't tend to flowers around the building because they're the private property of those who live on the ground floor. I don't dare touch them!'

The more individualistic utilisation of private financial resources appears to be a direct consequence of the situation of displacement across different systems and ways of conceiving of property that in many cases results in tenants opting for inactivity because they are unsure who should do what. This is evident in doubts expressed by Azra, a 50-year-old tenant of Grbavica, who hesitates to clean green spaces around her building because she is not sure if she is in charge of it and wonders if this should be a task for the tenants or for workers paid by the municipal council. Similar disorientation has been generated by an over-reliance on post-war humanitarian aid which replaced public institutions in providing financial and technical support for building reconstruction. Selma, for example, after having declared to her neighbour that she was not interested in paying for repairs to the lift because she preferred to use the stairs, told me that she and other tenants were waiting for donors to repair the lift. (In fact, following the implementation of private property, flat owners became financially responsible for all internal repairs, including the lift.)

Notwithstanding this, the quarrels about building management suggest that care of shared spaces is still considered a cultural value in the post-war setting. In both neighbourhoods, residents are categorised according to a moral hierarchy that distinguishes those who are *fini ljudi*, that is, those who are respectful of social conventions and the common good and those who are not. Although no longer framed in terms of socialist values of solidarity among the tenants challenged by wartime distrust, the maintenance of shared spaces emerges as a cross-ethnic value which is the background for a decent life in apartment blocks, especially after the wartime devastation and suspension of the rules of law and social order. Everyday life in the building highlighted an ongoing cultural redefinition of a modern model of behaviour in urban space, one embodied neither by the socialist infrastructure, nor properly represented by the formalisation of individual economic and legal responsibility for common spaces imposed by private property. In a situation characterised by a changed legal system and increasing economic difficulties and inequalities among households, contrasts and uncertainties around management issues highlight the daily cultural attempt to negotiate (between past and present systems) the boundary between individual and institutional economic competences in common spaces.

Neighbourliness in post-war globalisation

Scholars explain that before the war, being part of a network of neighbours in BiH entailed interaction in informal contexts according to a set of social norms, such as visiting neighbours' homes for funerals, births and weddings, or just for a chat and a coffee (Bringa 1995: 67; Sorabji 2008: 107). These neighbourly ties of mutual assistance and respect are sometimes referred to as *komšiluk*, a word of Ottoman origin that indicates the place of residence of neighbours linked by spatial proximity. It has also symbolised mutual and prompt help determined by living next door, as witnessed by popular expressions reported by scholars: 'a neighbour is closer than one's shirt' (*komšija bliži od košulje*) (Halpern 1958); 'Your neighbour is more important than your brother, since your neighbour lives next door while your brother may be far away' (Stefansson 2010: 69). In this context, the role of *prva komšija*, 'next-door neighbour' (literally, 'first neighbour'), acquired considerable social importance.

Under socialism, *komšiluk* was politically presented as an idyllic context of sociality among households of different nationalities united by sharing socialist citizenship (Sorabji 2008). 'Neighbourhood' in socially owned blocks ideologically embodied the concept of 'brotherhood and unity' and, ultimately, of socialist modernity. My interviewees confirmed that, by contrast to neighbours of *mahale*, solidarity among residents of socially owned buildings was established more by participation in the same workplace and its associated recreational activities than by mutual visiting of each other's homes.

Although some of my interlocutors reaffirmed their devotion to *komšiluk* values and prescriptions in the post-war period, these have been revisited as a consequence of the different ways of perceiving social proximity with neighbours after displacement. As already noted, the ethnic diversity of residents in socially owned buildings has diminished after the war but it has not been completely eliminated in either Grbavica or Lukavica.

The management of ethnic difference among neighbours has become particularly complex following the war. As other anthropologists have observed, inter-ethnic relations in the post-war period are not impossible but are lacking in spontaneity and are sometimes avoided because they could generate tensions

(Helms 2010; Stefansson 2010). As a result, only a few inhabitants continue to invite each other for religious celebrations, paying due respect to neighbours' cultural specificities in matters of food and other customs. There is always a risk that someone will forget the diversity of those present and express their antipathy and even hatred of other 'enemy' national groups. As I was able to observe, the prevailing feeling in this situation was not the fear of personal attack but the shame and embarrassment for being identified with the enemy and thus as unwelcome guests. Residents consequently avoid offering their personal opinions about the conflict and about political-religious issues, choosing instead less controversial topics such as the intolerance of ill-mannered rural neighbours.

The redefinition of the institution of *komšiluk*, namely the 'normal' way of practising informal relations with neighbours, is not only influenced by the change in inter-ethnic relations that occurred after the war. In Grbavica and even in Lukavica, where the majority of inhabitants belongs to the same national group, the tragic events of the war and the frequent turnover of residents make it difficult for the inhabitants to open the door to neighbours who are almost unknown. It is not surprising, then, that those who visited were not always residents in their post-war neighbourhood. Many of my interlocutors confessed that they did not frequent neighbours' houses as much as they did before the war. Many of them described their relations with neighbours as *Nema poverenja*! ('There's no trust!'), and claimed that neighbours are no longer willing to offer help if asked. Others described residential buildings as dangerous and as no longer able to provide material or social protection. But security concerns are not the only reason for the transformation of *komšiluk*. It is also influenced by the fact that one's neighbours are no longer necessarily one's co-workers from the same firm. Now, after the war, socialising with neighbours is limited to tenants' meetings.

Displacement is a further element influencing residents' perceptions of proximity and their willingness to engage in informal interaction with neighbours. Some of the older generation still feel 'closer' to their pre-war neighbours who have moved away than to those who now live beside them but whom they do not really know. In a few cases this has led them to disregard the strict ethno-national divisions and taboos, and to visit their pre-war neighbours for family celebrations or coffee on the other side of the line. By contrast, some of the younger inhabitants who experienced displacement but returned to live in their pre-war home stated that they were too young when they were forced to leave and have no memories of the families who had remained in the building. They often confessed that their post-war neighbours of the same age are 'foreign' to them. Yet they retain vivid memories of the people they met in the place of displacement and with whom they established enduring friendships, visiting them frequently in other neighbourhoods of the city. Hospitality and informal interaction at home are thus reserved for people with whom social relations were established in the past or in the present. In this sense, the experience of displacement has played a critical role in changing the cultural norms that define the importance of housing proximity in social interaction. In post-war Sarajevo, as elsewhere, new technologies and means of communication (at least the cheaper types, such as texting and smartphone chat) are often used, especially by new-generation Sarajevans, to maintain relations with pre-war or wartime neighbours 'displaced' all over the city and sometimes even abroad. In this context, the residential proximity that characterised the next-door neighbour (*prvi komšija*) is no longer central to the perception of social proximity, which now extends to those who are spatially (in the city or abroad) and temporally (pre-war or wartime) distant.

In some cases economic hardship of post-war and post-socialist Bosnia and Herzegovina also imposes restrictions on pre-war *komšiluk* habits like the ritual practice of hospitality in domestic settings. Low family budgets and poor housing conditions are frequent reasons for avoiding domestic interactions with neighbours, especially for special occasions, when greater financial resources are needed to offer refreshment. For example, more families are now forced by economic circumstances to celebrate *tevhid* and *mevlud* in mosques rather than at home.[8] This kind of non-traditional choice would have been highly disapproved of by the neighbourhood community in pre-war times. Before the war the hosts themselves would have perceived it as shameful because, as Bringa notes, offering hospitality to guests in Bosnia has always been correlated to the honour of the host (Bringa 1995: 69).

I should emphasise that the increasing popularity of meeting in public places has emerged as a result of a new rhythm of work and post-war transnational cultural dynamics, and this has had a disruptive effect on *komšiluk* by introducing new ways of practising neighbourliness not based on spatial proximity and not strictly regulated by the socially binding reciprocity of domestic visits and drinking coffee at home. Nonetheless, in public places economic reciprocity is also displayed in paying for a round of drinks for the friends one has invited. Meetings in public places are preferred because they shift interaction from the restrictions of domestic space into urban cosmopolitan contexts like the city centre, which conveys a sense of belonging to a more global space. Croegaert (2011), who analysed the case of Bosnian migrants to the United States, argues that changes in practices of drinking coffee and organising sociability are enacted by people who have experienced displacement. As she explains, 'Because food practices involve multisensory encounters, activities like coffee preparation and drinking offer potent resources for formulating spaces that may both challenge and co-opt models of organizing time and social well-being and belonging' (Croegaert 2011: 473).

In Sarajevo this change is visible in the curiosity shown by the inhabitants for the new cafés and fast-food venues and in the increasing consumption of Nescafé (*Nes kafa*), an *instant* coffee that in many meeting places has replaced the traditional Bosnian *slow* coffee that has historically symbolised the hospitality and conviviality associated with neighbourliness.

The shifting borders of BiH coupled with border-crossing displacement have disrupted a model of sociability centred on local communities, mutual home visits and the ready availability of inter-ethnic mixing at work and in the neighbourhood. As participant observation in this mobile context has revealed, apartment-block residents who invest scarce resources in the neighbours who live next door are often frustrated by a lack of reciprocity and mutual hospitality.

Conclusion

Yugoslav border reconfiguration in the Bosnian capital resulted in a violent negotiation over IEBL positioning, animated by ethno-nationalist projects that required enclosure of a pure ethnic space-time and the clear-cut affiliation of persons to be achieved through enforced mobility and the stable territorialisation of identity. For displaced people living in post-war Grbavica and Lukavica, neighbourhoods which were located on opposite sides of the IEBL, the pre-war socialist order involving inter-ethnic cohabitation of members of the working class on the basis of their employment and socio-economic conditions was disrupted by a process of ethnic displacement.

Yet these changes brought about by the moving of borders and enforced mobility failed to produce ethnically oriented everyday interaction. Instead, they created a sense among residents of downward socio-economic mobility and a feeling of having stepped back in time by generating unwelcome resemblances to the stigmatised rural Other. So too the introduction of private property and individual home ownership has not been accompanied by the complete disappearance of the value put on the management of common space in communal buildings, with its consequences for neighbourly relations. The forced movement of populations, the destruction of the socialist system of production and the inclusion of housing in the market economy made post-war buildings more ethnically homogeneous but more heterogeneous in the patrimonial and socio-economic status of inhabitants. New class inequalities interacting with the redefinition of duties among tenants in the private property system generated uncertainty about communal responsibilities and a concomitant categorisation of neighbours into those who care for the common good and those who do not. Notwithstanding this, neighbourhoods and hospitality seem not only to have lost centrality in daily informal interaction, but the absence of opportunities to socialise among building inhabitants caused by displacement, new housing systems and the commitment to a new concept of modernity rooted in a globalised society create changes in affective and moral maps that work in post-war buildings to decouple neighbourliness from housing proximity, and from the mutuality entailed by hospitality in domestic space.

This analysis of neighbourliness highlights trans-ethnic patterns of self-identification among Sarajevans scattered across the line. Cultural production of neighbours and the establishment of social taxonomies and cultural hierarchies have altogether outlined the centrality for displaced Sarajevans of the identification with an urban community whose values had been sometimes overstated to the detriment of the ethnic divide. This identification even ended in nostalgia for an idyllic pre-war urban inter-ethnic neighbourhood.

Palmberger (2008) has demonstrated that nostalgia is not simply past-oriented. Indeed, nostalgia for the urban community of neighbours is not aimed at recon-structing the inter-ethnic cohabitation of the past in the present. On the contrary, in a completely changed context of interaction, nostalgia lies at the core of a future project of modernisation.

In Sarajevo, displacement has been experienced as de-modernisation, de-urbanisation and de-Europeanisation (see also Jansen 2009) and the production of the 'modern self', driven by the need to reformulate life strategies after displace-ment in space and time, entails for Sarajevan neighbours the enactment of affective and embodied practices of daily interaction which convey temporal synchronisation and spatial inclusion in an urban context perceived as more European and global.

The material presented here shows that (geo)political borders reshaped by daily interaction in two Sarajevan neighbourhoods do not appear as clear-cut lines between past, present and future configuration of territory and power, values and identity affiliations. Through social practice borders are negotiated in the geo-graphical and historical space of apartment blocks where different systems meet, linger, melt and change. The reconfiguration of borders and the relocation of people around them expressed through the changing practices of neighbourliness give rise to a ceaseless remaking of socio-cultural categories to organise increasing complex-ity and instability of the whole system.

Notes

1 Significantly, the two neighbourhoods are administratively identified as *Mjesne zajednice* Grbavica II and Lukavica centar. *Mjesne Zajednice* are administrative divisions set in the parts of Sarajevo urbanised during socialism. As already underlined by other anthropolo-gists (Bringa 1995: 55; Sorabji 2008: 100) and as I myself observed, the extension of the neighbourhoods perceived by their inhabitants only partly overlapped with administra-tive divisions.

2 'Socially owned' was the official designation of these buildings in former Yugoslavia. It was meant to underline that properties were owned by the working people and not by the state, an ideology that was very specific to the Yugoslav 'self-management' system. Article 24 of the Law on Housing Relations (*Zakon o Stambenim odnosima*) adopted in 1984 specified that a socially owned property could be allocated to employees after taking into account his/her housing and patrimonial condition, the numbers of his/her family members and years of service.

3 The privatisation process involved both my interlocutors who had decided to return to their pre-war flat and those who had decided to sell their apartment and move to the other side of the IEBL. Legally one could sell one's socially owned apartment only after having acquired private ownership of it.

4 Vojska Republike Srpske (Army of the Serb Republic).

5 Stefansson (2007: 76) points out that, despite the tendency to stereotype *Bošnjak* displaced persons as country folk, many of them came from big Bosnian cities like Banja Luka or Mostar.
6 Other scholars have also highlighted cross-ethnic patterns of divide in BiH (Maček 2001; Stefansson 2007). See also Henig (2012), who deals with post-socialist influence on neighbourly relations in a rural context.
7 For further information about housing entitlements in shifting political systems, see Lofranco 2013.
8 Islamic commemoration of the deceased and celebration of the Prophet Mohammed's birth.

References

Appadurai, A. (1996) *Modernity at Large: Cultural Dimensions of Globalization*. Minneapolis: University of Minnesota Press.
Appadurai, A. (1998) 'Dead certainty: ethnic violence in the era of globalization', *Public Culture*, 10(2): 225–247.
Appadurai, A. (2006) *Fear of Small Numbers*. Durham, NC: Duke University Press.
Ballinger, P. (2003) *History in Exile: Memory and Identity at the Borders of the Balkans*. Princeton, NJ: Princeton University Press.
Barth, F. (1969) *Ethnic Groups and Boundaries*. Boston: Little, Brown.
Baškar, B. (2012) '*Komšiluk* and taking care of the neighbours' shrine in Bosnia–Herzegovina', in D. Albera and M. Couroucli (eds), *Sharing Sacred Space in the Mediterranean*. Bloomington: Indiana University Press, pp. 51–68.
Brandtstädter, S. (2007) 'Transitional spaces: postsocialism as a cultural process: introduction', *Critique of Anthropology*, 27: 131–145.
Bringa, T. (1995) *Being Muslim the Bosnian Way: Identity and Community in a Central Bosnian Village* Princeton, NJ: Princeton University Press.
Croegaert, A. (2011) 'Who has time for ćejf? Postsocialist migration and slow coffee in neoliberal Chicago', *American Anthropologist*, 113(3): 463–477.
Green, S.F. (2009) *Lines, Traces and Tidemarks: Reflections on Forms of Borderli-ness*, COST Action IS0803 Working Paper 1. www.eastbordnet.org/working_papers/open/documents/Green_Lines_Traces_and_Tidemarks_090414.pdf. Accessed 9 August 2016.
Halpern, J. (1958) *A Serbian Village*. New York: Columbia University Press.
Helms, E. (2010) 'The gender of coffee: women and reconciliation initiatives in post-war Bosnia–Herzegovina', *Focaal*, 57: 17–32.
Henig, D. (2012) '"Knocking on my neighbours' door": on metamorphoses of sociality in rural Bosnia', *Critique of Anthropology*, 321: 3–19.
Jansen, S. (2005) 'National numbers in context: maps and stats in representation of the post-Yugoslav wars', *Identities*, 12(1): 45–68.
Jansen, S. (2009) 'After the red passport: towards an anthropology of the everyday geopolitics of entrapment in the EU's "immediate outside"', *Journal of Royal Anthropological Institute*, 15(4): 815–832.
Lofranco, Z. T. (2013) 'Minorities and housing entitlements in shifting political systems: legal provisions and the experience of displaced Sarajevans', in M. Buttino (ed.), *Changing*

Urban Landscapes since 1989: Eastern European and Post-Soviet Cities. Rome: Viella, pp. 179–209.

Maček, I. (2001) 'Predicament of war', in B.E. Schmidt and I.W. Schröder (eds), *Anthropology of Violence and Conflict.* London: Routledge, pp. 127–224.

Maček, I. (2007) 'Imitation of life: negotiating normality in Sarajevo under siege', in X. Bougarel, E. Helms and G. Duijzings (eds), *The New Bosnian Mosaic.* London: Ashgate, pp. 37–57.

Palmberger, M. (2008) 'Nostalgia matters: nostalgia for Yugoslavia as potential vision for a better future', *Sociologija,* 50(4): 355–370.

Pelkmans, M. (2006) *Defending the Border: Identity, Religion, and Modernity in the Republic of Georgia.* New York: Cornell University Press.

Sorabji, C. (1989) 'Muslim Identity and Islamic Faith in Sarajevo' Ph.D. thesis, Department of Social Anthropology, King's College, Cambridge.

Sorabji, C. (2008) 'Bosnian neighbourhoods revisited: tolerance, commitment and Komšiluk in Sarajevo', in F. Pine and J. Pina-Cabral (eds), *On the Margins of Religion.* New York: Berghahn, pp. 97–112.

Stefansson, A. (2007) 'Urban exile: locals, newcomers and the cultural transformation of Sarajevo', in X. Bougarel, E. Helms and G. Duijzings (eds), *The New Bosnian Mosaic.* London: Ashgate, pp. 59–78.

Stefansson, A. (2010) 'Coffee after cleansing? Co-existence, co-operation and communication in post-conflict Bosnia and Herzegovina', *Foocal,* 57: 62–76.

We Are All Neighbours (1993) (film), dir. D. Christie and T. Bringa. Granada Television, 1993.

3

Border crossings, shame and (re-)narrating the past in the Ukrainian–Romanian borderlands

Kathryn Cassidy

In April 2008, I celebrated my birthday in the village of Diyalivtsi,[1] where I had been living since October 2007, while carrying out research on informal economic practices in the Ukrainian–Romanian borderlands. My host, Rodika, and I had spent some time preparing food and drink for visitors and the first to arrive were our good friends and neighbours Luchika and her daughter Zhenia. Luchika and her son-in-law Dima were both cross-border small traders of cigarettes to Romania, and until the birth of her son, Zhenia had also been involved in the trade. While we waited for others to arrive, Luchika entertained us all with stories about the Romanian border guards and customs officials from the nearby road crossing. One of the guards had been given the nickname King Kong, due to his size, and Luchika had us all laughing with her impressions of him asking how many cartons of cigarettes she had and sending her back to 'try again'. This was not the first time I had heard such stories since I had moved to Diyalivtsi. In fact, the trading of cigarettes and other products to Romania was often present in village life; in conversations over the fence with neighbours, in performances for St Andrew's feast day at the village school and during drinks and birthday celebrations in the village sauna. The significance of cross-border small trade in the village was not limited to its role in sustaining and reproducing local households,[2] but lay also in the way in which Diyalivtsyany[3] infused discourses surrounding the trade with meaning and its influence on their changing perspectives of the past.

Nonetheless, whilst we laughed along with Luchika, different emotions often emerged when discussing border crossings in private. In fact, on another occasion Zhenia came to visit Rodika in tears after an argument with her husband, Dima. 'Dima has gone back to his mother again. We had an argument. She said that we are a poor family and if he had married someone else he wouldn't have to cross the border. She says we are below them … their family don't do this.' The implication of the trade as being beneath Dima's family, who had returned to the village after successful periods of migrant labour in Spain, reflected broader feelings of cross-border small trading as bringing shame upon a household. The specific dimensions of how villagers expressed this shame within their local community will be explored in this chapter, through a focus on the relationship between these representations of the trade, its influence on how the past was narrated and the transtemporality of shame. Research into cross-border small trade rarely acknowledges the role of emotions other than the fear felt by traders in border crossings themselves (Konstantinov 1996). However, in other fields of research on transnationality, particularly migration, emotional aspects have emerged as a key area of research (Keough 2006). This book focuses on what it is people feel they have crossed and done when crossing borders and, in doing so, seeks to take an approach which not only acknowledges the importance of contextualisation of border crossings but also recognises an epistemological shift. This shift necessitates a methodological approach that combines observation at the border during crossings and interviews about border crossings with a grounded, situated approach that enables an understanding of narratives and representations of border crossing in everyday life away from borders themselves. In this chapter, I draw on 15 months of ethnographic fieldwork in the Ukrainian–Romanian borderlands, which included more than 6 months of participant observation in Diyalivtsi, a village in the Chernivets'ka region of Ukraine, just 4 km from the main road between the region's two main urban centres – Chernivtsi and Suceava. I begin this discussion with a brief introduction to cross-border small trade (CBST) in the Ukrainian–Romanian borderlands. In the second section, I explore conceptualisations of shame drawing on literature from the humanities and social sciences. Finally, I complete my framing of shame and CBST in the Ukrainian–Romanian borderlands by considering memory and transtemporalities. The ensuing discussion in the final section of the chapter then moves to focus on the role of shame in shaping representations of CBST and narrations of the past in this region of Ukraine.

Cross-border small trading in the Ukrainian–Romanian borderlands

The Ukrainian–Romanian border can be seen to represent what classically has been termed the emergence of the 'golden curtain' (Allina-Pisano 2009) in Europe, i.e. the appearance of new inequalities between those post-socialist/post-Soviet countries, which have or have not achieved greater integration within the global economy primarily through membership of the European Union (EU). In the Ukrainian community of Diyalivtsi, which is only 1 km from the Romanian border and just 4 km from the region's major road crossing with Romania, less than one person per household was in formal employment.[4] In the years before 2007, when Romania joined the EU, the country saw a steady rise in consumer prices. These outstripped those of neighbouring Ukraine and led to opportunities for local people to replace migration, the solution to high unemployment from the mid-1990s, by cross-border small trading, particularly of cigarettes,[5] to nearby settlements in Romania. Romania's relatively late accession to the EU and higher levels of poverty at the end of state socialism meant that these types of opportunity were much slower to develop in this region than in other parts of Ukraine or indeed the region as a whole. Therefore, whilst CBST was already observed to be in decline in much of post-socialist central Europe by the late 1990s (Sword 1999: 151), the trade has proven to be more resilient on the borders of the former Soviet Union, due to weak global economic integration (Williams and Balaz 2002). The proximity of the border in Diyalivtsi transformed the village and meant that by the time I moved there in 2007 for fieldwork, cross-border small trading was central not only to particular households, but to the village and regional economies as a whole. Very few households in the village possessed a family member who was not or had not been involved in this type of trading.

There has been a plethora of work exploring the emergence of this small trade across Europe's borders in the period since 1989/1991. Much of this work has focused on the trade itself and the unfolding of sets of practices within the crossing of the border. For example, whilst Williams and Balaz (2002) explore structures and power relations in the trade, Konstantinov (1996) links the trade to the now highly problematised concept of 'transition' in the region, and Polese (2006) uses CBST as a means to illustrate the weakness of post-Soviet states. Much of this work was based on observations of border crossings, where traders often feel under pressure and we do not get a sense of the broader meanings being ascribed to the trade and associated journeys. Long-term ethnographic work in Diyalivtsi enabled me to understand the ways in which traders not only reflect upon and discuss more openly their own experiences of the border, but also 'perform' aspects of these economic practices to their friends and neighbours. Only in such a context can a researcher gain insight into the emotional geographies of the trade, as they become displaced from the border itself and infused into the everyday life of the traders' homes and communities. In this chapter, I illustrate the depth that such an approach can bring to the understanding of emotions in the context of clandestine and covert activities by focusing on shame.

On shame

Before entering into more detailed discussion of shame in Diyalivtsi, I consider some of the key themes in the existing literature. I begin by reiterating Probyn's (2005) point that what shames us is absolutely central to our thinking about who we are and how we represent ourselves. As such, when trying to understand Ukrainian cross-border small traders' representations of their border crossings, we need to explore if and how shame plays a role in these crossings. In the following section, I will elucidate how repetitious encounters that lead to feelings of shame across much of a particular community undoubtedly have the potential to become highly meaningful in how that community constructs a collective sense and/or understanding of its place in the world. This means that I will also be engaging in another prominent area of discussion in the literature on shame (Probyn 2005; Ahmed 2014) by exploring the relationship between individual and collective shame, which necessitates consideration of the power relations shaping encounters that lead to shame. Our interactions with others cannot be seen to be free but take place within a framework of limitations and constraints, as I will illustrate later. Ahmed (2014: 102) has explored the relationship between collective and individual shame in her analysis of colonial pasts and the process of nation-building (see also Probyn 2005: xiii). However, this coming to terms with a shameful collective past through acknowledgement contrasts starkly with the situation for the Ukrainians, whose experiences I draw upon here. In this context, I emphasise how shame in the present can lead to re-engagement with the past and displaced re-enactment of the present in a way that seeks to challenge rather than acknowledge that shame. In the ethnographic material that follows, I will describe how this is a collective narrative action of the traders and the communities in which they live, rather than the political appropriation that Ahmed describes.

Whilst Probyn acknowledges that there will always be multi-scalar effects arising from shame, it is important to note the relationships between these scales and how these shift and change over time. Although we may consider, as Probyn does, that there is an immediate reflexivity to shame, which she argues can be transformative if acknowledged, in the example I explore here there is a longer-term reflexivity to shame, which is forced by the repetition of shaming acts over a period of months and years. In exploring this, I will nuance the assertion that admitting shame is in itself shaming. As the narratives employed by the traders of Diyalivtsi and Chernivets'ka oblast (administrative division) will show, in retelling their experiences of the border, they can admit shameful actions in context of a broader narrative, which brings no shame to themselves. Rather than making the traders 'feel small and somehow undone' (Probyn 2005: 2), the ways of retelling these shameful acts actually empower them to redefine what is happening in their border crossings. So whilst shame may not be talked about in most societies, its prominence in the everyday life of Diyalivtsi and other parts of the region engenders and perhaps even necessitates a need to find a way to talk about it. Yet, I do not go so far as to suggest that this removes lingering shame within the traders (Johnston 2007: 32). In fact, the ongoing repetition of the narratives that arise from the shameful acts of trading would suggest that this remains and needs to be expressed in order to be borne.

Central to any consideration of shame has to be the notion of interest and the ways in which shame 'highlights different levels of interest' (Probyn 2005: x). In short, we cannot be shamed if we are not interested in someone or in eliciting some form of interest or reaction from a person. This is one of the key themes of the following section, where I emphasise the complexity of this notion in CBST. I will argue here, in order to problematise some of Probyn's assumptions, that we are not always free to determine or decide in whom we show interest and that interest, to some extent, can also be feigned. Nonetheless, this interest is still about a desire for connection or communication and is therefore bound up, at least in the moment of its expression, in mutuality and reciprocity. I will explore what this means for understanding shame as an involuntary affect and the implications for any resultant non-reciprocity. In terms of temporality, we can also see shame as being connected not solely to the past, but also to a fear of regretful futures (Sykes 2002: 22). It is a shame relating to the fear of not using our own potential agency to shape a still unformed future. There is an inherent tension in such a proposition, as it posits the burden for such a future on the individual. However, we need to reflect on the differing potential for individuals to affect a meaningful influence over their own individual and collective futures.

If shame gives us this insight into our relations with others (Probyn 2005: 35), then in Diyalivtsi narratives of the shameful acts of border crossing can be seen as a collective acknowledgement of the shame of others in creating conditions for the shameful interactions present in border crossings. The feeling of shame does not reveal the 'truth' behind these relations; instead we learn only from the ways in which shame emerges in the need to create such discourses. There is an active agency to deny the evident shame in the crossing and to reposition it at a different level and on a different body – the body politic. This consideration of the body politic is also evident in Ahmed's work on shame. Ahmed theorises how the nation is shamed both through the behaviour of those subjects who do not live up to the national social ideal, but also in its treatment of others. However, I argue here that the nation can also be shamed by its own subjects for its treatment of them – the failure of the political elite to live up to a social ideal.

In order for shame to arise there has to be a sense of oneself within the interlocution in which it arises. So, whilst we can feel guilty about the things we do – perhaps eating or drinking too much, or overreacting to a particular situation – the experience of shame happens only in a scenario in which we are invested. The shame itself will bring into our consciousness this compromising of self. In fact, we may not know this part of ourselves until shame appears, signifying a development in our self-understanding. We will have knowledge of where it has arisen in the past, and if we have followed Probyn's advice we may have reflected on it, coming to understand, at least in part, why it has emerged. Armed with such knowledge we may think we can avoid shameful situations in the future, but inevitably we have more to learn as the self develops, and as opportunities arise for us to encounter shame in new spaces. Kosofsky Sedgwick (2003) powerfully argues that it is in our communication with others in failing to elicit the positive note we were hoping for that we find our blushes return. Given this changing nature of shame within ourselves, we can see how such an affect could be viewed as differentiated across people and cultures. Shame, as such, is therefore situated in our knowledge, imagination and social positioning.

Remembering and transtemporality

In considering some of the literature on shame, it is clear that questions of time and transtemporality are particularly important. Shame is inherently linked to our presents, pasts and futures and their mutual co-construction. In the section that follows, I focus on how border crossings are remembered and represented within the context of village life in Diyalivtsi. The narratives of border crossing, which emerged during my time in Diyalivtsi, clearly became linked not only to the actual crossings themselves but to the ways in which the villagers understood their own recent history and shaped their understanding of their current situation. As Lambek and Antze (1996: xii) have suggested, memory is spatial as well as temporal in the sense that space is created between the border crosser and their memory of the crossing. In gazing on this space, the memory itself becomes distinct from the context in which it was created. It is this gaze and the remaking of it within the social context of Diyalivtsi that will be explored later. Therefore, just as memory might be imagined as a practice (Lambek and Antze 1996), so might we consider how this process of retelling by Ukrainian traders shapes the object (the border crossing) itself.

As with the discussion of shame, the consideration of this process brings us into the heart of exploring the mutually constituted relationship between individual and collective. The people of Diyalivtsi draw heavily not only on collective representations of the past, but also on existing collective narrative forms to explore the events they describe. In doing so, whilst the traders do speak of events passed, they also engage in the construction of future objects, as there will be more crossings within the next few days for almost all of them. This is different, then, from the process of loss analysed by Lambek and Antze, since border crossings for the Ukrainian traders cannot be envisaged as 'definitively past' (1996: xiii).

To understand fully the relationship between the individual and collective in memory, we must pay attention to the social relations and discursive spaces shaping the production of these memories (Hacking 1995), which is the focus of the ethnographic material presented below. In fact, what we see is that a fundamental shift in institutional forms (after 1991) leads to a radical transformation in memories of the Soviet period, or as Foucault (1997) would see this, the discursive production of the subjects themselves, the Diyalivtsyany. In this way, we see how the process of border crossing dislocates earlier narratives of the Soviet period and creates the space for new and emergent memories. So, in the material which follows, we will see all three of the elements of the process with which Lambek and Antze are concerned: the production of memory in discourses; its further invocation within broader discourses; and the narrative organisation of memory within its expressional form (1996: xv).

Yet whilst Lambek and Antze posit that memory should support identity while its gaps or uncertainties undermine it (1996: xvi), what is explored here is how the present undermines identity and how this necessitates the creation of a space for alternative narrations of the past and present that can serve to reinforce exist-ing views of identity. In any case, memory (after Nora 1989) becomes objectified through differing cultural forms, and as we shall see in the case of Diyalivtsi, the use of anecdotes, in particular, is central to any understanding of memory. Such narra-tives are not shaped within a lone voice but as a multi-dialogical process between the teller and the institutional and collective context to this retelling. Our gaze on the past is, therefore, situated (Stoetzler and Yuval-Davis 2002) and organised around a subject (Lambek and Antze 1996). At the same time, it is also possible to think of the self, that subject, as emerging through these stories and narrations. As such, narratives of the past must make space for the differentiated individual, so that all meaning and sense of identification is not lost.

The view that memory is therefore a focus for struggle centred around power will evidently be seen, as the villagers of Diyalivtsi use narratives of border crossing not only to re-engage with the past, but also to construct views of it which chal-lenge those produced on a national level in Ukraine since 1991. In a sense, such a challenge strikes at the very heart of this 'nation-building process', also referenced by Ahmed in relation to shame. For the Ukrainian state, this has predominantly involved a view of the Soviet period as one of occupation or oppression by Russia, devoid of positive outcomes and experiences. The relationship with the Soviet past, which emerges in the narratives of the villagers of Diyalivtsi, in contrast to that of the official level, is much closer to Hirsch and Spitzer's view of nostalgia, i.e. the loss of something positive, 'in which the absent/gone is valued as somehow better, simpler, less fragmented, more comprehensible, than its existent alternative in the present' (2003: 82).

So work on memory can be seen to have challenged the very notion of the lin-earity of past, present and future. Feminist theorists (Grosz 1999; Radstone 2007) have also been at the forefront of critiques of linear assumptions of time, which are central here to understanding transtemporality in everyday experiences of the border. Radstone suggests that her exploration challenges the underlying linearity in accounts of cultural periodisation. I employ Radstone's view to explore the nar-rative accounts of CBST in Diyalivtsi. What emerges, as Radstone suggests, are not additive cause-and-effect relationships but contextually framed intertwinings of past and present. In considering transtemporality within the bordering context, it is also useful to draw upon Green's (2009) insights in her discussion of the relationship between borders, lines and time. In attempting to grasp the transtemporality of state borders, she makes particular use of the work of Jacques Derrida on traces. Unlike other theorists who have abandoned 'linear concepts' altogether, Green contends:

> I will tentatively suggest that some sense of line – denaturalised, made multiple, non-dichotomous, formed in trajectories and historically contingent – is still important for understanding a sense of borderli-ness. However, it is crucial that this sense of line not only evokes spatial location, but also time: one of the problems with line is that it appears to be a static entity, fixed in place, without time. (Green 2009: 3)

The contention that a trace, according to Derrida, could be seen to invoke something that never existed, i.e. has been imagined, in order to make sense of the present, is particularly useful and evident in the final section of this chapter. The Diyalivtsiany construct particular views of the Soviet period to make sense of their own actions in CBST. In doing so, however (and this is particularly pertinent to narrative analysis), such an invocation can also give meaning and understanding to pasts and futures. Green, therefore, concludes that 'Borders are replete with the traces of entities that have never existed. One could easily argue that the concept of nation is classically one of those entities' (Green 2009: 13).

If borders are replete with such traces, it seems clear that in processes of bordering, which are embedded in everyday experiences, we can also uncover traces of these imagined entities. The concepts of time and temporality are thus captured in these ideas of lines and traces. We can also look to Massey's work on space to understand the 'timeliness' of borders. Where Massey's work is particularly useful to our approach to situated, everyday bordering is in exploring the multiplicity which we have highlighted in our discussion of situatedness and in incorporating a sense of dynamism and change. Whilst Derrida sees spaces as 'dead time' (1997: 68), or in which time is stopped, Massey argues that space is entirely lively, constituting a 'simultaneity of stories so far' (Massey 2005: 12). Thus, space is the outcome of multiple relations, unpredictable happenings and everyday activities. This is because, Massey argues, the mere fact of being positioned means a difference from being positioned elsewhere.

Shame and crossing borders between Ukraine and Romania

I turn now to the ethnographic material from my research in the Ukrainian–Romanian borderlands to explore the transtemporality of shame. It is important to establish that Diyalivtsyany did express shame surrounding their engagement in the trade and particularly relating to their behaviours and use of female bodies to attract attention from Romanian border and customs officials during border crossings. Within public spaces, border-crossing narratives rarely recognised this feeling, thus opportunities for insight into expressions of shame generally came in smaller group conversations or within villagers' homes, such as the situation described in the introduction in relation to Zhenia's tears following her argument with Dima. Zhenia spoke to me on a number of occasions of the discomfort she had felt in trading across the border and the relief of being able to stay at home once she had become pregnant with the couple's son. Sveta, a woman in her late thirties who lived in Diyalivtsi, showed more visible signs of shame one day when Luchika and I talked to her about trading at her courtyard gate. As Sveta stood there, Luchika explained to me how her friend was very popular with the male border officials because of her buxom figure, at which Sveta blushed, looked down at the ground and tried to move the conversation on to the forthcoming show at the village hall. Whilst

Zhenia's mother-in-law had seen the cross-border small trading as a whole to be shameful, reflecting poor economic status, Sveta's blushes appeared to relate to the description of her behaviour during the border crossing. There was also a sense that trading was shameful not only because it highlighted the poor economic status of particular families in the village, but also because it evidenced on a day-to-day basis Ukraine's own reduced economic conditions in relation to neighbouring Romania. I thus seek to explore shame as relational across these scales, as well as temporally in relation to Diyalivtsyany narratives of pasts, presents and futures. Consequently, I have divided this discussion into three sub-sections. The first explores shame surrounding the sexualised performances of female bodies, which formed the basis of many crossings and to which Luchika referred in her discussion of Sveta's success. This section seeks to explore how shame is complexly bound up in these attempts to attract sexual attention from Romanian border guards and customs officials. The second section focuses on the phenomenon evident in Zhenia's account of her relationship with her mother-in-law and the view that trading across the border in itself is shameful to the individual as it highlights a low economic status and lack of other employment/income opportunities. Here, I explore how this relates to narratives of and encounters with politics and power. The final sub-section is concerned with how this process of shame-driven present narrative construction necessitates revisions to how the Diyalivtsyany talk about and construct a shared understanding of the Soviet period.

Shame and the everyday sexualised performance of CBST

The sexualised performance involved in CBST at the Ukrainian–Romanian border can be seen to be part of a wider 'sexuality of organisations' (Hearn and Parkin 1987: 3). As in other workplaces, male and female bodies are controlled to (re) produce (in this case primarily Romanian) gendered power relations. According to Hearn and Parkin, this process is evidenced through 'a mass of sexual displays, feelings, fantasies and innuendoes, as part of everyday organizational life' (1987: 3). Therefore, after Crang (1994), the informal spaces of CBST at the Ukrainian–Romanian border reflect other workplaces, in that they are sexualised through the adoption of sexualised work roles. I have previously written about the role of gender in cross-border small trade (Cassidy 2013), focusing on this sexualised performance of the female body and the creation of gendered spaces that prevent female traders from expanding their endeavours and lead to higher profitability for male traders. In this chapter, I want to take a slightly different look at this sexualised performance and consider how it generates shame in both the male and female traders who participate in it. For the people of Diyalivtsi, arousing the sexual desire or interest of the male Romanian border and customs officials lay at the heart of their endeavours. This meant that female border and customs officials were always to be avoided and were often depicted as outsiders in narratives of border crossing, as Luchika explained: 'You can always rely on Adi; I try to go to him. I never go to that woman, what's her name? She is really strange and she's always reporting us, as well as her colleagues.'

This arousal of interest is central to Probyn's analysis, as well as the ways in which shame 'highlights different levels of interest' (Probyn 2005: x). I suggest that the feigning of interest by Ukrainian traders offers a challenge to understanding the production of shame as the 'firing up' of affect (Tomkins, cited in Kosofsky Sedgwick and Frank 1995: 5). Such an affect would be involuntary, and in this understanding, it helps us to prioritise and determine where to focus our attentions. So in cross-border small trading the feigning of such interest does not have this prerequisite affect and it is the rational mind which dictates the process, as a conversation I overheard in Diyalivtsi between Luchika and Rodika, my host, demonstrates. Luchika was trying to persuade Rodika to start trading cigarettes across the border to generate much-needed income in her single-parent household:

> You've got large breasts. You'll have no trouble getting through the border. They like that, the men at the border. You know Sveta? She's just like you. When she started at the border she kept making mistakes, as she didn't know what she was doing. But she was bending down to pack her bag and one of the men noticed her breasts and he helped her. Now she uses them all the time and she has no problems at customs.

This being the case, then why would Diyalivtsyany feel any shame resulting from a spurning of their feigned interests? The answer, of course, lies in the complex social relations and norms, which govern such performances of interest (after Epstein 1984: 48), and also the intersection with the overall activity of trading. Or, perhaps, as Probyn has suggested, this is one of the many forms that interest could take (2005: 15). Whilst the interest in terms of seeking sexual relations with the border official may be feigned, the interest in gaining a 'real' response to the performance is genuine. We have to question whether this differs from an openly flirtatious individual, who frequently seeks the reciprocity of others' interest more out of habit than as a step to establishing relations with the other.

However, when I write of the shaming sexualised performance of cross-border small trading, I am also reminded of Kosofsky Sedgwick's conclusion that shame is in itself performance (2003: 38). Through this performance the subject is somehow brought into being at the very moment of being seen and acknowledged by another. If we think of Luchika and her description of Sveta's border crossing, we see how it is in that acknowledgement of her breasts, this 'noticing' that we sense his interest and perhaps even imagine Sveta's blushes, or as Kosofsky Sedgwick would describe them, her 'blazons of shame' (2003: 36). Yet it is these very signs of shame that open up a bridge – a form of communication – to our interlocutor. So whilst no sexual acts took place, flirtation on the part of female traders and discourses that drew attention to female companions on the part of male traders left them open to shame if their advances were not reciprocated and the necessary interest was not generated by their actions at the border. Whilst bribes were also often paid, such sexualised performances could also serve to encourage the acceptance of the bribe and to smooth passage through the border. Although many traders appeared confident in these performances at the border, smiling with the officials, laughing and joking, their actions and comments away from the border often gave a different sense of how such encounters invoked shame and made them feel uncomfortable.

This process raises questions concerning the visibility of shame; that is, an understanding which extends beyond the initial blush of shame to incorporate Probyn's suggestion of how we acknowledge and reflect on shame (2005). In fact, what was apparent from how experiences of CBST entered into popular narrative in Diyalivtsi was that little of this type of reflection had in fact taken place and the emergent stories told as jokes/humorous tales within the village generally failed to reflect at all on what brought this shame, but instead constructed a particular version of events that sought to reinforce the inferiority of the Romanian border guards and officials involved. This process was also reflected in how shame shaped narratives of the past. In almost all of these narratives, the Romanian officials become comic, slow, ignorant individuals, duped by the quick wits or audacity of the Ukrainian traders. For example, the references to 'King Kong' reflect this tendency – King Kong is portrayed as big and powerful but easily distracted by the sexualised performance of the traders. Officials who try to obstruct the trade lack intelligence and are dehumanised and unnamed, whereas those who permit the relatively easy passage of traders and goods become 'good guys', like Adi, who is referred to by Luchika in the earlier quote. In fact, Adi was the only official whose real name I heard used in the time I spent in Diyalivtsi and Chernivtsi.

The final aspect of shame relating to sexualised performance referred to above was the involvement of male traders, which challenged normative gendered relations within the local community. This was illustrated by a conversation I had with Zhenia, Luchika's daughter, who until the birth of her son had crossed the border on a regular basis with her husband to trade cigarettes.

> I used to cross the border as well, you know? There was one border guard there who really liked me. He knew I was married, as I used to cross with my husband, but he didn't seem to care. Dima encouraged him when he used to comment on me and he was always asking about me after I stopped crossing. I was glad after I had [my son] as I didn't have to cross any more. I didn't like how it felt.

I observed such practices on a number of occasions when travelling with Kostia, a trader from Chernivtsi. On one such trip in 2008, Kostia mentioned a young woman, who had been travelling in Kostia's minibus with her husband. When they reached the border, the customs official commented on the 'pretty girl' and Kostia encouraged the official to approach his minibus and inspect her more closely. The official did not speak to the young woman, but commented only to Kostia, who like many other drivers would seat younger women in the front of the minibus, whilst older women and men sat in the back. However, as with Zhenia's description, there was also an underlying shame, which was revealed by traders, such as Kostia, away from the border, about their part in these encounters. Many tried to 'undo' their role in discussions afterwards, placing the responsibility for the encounters firmly on the Romanian officials: 'Did you see the way that man [customs official at the border] talked about you? These Romanians are always after Ukrainian girls. They are really terrible. They are all married but they just don't care.'

In his narration of the story, Kostia does not acknowledge his own role. In fact, he actively speaks only of the Romanian official and removes himself completely. The objective of such a comment is clearly to redefine what was observed, to place the emphasis on the official and to avoid feeling shameful himself. Kostia knows that his own behaviour has been witnessed, but in framing the encounter in such a way, he does not need to acknowledge or reflect on this. It is the action of the official which is shameful, and to emphasise this he refers to the man's marital status. Ahmed (2014) argues that on a national level an apology for past shameful actions is to be avoided, as it could be seen as a declaration of responsibility. We can also understand why the villagers in Diyalivtsi never apologise for their behaviour at the border in a similar manner, as a lack of admission of responsibility. The shame that was felt in the act did not need an apology within their society because they all understood that the structural conditions which had brought about the act were not of their own making. At the same time, this does not mean that they do not regret the things they have to do in border crossing, but as Spelman (1997: 104) points out, such regrets do not assume responsibility.

Clandestine and covert activities offer a unique context to Darwin's observation regarding hiding and turning away in shame (cited in Probyn 2005), as cross-border small traders are already hiding. So whilst they may feel the urge to turn away, run or hide even in their border crossings, many stand and willingly face the shame of their encounters with Romanian border and customs officials. Therefore, in uncovering themselves in the process of cross-border small trading, as Luchika describes, female traders become open to shame, but they hide or cover the goods they are carrying across the border. At the heart of shame lies a juxtaposition of self and other, in which shame is of myself but in relation to how I appear to others (Sartre 1956: 221–222). Ahmed extends this to suggest that shame is bound up in a sense of who we are and not what we have done. However, in CBST, the actions of traders are intended to portray a particular sense of who they are – for female traders this means sexually available, so shame arises in this misrepresentation, as most female traders are not actually sexually available. Far from acting as a deterrent in this case, then (Ahmed 2014: 106), subjects collectively break the social ideal within CBST in order to enable and improve their opportunities at the border.

The source of shame for the cross-border small traders in their sexualised performance is evident in both Kostia's and Zhenia's narratives, i.e. social norms of gender relations, particularly after marriage. For the people of Diyalivtsi, gender relations are dominated by heteronormative assumptions and could be seen as restrictive in terms of conversations, never mind flirtations or any kind of attempt to demonstrate or gain the interest of a member of the opposite sex. As such, lone women were generally absent from social spaces within the village, such as the bar/restaurant or sauna, apart from during particular celebrations or events. Any man or woman who traversed these boundaries of restrictive gender relations would find themselves much gossiped about within the village in order to bring their behaviour back in line with these norms. This process of shaming was therefore also the basis of the shame when the traders sought the sexual attention and interest of the Romanian border officials in their crossings. Of course, the results of shaming for an individual or a community can be both stigmatising or reintegrative (Braithwaite 1989). However, in the case of cross-border small traders, within the local community and as a result of the re-narration of their border crossings, we could argue that the result is neither. The broader context to their shame means that they are able to avoid at least local-level stigmatisation to a certain extent, yet the need to continue to reproduce their households means they are not able to reintegrate into the norms of socio-economic life.

Shame and narratives surrounding the 'body politic'

As I began to suggest above, shame in the Diyalivtsi context was linked for a number of reasons to the local and wider political context. Evidently, shame implies some form of contact, and this is interesting in the Ukrainian–Romanian setting. After 1989, Romania's many years of isolation under Ceaușescu ended, and following the collapse of the Soviet Union in 1991, the border opened up for the first time in decades. Whilst initial contact was out of curiosity, for most Ukrainians it confirmed the narratives they had developed about the poor economic conditions in their neighbouring country: as Rodika said: 'People here don't live like poor people. Our way of life is not poor like it is there in Romania.' As this situation has changed in the two decades succeeding the collapse of socialism, so we have seen significant changes in the borderlands as a contact zone; in fact, a whole shifting of the zone itself. Border crossing in the 1990s and early 2000s did not involve shame for Ukrainians. By 2007, rather than being a curiosity, crossing had become a material imperative for the villagers. Tales of border crossing no longer centred on nights spent in local discos but instead focused on the difficulties of negotiating customs with cigarettes, as my neighbour Luchika explains: 'You know that sometimes they will send you back many times. I have to go and leave some cigarettes and try again. I always tell them I have three cartons and I pretend I don't speak Romanian if they ask anything else. Sometimes it can take six attempts, but I get through eventually.' If the narration of shame has the ability to disperse its effects across space to different places, then geographers need to consider this mobility of shame; its transcalarity and the ways in which it is displaced and the resulting relations of shame.

It is the broader understanding of CBST as a shameful occupation illustrated by Zhenia's narrative relating to her mother, which shaped the way in which villagers developed particular narratives surrounding their understanding of power relations and politics. So whilst shameful acts of border crossing do not threaten the social relations of Diyalivtsi – i.e. they reflect the existing stigmatisation of poorer families, such as Zhenia's – what they do reveal is their centrality in forming a basis for a new set of relations that strengthens the collective identity of the numerous households involved in the trade. The articulation (Crimp 2002: 66) of these narratives creates borders in the local context not only between those who trade and those who do not but also between the villagers and the political elite, who are generally portrayed on the national level, and thus create a separation between who they are and what it is to be Ukrainian. As the political and social elite in Kyiv are discredited, so are their attempts at 'nation building'. Nonetheless, it is in this process that we see evidence of the particularity and generality of shame and how it can be moved from one to the other; transformed from the particular shameful act of individual traders to a broader shame of Ukraine's political elite and its corruption that has led the villagers of Diyalivtsi to such actions. As Probyn might suggest, evident here is 'shame's passage from the physiological level to the sphere in which it becomes political' (2005: 79). She argues for a shame that is felt in individual bodies but also in the body politic. However, what happens in the case of Ukrainian cross-border small traders is that even as a collective they do not have the power to bring about this affect in the body politic. In fact, the body politic can stand amongst them, unshamed, even in full knowledge of their individual shame. In discussing this, I am reminded of the visit of Yulia Tymoshenko to Chernivtsi in September 2008, following severe flooding in the region that had closed the city's large market and source of much income for the region. As she stood on her raised platform in the middle of the flooded market and asked the people what they would have her do to help them, it struck me that here was a body both her own and representationally the body politic that was untouched by the shame, which the Diyalivtsyany and others placed on her in their everyday lives.

The only time during fieldwork that I encountered anyone within the village setting onto whom such a view of politics was projected was when I was summoned one morning to visit a neighbour, 'the policeman', who was rarely seen within the village. He and his wife lived a few doors down on the opposite side of the road, and whilst she was often to be seen out and about in the village, grazing their cow, making purchases in the shop, I had only ever seen him emerge from their courtyard to go out in his car and travel further afield. It became clear when speaking to him that he had little regard for the other villagers. He had been a mid-level policeman in the region prior to his retirement and Maria was his second wife. He had moved to Diyalivtsi after they married. They had one of the village's few 'original' two-storey homes[6] and on the Sunday I visited, I was informed of his views on Ukrainian politics. Dmitriy was a supporter of Yulia Tymoshenko, whose party at that time was called Bloc Tymoshenko, and he proudly showed me the notebooks and other branded stationery and pamphlets he had from the party. He was keen to impress upon me what an amazing woman and politician she was. However, more important than Dmitriy's political views was the reaction of my host Rodika when I returned home after the meeting with Dmitriy. 'What did he have to say? Did he talk to you about politics? It's all right for him to occupy himself with politics. He was a policeman, you know? So he has a big pension. He doesn't have to fight for money.' What is interesting here is that those involved in politics are removed from the shame of the everyday border crossing experiences of many of the others in Diyalivtsi and trading in general. Dmitriy is not present in the village narrative-making about trade because he does not participate or feel the shame associated with it. He is free to develop his views of politics separately from the trading activities, which otherwise dominate village life.

Among the issues that repeatedly emerged in Diyalivtsi and beyond were narratives that reflected upon the limited opportunities to create stable futures within Ukraine. In the context of shame, we can understand this as the ways in which the traders may have used their shameful activities in the present to overcome the potential shame and regret of not having done more for the future (after Sykes 2002). A discussion I had with Kostia about his house and his son perhaps best reflects this process.

> Yes, my house is outside Chernivtsi. I am building it. There are two floors and a large balcony ... I know there is only me, my wife and my son, but I have to build something for him as well. Who knows what there will be in the future? What if it is still the same? I want to be sure at least he has a house ... somewhere to live. I was always told that this was a safe thing to invest money in ... a house. Other things, I don't know ... I can't control, I suppose.

Kostia's own wife was not involved in CBST and his comments also link to some of the broader gender relations shaping and being shaped by trading. Lehtinen (1998: 56) argues that shame is gender-specific, with women feeling shame inwardly and men outwardly. In the case of cross-border small trading, it is difficult to compare gendered aspects of shame, since the role of male and female traders is different. Women 'know' shame differently in border crossing, because their bodies become the sites of 'interest', so whilst men may engage in the performance, the shame they feel from failure to engage 'interest' in their female companions is not felt at an individual level to the same extent as that of female traders focusing on themselves, and their own bodies. Nonetheless, it could be argued that the broader shame of the act of crossing the border itself could be felt more acutely by male traders because of gendered social norms, which place an emphasis on their role as 'breadwinners'.

Interestingly, Tomkins (cited in Kosofsky Sedgwick and Frank 1995) posits that those who have earlier been an object of shame find it easier to re-experience this later in life. It is almost as if their connection to shame has been established and needs only to be tapped into at a later date. So, for men like Kostia, who had earlier experienced the shame of not being able to provide for his family in Ukraine, the shame of CBST now forming their main occupation would be experienced more readily:

> I used to work in construction with a guy here, but I got tired of working and receiving no pay. Sometimes we would get paid and at other times we wouldn't and I couldn't rely on them. The boss was no good, a drunk. I had to find a way to get money on my own and not to have to rely on people like him. The construction sector is full of them.

Later, Kostia had also struggled as a migrant construction worker in Portugal: 'Many of the Ukrainians there didn't behave themselves whilst we were there, drinking and … you know. They had a bad reputation there. We tried to just get on with things and ignore them, because we didn't want people to think we were like them.' Shame in border crossing therefore reflected not only the shameful acts of sexualised performance but was relational to a broader shame of having to make such trips to Romania, 'the poorer neighbour'.

In the Ukrainian context we are dealing with a situation similar to that discussed by Blagg (1997) in his study of the Australian justice system's inability to employ reintegrative shaming with aborigines. The system's ability to shame is compromised by its own shameful past treatment of aborigines. Similarly, the shaming agency of the Ukrainian state is compromised by high-level corruption. But shame is not always to be feared. Perhaps the fear arises in the moments before the shaming activity and in the moments before the retelling of that activity, but its burden is lessened by repetition in cross-border small trading and by the reframing of what has been done in the narrative social settings of Diyalivtsi. In such a way, the possibilities for reproach are diminished and, therefore, become less feared. In answer to Probyn's question about how to voice shame without 'reshaming' the objects of shame (2005: 101), I am suggesting that anecdotes and storytelling enable such a 'non-shaming' voice. They are often very public, but fit in with existing oral tradition. This creates at least a normative format, even if the content of the narratives confirm shameful acts.

Through these narratives and anecdotes and also through their widespread collective experience, the fear of contempt associated with admitting shame (Piers 1971) can be alleviated at least within the immediate community. The failure of others to respond to the anecdotes or tales with a smile or laugh could lead to further social isolation (Johnston 2007: 37), but as Luchika's example demonstrates, this was not the case with traders in Diyalivtsi. These narratives had the sense of being well worn, and there was a confidence in the telling of these stories. This perhaps reflects the situation of others in the village who have not been involved in the trading, but may be prone to the shame of others (Kosofsky Sedgwick 2003: 14). 'But in interrupting identification, shame, too, makes identity. In fact, shame and identity remain in very dynamic relation to one another, at once deconstituting and foundational, because shame is both peculiarly contagious and peculiarly individuating' (Kosofsky Sedgwick 2003: 36).

However, unlike Kosofsky Sedgwick (2003: 37), I do not see the relationality emerging from shame as being entirely uncontrollable. The Ukrainian traders I encountered were able to gain some control over the impact of shame within their own communities, even if the impression left at the border was not the one they would have sought. There was a stigma that remained in place across the border, where the traders' ongoing activities fuelled stigmatising discourses about Ukrainians within Romania (Cassidy 2013). However, there was a relationship, which emerged in narratives concerning politics/power and the structural conditions leading to the proliferation of trading. In shifting the blame for trading onto 'the body politic', traders not only alleviated some of the social stigma associated with involvement in the trade locally but also began to link the trade to providing for more stable futures in the context of current instability. This gave a sense that addressing concerns and fears over their families' and communities' futures overshadowed the shame of trading. The economic benefits of the trade were of particular importance to male traders, as Kostia explained, who had struggled to meet the needs of their families through regular employment and migrant work overseas.

Shame and re-narrating the past in contemporary Ukraine

In this final section, I posit that the trade also formed the basis of nostalgia for the Soviet period in Diyalivtsi, which centred around people's ability to work and provide for their families. One day, I was watching a programme about furniture-making in the Soviet period with my host Rodika and she was keen that I understood the quality of the furniture produced at the time. 'Look! Such lovely furniture, and really good quality. I could afford to furnish my house in those days. I could afford everything I needed on my own salary.' Any problems associated with the Soviet period were seemingly under-communicated in Diyalivtsi. A conversation with Zhenia revealed her frustration with how the era is portrayed in the village: 'These people have just forgotten how bad it was. They have forgotten about all the beatings from the brigadier and how we couldn't do anything or go anywhere. All they remember is how much cheaper things were and how stable life was if you went to work, came home and didn't try and change anything.'

As we see in Zhenia's account, the creation of such memories involves having to split such positive aspects from the negative and traumatic elements of the period (Hirsch and Spitzer 2003: 84). For Hirsch and Spitzer, exile denoting temporal and geographical distance enables such a process. In Diyalivtsi, the present situation not only enables but also necessitates and demands that attention be given to the past. In fact, as border crossings continued in the present, such a need, for some, becomes urgent. In Hirsch and Spitzer's work they had to return to the physical location of their memories, a process which both authenticated and challenged the narrative. However, the villagers of Diyalivtsi still inhabit the same location they did during the Soviet period. Consequently, challenges to their narratives, such as Zhenia's, do not necessarily spell the demise of a dominant narrative, when the need for it is deemed to be greater than these tensions and contradictions. In other words, Zhenia points out that such a positive view of the Soviet period is evidently false, and blames this on 'forgetting'. However, I am suggesting that it is the shame felt in present experiences, derived from cross-border small trading in particular, which not only shapes positive narratives of the past but makes them more important in alleviating shame in the present. This is not an act of 'forgetting' but a purposeful, collective 're-making' of the past.

If ancestral shame can be transgenerational, then so a re-evaluation of a past that counters wider national shame can be reimagined in the present. If pasts take on new 'detail and color' (Probyn 2005: 110) when we explore them in terms of emotion, then we also need to consider that the emotions we feel in the present can shape these details and colour of the past, e.g. what once seemed very negative, something that at the time was to be escaped, can be reimagined as a past with at least some positive elements in the light of a compromised and shameful present. For Ukrainians, just as in colonial settings, this is possible given the recent Soviet past. Such an interpretation really begins to break down and challenge the focus on 'nostalgia' that has been ubiquitous in research on post-Soviet space (Nikolayenko 2008). Whilst such work has acknowledged that views of the Soviet period may have been shaped by economic difficulties associated with post-Soviet (and post-socialist) spaces, none has recognised the presence of shame in this reworking of the past; what we may consider to be a productive (after Warner 1999) outcome of the shame experience in border crossing.

However, the ways in which this narration then interlinks with views of the Soviet period create a much greater sense of how the narrator and the people of Diyalivtsi may become 'alienated tourists' of their pasts (Lambek and Antze 1996). What I posit here is that there is not one temporality to pasts, but many, and that in their narratives the traders and villagers of Diyalivtsi draw connections and move between these spaces within the context of everyday life. In some ways, this is part of Lambek and Antze's 'hermeneutic spiral of interpretation' (1996: xix), whereby one dominant view of the past is re-explored in the context of present events to be replaced by a new, emergent narrative. Away from the border and their trade, Diyalivtsyany are able to layer these past events into a narrative infused with meaning that shapes their consciousness of the present.

Part of this process of alienation links to the relationship with the Ukrainian state discussed in the section above. As Dima, a local shopkeeper, explained to me: 'These Ukrainians cannot run our country, they don't get anything right. I think we will probably just go back to how things were, you know? The East will go back to Russia, the West to Poland and us to Romania.' Therefore, as Blagg (1997) suggests in relation to the Australian state's ability to reintegrate aborigines, so the Ukrainian state's ability to rally its subjects behind an 'ideal' it creates is compromised as well through the shame that is displaced onto it in the narratives assigned by border traders. This does not mean that the desire for the ideal or pride in the nation is diminished, but instead that the belief that the political elite are the people who can lead the nation to this ideal is questioned. Rather than apologise for the past, which is the colonial perspective from which Ahmed takes her position, Ukrainian traders simply seek to see this elite do better in the present. In spite of regime change in Ukraine – each promising to do better than the last – there is no shift in the material situation in Diyalivtsi, so the shame of border crossing continues. If, as Johnston suggests, pride and shame can be viewed as co-constructed (2007: 33), then we can also understand this co-construction to take place across time and space. Unlike Ahmed's analysis of shameful pasts being appropriated for prideful nationalistic presents, the Ukrainian situation I analyse can be seen to be a co-construction of a prideful past in the context of a shameful present. This can then be linked to feelings of shame and pride in relation to potential futures. The point here is that we cannot understand this process of co-construction outside temporal shifts and change.

Conclusion

In this chapter, I have argued that in order to understand the border crossings made by traders in the Ukrainian–Romanian borderlands, we need to consider both shame and transtemporality. I have argued that shame emerges from attempts to elicit sexual interest from Romanian officials by both male and female traders, even though the interest on the part of the traders is feigned and does not reflect real attractions to their interlocutors. However, in both cases, narratives emerge away from the border, which seek not to reflect on the shame of such activities, but to place them in broader political and economic contexts, which transfer the shame to the body politic. At the same time, the use of existing comedic narrative forms of story-telling, particularly anecdotes, helps to alleviate the shame of admitting the activities within the context of the local society, where such performances would usually lead the traders to be the subject of stigmatisation, as they go well beyond the boundaries of what are considered to be appropriate interlocutions between men and women. Therefore, friends and neighbours, who could also become stigmatised on a broader level through the trade, are able to contribute to the repositioning of the activities through laughing along with the stories and agreeing with the emphasis and analysis given. Nonetheless, whilst this shifting of the individual to collective is successful on a local level, the traders and community of Diyalivtsi lack the power to impact on or give rise to shame in their intended targets – national-level politicians and 'the body politic' as a whole. However, as the shame becomes relational through narrative across the levels discussed above, so we can also gain insight into how this present shame shapes views of the past and links to the academic literature on memory. The Soviet period is reviewed in the context of the shame felt as subjects of a state, which does not acknowledge its role in creating the shame of every day in CBST. What emerges are narratives of the past that split the negative aspects of life in the Soviet Union from those which are considered to be positive. Such revisions do not go unchallenged, as we have seen, but were still able to become dominant in Diyalivtsi because of the collective effort to displace and try to move away from the individual and collective shame arising from CBST.

Notes

1 Diyalivtsi is a pseudonym for the village in the Chernivets'ka region in which I carried out participant observation in 2007–8.
2 The economic importance of the trade was considerable, with almost all households having been touched to some extent either directly or indirectly by these activities (Cassidy 2013).
3 Inhabitants of Diyalivtsi.
4 According to statistics collected by the village council and dated August 2005.
5 In June 2008, cigarettes costed from as little as 30 cents (0.3 euro) per pack of twenty in Ukraine but retailed in Romanian shops across the border from around 1.5 euros per pack of twenty.
6 Most two-storey homes had been built after 1991, as a result of funds generated from migrant labour or CBST. The handful of older two-storey homes belonged to those who had occupied positions of authority/power during the Soviet period, such as the head of the collective farm.

References

Ahmed, S. (2014) *The Cultural Politics of Emotion.* 2nd edn. Edinburgh: Edinburgh University Press.

Allina-Pisano, J. (2009) 'From iron curtain to golden curtain: remaking identity in the European Union borderlands', *East European Politics and Societies,* 23(2): 266–290.

Blagg, H. (1997) 'A just measure of shame? Aboriginal youth and conferencing in Australia', *British Journal of Criminology,* 37(4): 481–501.

Braithwaite, J. (1989) *Crime, Shame and Reintegration.* Cambridge: Cambridge University Press.

Cassidy, K. L. (2013) 'Gender relations and cross-border small trading in the Ukrainian–Romanian borderlands', *European Urban and Regional Studies,* 20(1): 91–108.

Crang, P. (1994) 'It's showtime: on the workplace geographies of display in a restaurant in southeast England', *Environment and Planning D: Society and Space,* 12: 675–704.

Crimp, D. (2002) *Melancholia and Moralism: Essays on AIDS and Queer Politics.* Cambridge, MA: MIT Press.

Derrida, J. (1997) *Of Grammatology,* trans. G.C. Spivak. Baltimore, MD: Johns Hopkins University Press.

Epstein, A.L. (1984) *The Experience of Shame in Melanesia: An Essay in the Anthropology of Affect.* London: Royal Anthropological Institute of Great Britain and Ireland.

Foucault, M. (1997) 'The ethics of the concern for self as a practice of freedom', in P. Rabinow (ed.) (trans. R. Hurley), *Michel Foucault: Ethics, Subjectivity and Truth, the Essential Works of Michel Foucault 1954–1984,* Vol. 1. London: Penguin.

Green, S.F. (2009) *Lines, Traces and Tidemarks: Reflections on Forms of Borderli-ness,* COST

Action IS0803 Working Paper 1. www.eastbordnet.org/working_papers/open/docu ments/Green_Lines_Traces_and_Tidemarks_090414.pdf. Accessed 9 August 2016.

Grosz, E. (1999) *Becomings: Explorations in Time, Memory and Futures*. Ithaca, NY: Cornell University Press.

Hacking, I. (1995) *Rewriting the Soul: Multiple Personality and the Sciences of Memory*. Princeton, NJ: Princeton University Press.

Hearn, J. and W. Parkin (1987) *'Sex' at 'Work': The Power and Paradox of Organization Sexuality*. Brighton: Wheatsheaf.

Hirsch, M. and L. Spitzer (2003) '"We Would Not Have Come Without You": generations of nostalgia', in K. Hodgkin and S. Radstone (eds), *Contested Pasts: The Politics of Memory*. London: Routledge, pp. 79–95.

Johnston, L. (2007) 'Mobilizing pride/shame: lesbians, tourism and parades', *Social & Cultural Geography*, 8(1): 29–45.

Keough, Leyla T. (2006) 'Globalizing "postsocialism": Mobile mothers and neoliberalism on the margins of Europe', *Anthropological Quarterly*, 79(3): 431–461.

Konstantinov, Y. (1996) 'Patterns of reinterpretation: trader-tourism in the Balkans (Bulgaria) as a picaresque metaphorical enactment of post-totalitarianism', *American Ethnologist*, 23: 762–782.

Kosofsky Sedgwick, E. (2003) *Touching Feeling: Affect, Pedagogy, Performativity*. Durham, NC: Duke University Press.

Kosofsky Sedgwick, E. and A. Frank (1995) 'Shame in the cybernetic fold: reading Silvan Tomkins', in E. Kosofsky Sedgwick and A. Frank (eds), *Shame and its Sisters: A Silvan Tomkins Reader*. Durham, NC: Duke University Press, pp. 496–522.

Lambek, M. and P. Antze (1996) 'Introduction', in M. Lambek and P. Antze (eds), *Tense Past: Cultural Essays in Trauma and Memory*. London: Routledge, pp. xi–xxxviii.

Lehtinen, U. (1998) 'How does one know what shame is?', *Hypnatia*, 13(1): 56.

Massey, D. (2005) *For Space*. London: Sage.

Nikolayenko, O. (2008) 'Contextual effects on historical memory: Soviet nostalgia among post-Soviet adolescents', *Communist and Post-Communist Studies*, 41(2): 243–259.

Nora, P. (1989) 'Between memory and history: Les lieux de mémoire', *Representations*, 26: 7–254.

Piers, G. (1971) *Shame and Guilt: A Psychoanalytic and a Cultural Study*. New York: Norton.

Polese, A. (2006) 'Border crossing as a daily strategy of post soviet survival: the Odessa–Chisinau elektrichka', *Anthropology of Eastern Europe Review*, 24(1): 28–37.

Probyn, E. (2005) *Blush: Faces of Shame*. Minneapolis: University of Minnesota Press.

Radstone, S. (2007) *The Sexual Politics of Time: Confession, Nostalgia, Memory*. New York: Routledge.

Sartre, J-P. (1956) *Being and Nothingness*. New York: Philosophical Library.

Spelman, E. (1997) *Fruits of Sorrow: Framing Our Attention to Suffering*. Boston, MA: Beacon.

Stoetzler, M. and N. Yuval-Davis (2002) 'Standpoint theory, situated knowledge and the situated imagination', *Feminist Theory*, 3(3): 315–334.

Sword, K. (1999) 'Cross-border "suitcase trade" and the role of foreigners in Polish informal markets', in K. Iglicka and K. Sword (eds), *The Challenge of the East–West Migration for Poland*. London: Macmillan, pp. 145–167.

Sykes, K. (2002) 'The gift of shame: the invention of postcolonial society', *Social Analysis*, 46(1): 12–25.

Warner, C. (1999) *The Trouble with Normal: Sex, Politics and the Ethics of Queer Life*. New York: Free Press.

Williams, A.M. and V. Balaz (2002) 'International petty trading: Changing practices in Trans–Carpathian Ukraine', *International Journal of Urban and Regional Research*, 26(2): 323–342.

4

Travelling genealogies:
tracing relatedness and diversity in the
Albanian–Montenegrin borderland[1]

Jelena Tošić

> Oh, you come from our relatives in Albania. Welcome, welcome. Our door is always
> open to you. Are you hungry? Please stay for lunch. How are our relatives? Send them
> kind regards and tell them that we are looking forward to seeing them again soon.
> Come, stay for lunch. My son will be here in a minute. (cited from fieldnotes)

This astonishingly warm welcome was immediately followed by a breathtak-
ing moment. When Rustem – my co-traveller – and I entered the house of Ilija
Karadaglić's 85-year-old widow, Marija, in the village of Vranj (see Figure 4.1),
we really did not expect to find what was hanging on the wall to our left, so that it
would be the first thing visitors would see. It was the most complete version of the
Sarapa family tree we had seen so far and we were totally unaware of its existence.
The small genealogical fragment we had been carrying with us for weeks seemed
inconsequential compared to the magnificent and artistic genealogy comprising
twelve families and going back to the fifteenth century that had been compiled by
Colonel Vaso Vukičević in 1959 (see Figure 4.2).[2]

However, we were not the first visitors who, by following the 'genealogical' path,
had knocked on the door of the Karadaglić family. About thirteen years before, the
Ymeri brothers from Koplik in Albania – whose family tree we carried with us – had
crossed the Montenegrin–Albanian border immediately after its reopening in 1990.
The two brothers, who were well-known dentists about to open a private clinic on
the outskirts of Koplik, were fulfilling their father's last wish: to re-establish contact
with their relatives in Montenegro, contact that had been almost entirely lost by the
closure of the border in 1948.

In the course of my research on the coexistence of ethnically and religiously
diverse populations in the Shkodra region (see Figure 4.1), where I collected life
stories and family histories, I encountered several cases of family (re-)connection,
including the reconstruction of genealogies. Having framed my research as a
regional comparison (Gingrich and Fox 2002), I was drawn into this ongoing
'genealogical cross-border movement' and became both a 'witness' and at times

even an agent of family reconnection. I decided to trace the genealogical trajectories and relations and use them as a compass for capturing regional cross-border mobility and relatedness (Carsten 2000). In particular, however, I was interested in their interrelation with local diversity patterns, understood as modes of differentiation and accommodating difference (e.g. Vertovec 2009). In this sense, the Sarapa case proved to be highly instructive.

Indeed, the intra-regional comparison soon revealed a significant difference between two main migratory and hence 'genealogical trajectories' connecting Albania and Montenegro: one leading from Shkodra and its surroundings to Ulcinj, and the other one from Shkodra up to Tuzi and Podgorica (see Figure 4.1). While genealogies marked by migration between Ulcinj and Shkodra were clearly mono-ethnic and mono-confessional (Albanian–Muslim), the Sarapa genealogy – which included relations stretching across present-day Albania and Montenegro north of Lake Shkodra – featured an extraordinary diversity and inclusiveness that incorporated practically all local ethno-national, religious and ideological/political 'categories'. Here, people declaring themselves to be Albanians, Montenegrins, Serbs, Yugoslavs, Christians and Muslims, democrats or socialists – allegiances that entailed tensions and conflicts in other parts of the Balkans – were not merely relatives, but respected the individual freedom of self-denomination.

In this chapter I use episodes from my journey along the Sarapa genealogical pathway to explore the interrelatedness of human and border mobility and inclusivity of diverse population patterns. I will show how the narrative and biographical movement through, and the shared knowledge of, the border region within different time-spaces is constitutive of the openness to diversity that characterises this northern Montenegrin–Albanian borderland in the Sarapa case.

Furthermore, I will show how in the case of a particular inclusive kinship practice and genealogical representation, ethno-national and religious diversity – although prominently featured – are but two aspects of diversity understood in a multi-dimensional (Vertovec 2007, 2009) and intersectional (e.g. Yuval-Davis 2011) manner, where citizenship, cross-border migration background, gender, bilingualism and political and ideological positions also play a vital role. The chapter thus follows the call to take seriously the salience of ethno-nationalism in the Balkans, while accepting the need to go 'beyond' conventional analyses (e.g. Verdery 1994; Duijzings 2003; Bougarel et al. 2007; Tošić 2015a) and avoiding the reproduction of the Balkanist stereotype of the ethno-national 'powder keg'.

I conclude by suggesting that the kind of inclusive diversity pattern revealed through genealogies and modes of relatedness characteristic of the border region that is the focus here is one of the important factors for peaceful coexistence: that is, the lack of ethno-national violence. Moreover, I argue that the border legacy of peaceful coexistence should be considered within the ongoing process of EU integration, which – through its focus on minority rights – has so far strengthened rather than transcended ethno-national allegiance.

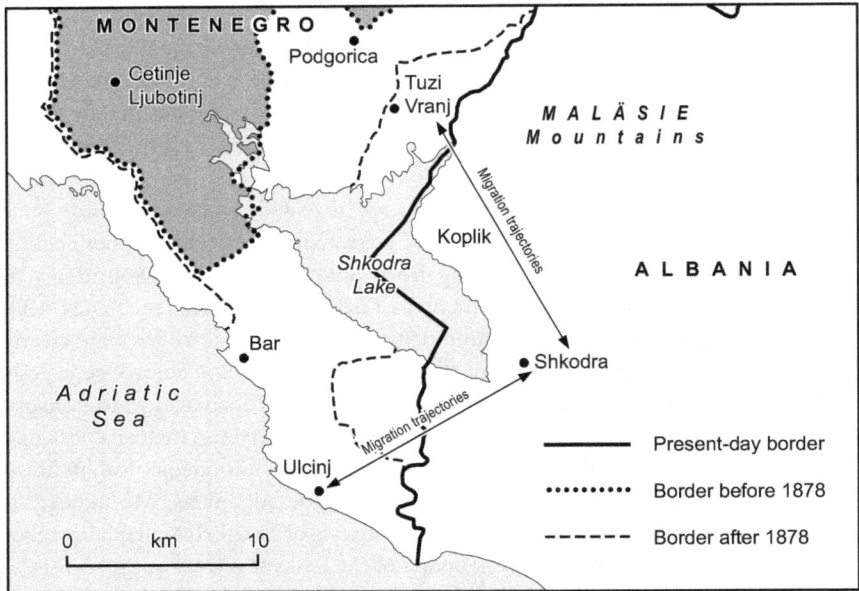

4.1 The Shkodra region: border movements, migration trajectories and localities

Moving and crossing borders: mapping genealogical time-space

The border between present-day Montenegro and Albania features several significant spatial shifts through time and different socio-political contexts. Although necessarily reducing the historical–spatial complexity of border movements, the map
in Figure 4.1 emphasises three distinct time-space border fixations. The dotted line
represents the border up to the Treaty of Berlin (1878), which not only recognised
Montenegro's independence, but extended to it significant territorial gains (as
indicated by the shaded area). The solid line indicates the present-day state border,
whose ground was laid at the beginning of the twentieth century.

The border was marked not only by time-space shifts, but also by shifting degrees
of porosity and enclosure, as successive border regimes transformed the landscape
in different ways. Under the Ottoman Empire in the mid-nineteenth century, the
area was a frontier rather than the border 'line' that came to typify post-Westphalian
Europe as naturalised, timeless and self-evident (see, e.g. Green 2009). Like other
'shatterzones of empire' (Bartov and Weitz 2013), this imperial borderland was
marked by permeability, brisk and diverse forms of mobility, 'flexible' governance strategies and ambivalent loyalties among the population (e.g. Reinkowski
2003; Blumi 2003). As Reinkowski argues, it was the distinctive dynamics of the
Ottoman–Montenegrin border that contributed to shifting identities, boundaries and allegiances among the local population. Local people found themselves

between the 'soft' margins of Ottoman rule on the one hand and, on the other, the political strategies of the Montenegrin rulers whose goal was to shift the border in their favour. Hence repeated border crossings, conversion to Islam or intermarriage were common social practices in the Montenegrin–Ottoman borderland.

After having been marked – although still permeable and contested – by more pronounced linearity due to the post-imperial rise of the nation-state in the Balkans and the emergence of contested national borders, the year 1948 represents a crucial rupture in the history of the Albanian–Montenegrin borderland. From 1948 onwards Enver Hoxha's totalitarian and isolationist regime transformed Albanian borders into almost impermeable 'death zones'. 'Even the birds were afraid to fly over the border' was a phrase I often heard during my fieldwork in Albania, which clearly expressed the collective trauma of a life marked by repression, fear and highly restricted mobility. The few individuals who could cross the border legitimately – for example athletes – were often covert 'messengers' carrying letters to relatives beyond. The even fewer individuals who managed to flee – whose families often did not even know of their plan – did not as a rule carry messages due to the clandestine and highly risky nature of their one-way journeys to 'free' and 'modern' Yugoslavia.

After the fall of the authoritarian socialist regime in Albania in 1990, the reopened border to Montenegro (at that time a Yugoslav republic) became the space of travelling goods and people both legally and illegally. Apart from the political and economic aspects of the reopening of the border after more than 40 years, a crucial socio-cultural dimension of the cross-border process was the (re)discovery and revival of family ties. Most of all Albanians, longing for reconnection with the 'outside world' after decades of almost hermetic isolation, reached out for their known and unknown relatives led by surnames and genealogical fragments. The Montenegrins, on the other hand, as in the case of the Sarapa 'genealogists,' as we shall see below, were as much driven by curiosity as by a desire for family reunion. Albania represented the ultimate socialist 'other' in contrast to Yugoslavia's open borders, freedom of movement and global non-aligned political agency.

The two main reasons for cross-border movement between Albania and Montenegro – family reunion and trade – were mutually constitutive. The kinship-led border crossers were joining the large-scale cross-border movement connected to the retail trade and smuggling, which was especially profitable during the international trade embargo on the Federal Republic of Yugoslavia. At the same time, these family ties to Montenegro and bilingualism were crucial for becoming a successful border entrepreneur. In many cases initial encounters between relatives led to regular border crossing for mutual visits and eventually to the (re)building of close personal and trade relationships that persist to the present day.

Genealogies, genealogists and diversity

Apart from exemplifying early anthropological 'mimicking' of natural science epistemologies,[3] the genealogical mode of thought has been the object of substantial critique in anthropology due to its tacit essentialist and binary (nature/culture) implications. However, the genealogical paradigm remains relevant in anthropology, since it 'not only figures centrally in organizing knowledge about the world alone but is also implicit in structuring those social institutions and relations that give our social world its form and meaning' (Bamford and Leach 2009: 2–3).

Following the many critiques of the genealogical method, my aim is not to reconstruct a historical genealogical 'truth'. Rather, I aim to explore how and when people narrate and (re)present their genealogical knowledge, and how they relate to each other while referring to it. In other words, I am principally concerned with what people actually 'do' with genealogies. The heuristic notion of 'relatedness' (Carsten 2000: 5) is a useful conceptual tool, since it makes graspable relations grounded on claimed and genealogically 'proven' 'natural' kinship connections, as well as those based on other kinds of relations (such as historical knowledge, trade relations and friendship) which evolve around the process of family reunion.

My epistemological approach is both emic and narrative-praxeological. In the first sense I have taken up the local prominence and similarity patterns of social organisation in the Montenegrin and Albanian part of the Shkodra region. The region is historically characterised by an exogamous patrilineage and tribal system,[4] a pronounced knowledge and socio-political relevance of relations based on reference to genealogical and symbolic kinship,[5] similar customary law patterns[6] and patriarchy (e.g. Djilas 1958; Kaser 1992; Morrison 2009).

In the second sense, I conceptualise the ethnographic reality of genealogy, which people were reconstructing and literally carrying around, as a narrative (and) agency space.[7] In other words, I appropriate the local prominence of the genealogical mode of representation and relatedness as a 'sensor' for inquiring into modes of accommodating various dimensions of social differentiation as well as the dynamics of life in a border region. Genealogy figures here as a 'boundary marker' (Heiss and Slama 2010), exemplifying specific modes of exclusion and inclusion, and as a medium of narrating the historical dynamics of population diversity in the Albanian–Montenegrin borderland.

The case of kinship (re)connection in the context of a transforming borderland immediately after the end of a highly restrictive border regime is a particularly interesting setting for inquiring into modes of dealing with difference. To begin with, it includes people who have in many cases never seen each other before, and who in spite of spatial proximity lived in radically different socio-political environments, have different educational and social statuses and mobility biographies and potentially refer to different readings and segments of family and regional history.

Genealogies themselves – as relational and historical narrative 'maps' – had a crucially different significance in the Yugoslav and Albanian parts of the borderland. While in Montenegro genealogical knowledge and 'activity' was not sanctioned, in Albania under Hoxha genealogies evolved almost as secret knowledge, an instance of which the local significance of genealogies in Shkodra – the present-day urban centre of northern Albania and one of the most important urban units in the Ottoman Balkans – can serve as a prime example. During my fieldwork I realised that the reconstruction of family history and genealogy was a way of reappropriating social status after the trauma of the Hoxha regime, which *inter alia* aimed at literally erasing urban middle-class identity. In Shkodra, which as one of the strongholds of the urban middle class was particularly targeted by the Hoxha regime, the dominant discourse of incorporation centred on urbanity. The prime 'other' of the urban resident (*cytetar*) is the 'hill dweller' and the peasant (*malisor* and *katundar*), who can, however, accommodate to the urban way of life. A crucial aspect of the latter – usually expressed through the metaphor of 'calmness' – is their alleged 'inherent' tolerance for ethno-religious diversity and the associated peaceful habitus of the urban dwellers (Tošić 2015b). The main collective agents of the urban middle-class discourse are the so-called 'old families' (*familje e vijeter*) whose existence and legitimisation depend literally on the production of genealogies. This is best exemplified by the work of Hamdi Bushati, whose two volumes on the history of Shkodra together with his genealogical booklet containing the family trees of the old families (Bushati 1998, 1999a, 1999b) graced the bookshelves of every family I visited in Shkodra. The following statements represent the quest of many Shkodra families to belong to the class of old families, a quest that motivated the reconstructive 'genealogical activities':

> 'We should have been in the book.' 'At the time we were asked to provide our genealogy, we still haven't reconstructed it.' 'Ours is a real old Shkodra family. You can find us and our family tree in Bushati's book.' 'Many old families were left out by Bushati.'

Hamdi Bushati's book, which is both held in high regard and seen as incomplete, became the encyclopaedia of old Shkodra families and as such expressed the middle-class discourse on urbanity and incorporation within which genealogies served as documents of old-family pedigree (Tošić 2015b).

By contrast, families in Albania with kinship ties to Montenegro had to hide their genealogies during the totalitarian Hoxha regime, since any link to Yugoslavia was likely to result in even greater surveillance than that experienced by other Albanian citizens and could lead, for example, to denial of access to higher education. Thus it is understandable why the Ymeri brothers waited for the end of the regime and the opening of the border before attending to their father's dying wish to reach out to their relatives across the border. As Bajram Ymeri remarked when explaining why genealogical information was top secret: 'No one was supposed to know. Otherwise we would have never been allowed to study! This would have been a huge problem for us!' The genealogists in this case were generally fathers and grandfathers, who communicated genealogical knowledge to their children surreptitiously and by word of mouth.

In Montenegro the situation was crucially different. Genealogical knowledge, although part of the standard cultural repertoire, never acquired such a huge significance, since it was never sanctioned. Within the Yugoslav context, the Montenegrin focus on kinship and local history was (and still is) both envied and ridiculed. In the manner of 'nesting Orientalisms' (Bakić-Hayden 1995), it was ascribed to the 'more traditional' and 'tribal' 'Montenegrin mentality' as opposed to the urban, individualistic and nuclear family mode of 'Yugoslav' and 'socialist' sociality.

The Montenegrin genealogists I encountered in the course of my Sarapa travels were usually older men who were interested in family history and who devoted their life to genealogical research after their retirement. Their prime motives were twofold: first, preserving the history of the family and situating it within the context of the history of Montenegro; and second, reuniting relatives and keeping relations based on kinship 'alive'. The historiographical work can be characterised as a transnational and systematic collection of sources (letters, documents, pictures, obituaries, historiographical references and notes made by different relatives) by a number of persons – sometimes in cooperation, but sometimes in competition – that resulted in meticulous private archives, genealogical drawings and internet sites (as in the Sarapa case).[8] 'I gathered all this because one should know about one's family. The young people are usually not interested', Jovan Vukičević – a retired director of a furniture factory living in a small 'socialist' flat in Podgorica with his wife – told us as he unpacked mountains of material on the Sarapa in front of our eyes. His genealogical and historical work, which became his main preoccupation after retirement, aims to preserve knowledge of the Sarapa as 'one of the best Montenegrin *bratstvo*'.[9] Jovan emphasised the uniqueness of the Sarapa, by pointing not only to their courage in resisting the Turkish invasion (from the fifteenth century onwards), but also by stressing the internal diversity and inclusiveness of this *bratstvo*. He saw no problem in being genealogically related to Muslims and Albanians. Nor did an 'unproven' genealogical connection prevent him from offering his potential relative, Isa Paljević, a job in his company, as we shall see below. Jovan's overarching 'genealogical' goal might even be characterised as 'setting right' the history of Montenegro in general and in terms of its inner diversity – in particular, in terms of the inclusion of Islam.

> The Turks were present in Montenegro, although we say we were never invaded. They were indeed here ... You will find very few Montenegrin families where no one converted to Islam. But people are hiding this fact, they think it is a crime ... I don't have a problem with that. It is a matter of individual choice. The important thing is, if someone is a good person.

The second of the two motives of 'genealogical agency' mentioned above – reuniting relatives and keeping kinship ties alive – also includes valuing diversity and inclusiveness as an integral part of kinship relations and family history. As Bajram Ymeri narrates the early days of his genealogical travels to Montenegro, he recalls how he and his brother were hosted by different families for weeks and were proudly introduced to still unknown relatives. The scene he repeatedly recalls as 'the most magnificent moment of family reunion' is when Stevan Karadaglić – one of the relatives with whom they had the closest relationship and who added the Ymeri branch to the Sarapa genealogy – presented the brothers to the assembled relatives following the funeral of his wife. 'I will tell you who these men are. They are our relatives from Albania. Every one of you should know that.' The Albanian-speaking Stevan in turn laid out in great detail the family history for the some fifty relatives gathered at his wife's funeral, giving special attention to the origin of the Ymeri branch of the Sarapa. Bajram Ymeri and his brother were close to tears. Their father's dying wish was finally fulfilled.

'This was all Turkey, you know': border legacies, conversion and genealogical inclusiveness

In order to contextualise fully the genealogical, narrative and relational framework this chapter emphasises, one must start from the 'beginning' – the founding myth of the Sarapa genealogy. This narrative is the overarching reference point for individuals recounting genealogical 'evidence' and is an integral part of the most complete genealogical representation of the Sarapa (see Figure 4.2).

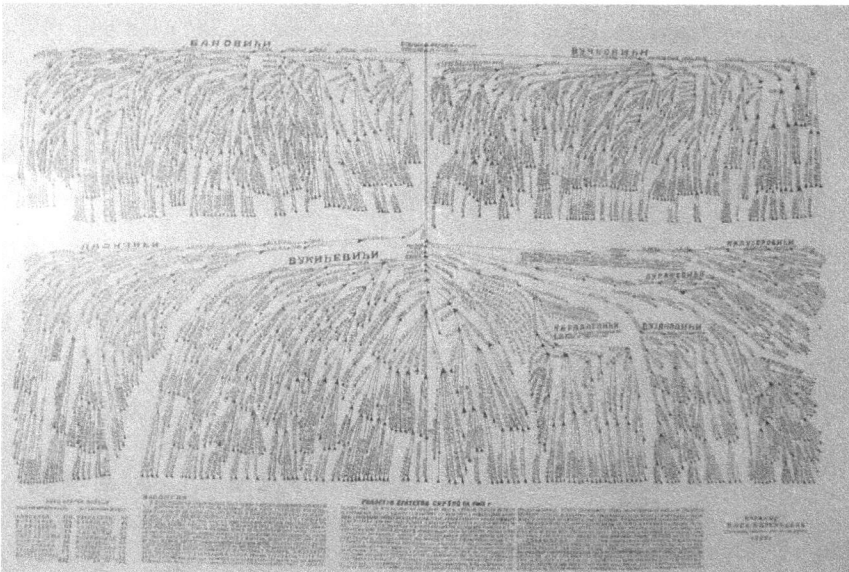

4.2 The Sarapa genealogy by Vaso Vukičević, 1959

The ancestor of all the Sarapa – Božina Sarap – from whom 12 families derive their origin today, is said to have come from present-day Bosnia (the village of Sarapovina) to Montenegro in 1465, two years after the Ottomans conquered Bosnia. The grand narration that all agree upon, regardless of confessional and national affiliation, is that Božina Sarap was one of the 'brave' men who came to the (still) not occupied 'Old Montenegrin'/Zeta lands (see Figure 4.1, shaded area) to fight against the Ottomans and protect both Montenegro and Christianity. After conflict and subsequent reconciliation with the local lord Ivan Crnojević,[10] Ivan granted Božina a piece of land. This is how Božina settled near Cetinje (the village of Boguti in the region of Ljubotinj), worked the land and remained a respected servant of Lord Crnojević. He built a church for Saint Nikola – whom the Sarapa venerate as their family saint (krsna slava) – next to which he was buried and where his descendants built a statue in 1930 in honour to the founder of the bratstvo.

As already mentioned, for centuries life in the Montenegrin–Ottoman borderland was marked by war and shifting borders. Božina's descendants, like all the inhabitants of this borderland, lived in a situation of ongoing conflict with the Turkish army and administrators determined to collect taxes. War against the Ottomans was not the only hardship for the locals, nor was the constant re-establishment of the Ottoman frontier the only mode of engaging with the shifting border. Blood feuds and poverty frequently led to cross-border migration to 'Turkey'. Virtually every genealogical narrative I collected during fieldwork identified blood feuds as the primary cause of cross-border migration. Flight across the border was often accompanied by a change of family name and sometimes by conversion to Islam, which would prevent being identified as a target by potential assassins. Without denying the possibility of the blood feuds' impact on historical migration dynamics, its narrative deployment illustrates an interesting interrelation and mutual constitution of the border and local social formations and systems of value. The border here functions, one could argue, as a way both to comply with and reproduce the local socio-legal organisation and to outwit it by 'camouflaging' patrilineal identity. Furthermore, the mutual relation of local social organisation and customary law and the opportunities afforded by a life in the imperial borderland enabled the emergence of inclusive diversity patterns, as we shall see in the case below.

The case of the Vukičević, a sub-branch of the Sarapa (see Figure 4.3), follows the narrative pattern outlined above in which a blood feud features as the cause of cross-border migration. In the mid-nineteenth century three brothers of the Vukičevići – Mijat, Božo and Paljo – fled across the border to 'Turkey' to save their lives.

Two of the brothers, Mijat and Božo, changed their name to Karadag, which in Turkish means Montenegrin, and their progeny are the present-day Karadaglić, who are Orthodox Christians and consider themselves to be Serbs.[11] The third one, Paljo, is said to have married a rich Muslim woman, and his offspring are the present-day Paljević (see Figure 4.4), who see themselves as Muslims and Albanians.

4.3 The Vukičević (Karadaglić and Paljević) branch of the Sarapa genealogy

Even if not all present-day Vukičević, Karadaglić and Paljević are involved in intense everyday relations, they know of and refer to each other as relatives. Although an important aspect of their practice of relatedness is a narrative one that transcends the present time-space context, genealogical relatedness and shared narratives can crucially shape relations in the present. Jovan Vukičević's decision to employ his (most probably) relative Isa Paljević can serve as a good example in this regard. For Jovan, this act represented a continuation of kinship solidarity between the Vukičević and the Paljević, an act that transcended both time and space. In a directly associated narrative, Jovan recalled how in 1941 when his father was on his way to the Albanian front to retrieve his horse, he was hosted by the Paljević in Tuzi. After sharing their knowledge about what was going on in Albania, the Paljević finally convinced Jovan's father not to go, and thereby actually saved his life.

The practice of symbolic kinship in public represents a crucial expression of relatedness among the Sarapa in the present time-space context. 'Standing in the line of family members' (*stajanje u redu*) at funerals exemplifies demonstrative kinship practice. In the following quote, Marko Karadaglić recalls how a guest at his uncle's funeral wondered how the Muslim Redzo Paljević could stand in the family line:

> You know, sometimes someone asks, like for example, when my uncle died and Redzo was standing in the line – you know, when someone dies, the relatives stand in the line – and someone asked me, 'How can Redzo stand in your line? He is a Muslim!' And I said, 'Of course he stands in our line, He is my relative!'[12]

The specific feature of this genealogy and the present-day practice of kinship based on it – the inclusion of Islam in a Montenegrin family tree, in which the apical ancestor (Božina Sarap) had once fought against Islam to protect Christianity – becomes even more astonishing when one considers the hegemonic historical image of conversion. The following verse from the famous 'Mountain Wreath', in which the Montenegrin Prince-Bishop and poet Petar II Petrović Njegoš speaks through Prince Danilo who cites the Ottoman Sultan, describes and harshly condemns the policy of Islamisation seen as the alternative for the failed military conquest by the Ottomans:[13]

> Montenegro I cannot win or tame,
> nor call it mine in any real sense;
> this is how one should deal with its people.
> And so began the devil's Messiah
> to offer them sweetmeats of his false faith.
> May God strike you, loathsome degenerates,
> why do we need the Turk's faith among us?[14]

The religious inclusiveness which the Sarapa genealogy exemplifies is unthinkable in some other parts of Montenegro, where families who converted to Islam are not to be found on family trees. Moreover, it is equally unlikely that persons declaring an identity other than Montenegrin, such as the Paljević who consider themselves Albanians, will be included in genealogies. They simply cannot be considered relatives.

How is the extraordinary inclusivity of the Sarapa genealogy and the kinship practice based on it to be understood and explained against this background? The specificity of the borderland dynamics described earlier – the legacy of the semi-permeable, contested and shifting border – is clearly one factor. That the history of the Sarapa unfolded in the former Ottoman–Montenegrin borderland is a crucial part of the explanation of its inclusivity and ambiguity. Hence it is not surprising that the genealogies and conversations I recorded described migrations across the old border to the Ottoman territory – as in the case of the Vukićević – and uses them to legitimise the transformation of ethnic and religious identity in the region up to the present day.

'This was Turkey, you know', my interlocutors kept on repeating, highlighting that conversion cannot undo kinship relations. Marko Karadaglić explained his view of the conversion of the Paljević as follows: 'They accepted this new religion, but they remained our relatives. Their ancestor, Paljo, simply turned to the new faith, but a relative stays a relative. Nothing can work without relatives. People turned to Islam because they were pressured, or some did it out of free will. It is their affair, their destiny. This is no problem at all.'[15]

Jovan Vukićević, for whom conversion represents an integral, although often silenced aspect of Montenegrin history, also explained the identity transformations of the Paljević by emphasising the border legacy. When I asked him how Paljo's children could be Muslims in a society where identity and religion are transmitted through the male line, his answer was familiar: 'I know it's strange, but this was Turkey, you know.'

Jovan also mentioned the process of conversion within Montenegro itself, illuminating the connection between border crossing and identity transformation. When a conversion occurred across the border on Turkish soil, it was neither a reason to exclude the relatives nor a disgrace to the family. However, within Montenegro, conversion was an issue, for it seemed to threaten to Islamise the country. Thus those who despite their poverty resisted conversion like the Vukičević were applauded, as Jovan proudly describes:

> They were decent, heroes and patriots. They protected Montenegro. Among them there were no renegades. You know, there were many people in Montenegro, who not only converted to Islam, but moreover caused great problems, great problems. They wanted influence, spread around, wanted to build mosques and to Islamise the whole region. We did not have such problems in our family.

This pronounced double standard in relation to judging conversion is constituted through border crossing: as long as relatives converted out of pressure and necessity upon emigrating to Ottoman territory and did not return to Islamise Montenegro, they remained relatives and their decision was understood rather than condemned.

Although converted relatives were often referred to as 'Turks' or as 'Turkicised' (*poturčeni*), they were thought of as our 'own Muslims' in contrast to 'real Turks'. A common refrain heard throughout the region expresses the crucial boundary between converts and historical migrants of the Ottoman period: 'Originally, there were no Turks around here.' Three notions of 'Turk' are implicated in this view. First, the 'authentic Turk', who is occupier, soldier, tax collector and Islamiser. This authentic Turk is seen as less threatening than the second kind of 'Turk', who is the local convert imagined as a passionate and enthusiastic 'internal Islamiser', an image exemplified by Jovan's narrative about the 'problem-causing' converts in Montenegro and who are seen as a threat to the confessional identity of the Montenegrin *bratstvo*. Finally, the 'legitimate Turk' is the border-crossing relative, who was either forced to accept the new faith or did so out of a quest for a better life in the new post-migratory socio-economic context.

The discursive association between the border time-space factor and the frontier orientalist mode (Gingrich 1998; Jezernik 2010) of differentiating between the legitimate, border-crossing convert and the threatening 'real' and 'problem-causing' 'own Turk' provides the ground for maintaining two strands of loyalty: kinship and nation/religion. One can thus simultaneously maintain two markers of identity regardless of conversion: the Christian orthodox faith and patrilineal belonging. This discursive strategy once again enables genealogical inclusivity as an important basis of identity dynamics in the Montenegrin–Albanian borderland.

Border crossers: beyond time-space and the ethno-national

Apart from inclusivity across ethno-national and religious lines, the Sarapa case also exemplifies a subversive ambiguity towards ethno-national diversity and a means to transcend it. Once again the border can be seen to underpin the ways in which local diversity plays out, as demonstrated by the case of another border-crossing family and branch of the Sarapa *bratstvo*, the Paljević.

Apart from sustaining close relations with relatives across the border, the Paljević are actively related and regularly perform symbolic kinship with their Christian relatives in Montenegro. Among my interviewees were two brothers, Isa and Sait Paljević, who like the Paljević in general, see themselves as Muslim Albanians. Although aware of their genealogical links to the Vukičević and Karadaglić, Isa and Sait did not possess a copy of the Sarapa genealogy. As Rustem and I unfolded before them the grand version of the Sarapa family tree (see Figure 4.2) and the sub-genealogy of the Vukičević /Karadaglić (see Figure 4.4), the brothers were stunned. After initial speechlessness Isa and Sait recounted the familiar genealogical narrative. However, their version included an interesting variation: the possibility that their ancestors had already been Muslim before crossing the border to 'Turkey'. When he visited Ljubotinj a few years later to see his family place of origin, Isa searched the cemetery and found what he was looking for: Muslim tombs. In spite of having made the point, which echoes Jovan Vukičević's claim that there

4.4 The Paljević branch of the Sarapa genealogy

were indeed converts in old unoccupied Montenegro, the brothers were in no doubt about their orthodox Christian origin. They thus favour the genealogical version that they share with their Christian relatives, in which the descendants of their ancestor Paljo became Muslims only because he had crossed the border to 'Turkey' where he married a Muslim woman.

Isa's and Sait's encounter with genealogy – perceived as a historical document and approached with visible respect and veneration – ignited a series of lively debates, which on different occasions involved other family members and friends. While these debates were fascinating because they provided the missing genealogical information of the Paljević branch, their primary significance lay in revealing the functioning and practice of fluid and ambiguous identity claims. For hours the brothers switched backwards and forwards between claiming their Montenegrin and Albanian identities. The long and challenging conversations, supported by food, coffee and laughter – but never marked with conflict or closure – again demonstrated the crucial significance of the origin across the historical border.

> *Sait*: 'Yes, we are Vukičevići from Cetinje, Montenegro, our ancestors were orthodox Christians, according to our origin we are *real* Montenegrins. But today we feel as Albanians. Our grandfather, father and uncles all married Albanian women and declared themselves to be Albanians. We cannot be something else. But our origin is Montenegrin. We are Albanians with a Montenegrin origin.'
>
> *Isa*: 'And after all, as one can hear in the parliament. One has the right to declare as one wishes to belong!'

Although the Paljević use ethno-national terms and reproduce the ethno-national pattern as the dominant way of framing difference, they also subvert it. They do this by insisting on embodying identities which, in many other parts of the Balkans, cannot be combined: they are both Albanians and Montenegrins; both Muslims and (former) Christians; nationals by origin and citizens of a liberal state free to choose their identity.

What enables them to do this? In this case, their family history along the shifting border plays a crucial role and functions as a platform on which to enact their identity. The notion of origin enables the Paljević to locate their Montenegrin identity in another genealogical time-space, beyond the historical Ottoman–Montenegrin border. This relocation of identity through reference to an origin beyond the historical border enables the Paljević brothers to be Christian Montenegrins by patrilineal and territorial origin without endangering their inherited Albanian Muslim identity. In other words, the reference to the historical border crossing is a brilliant way both to legitimate the ambiguity of ethno-national identity and stay in line with patrilineal ideology.

Moreover, in the Paljević case, the ethno-national aspect of diversity is not only ambiguous, but is also superseded by other aspects of identity and social differentiation, primarily by the fact that the Paljević are successors to a famous and respected

4.5 Beçir Tafa (*centre*), the Bajraktar of Tuzi, Montenegro
(Ulqini 2003:82)

family of Bajraktars. The title of the Bajraktar ('flag carrier') was a prestigious title – originating in the Ottoman military vocabulary – which the Ottomans granted to respected local families.[16] The photograph showing Isa's and Sait's grandfather, the Bajraktar Beçir Tafa (see Figure 4.5), was repeatedly and proudly presented, and remained ever close at hand during our conversations. In a narrative sense Beçir was sharing our table in the present, handing over his prestigious function from the beginning of the twentieth century.

This narrative movement across time and space into the nineteenth century is, however, not the end of the Paljević story of the interrelation of belonging and the dynamics of the border, for it is not only the historical border shifts and crossings that are of crucial relevance here. The personal experience of Isa and Sait with the more recent socialist border, or rather with its complete closure, are also relevant. Because of this bilingual competence and kinship networks, Isa's and Sait's father had worked as a driver and interpreter for the Serbian communists in Albania after the Second World War. When the border was closed in 1948 the Paljević were, so to say, trapped in Albania and remained living in Shkodra for many years. In Albania, they were again someone else: primarily Yugoslavs, and only in the second instance, Montenegrins. The main feature of their identity, apart from their language competence, was their Yugoslav citizenship, which they never wanted to relinquish in favour of Albanian citizenship. They considered themselves Yugoslavs and do so to the present day.

Upon returning to Montenegro, which they longed for due to the harsh living conditions in communist Albania and out of nostalgia, the brothers found their land had been confiscated by the very institution with which they had identified while in Albania: the Yugoslav state. But relatedness, in this case in the form of patronage, entered the scene. As already mentioned, Isa soon found work with the help of Jovan Vukićević, precisely because he was a 'Sarapa'.

One can argue that the key feature of the inclusivity the Paljević embody is the fact that they are both the progeny of border crossers and are border crossers themselves. Hence, both the legacy and personal experience of cross-border migration are the bases for flexible, context- and interest-oriented usage of ethno-national identity categories.

Finally, the case of the Paljević clearly shows the critical importance of a multidimensional approach to diversity in the Balkans where ethno-national belonging is merely one aspect of difference. In the Paljević case, cross-border migration background, historical social titles, social networks, multilingualism and citizenship are all clearly equally or even more important than the ambiguous ethno-national loyalty.

Gendering patrilineal genealogies

Women are nonexistent in patrilineal family trees, in so far as these embody ideological representations of the continuity of the male line. It was continuously surprising to me and my female interlocutors that women are completely omitted genealogically. I recall the moment of the genealogical interview with the husband of Lirie, one of my initial acquaintances and later close friend in Shkodra, when she literally cried out: 'This is outrageous! Why am I not visible in your family tree? I am your wife and we have two children!'

Although as a rule women themselves were neither in possession of nor pursued the reconstruction of genealogies, they often took the role of co-narrators of their spouse's family history. Moreover, upon being confronted with expressions of interest, they willingly revealed their often substantial knowledge of their own family history, while referring to and introducing male family members as the prime 'narrative agents'. In Lirie's case, it was her uncle who joined us in several conversations on Lirie's parents' family histories.

In another case narrative authority was again granted to men. As expressed through the opening quote of this chapter, Marija, Ilija Karadaglić's widow, repeatedly referred us to her son as the prime source for the history of the Karadaglić. However, during the genealogical conversations it turned out that she was actually more knowledgeable than he was. Marija had been an active listener and co-chronicler next to her husband and his brother. Although her son was irritated by his mother's spontaneous and passionate outburst of detailed knowledge, he valued her knowledge highly. He repeatedly lamented that he had not listened more attentively to his father's accounts of their family history.

In the case of the Paljević, however, women were almost completely silent. While at times sitting with us and listening to the narratives and heated debates about belonging, politics and regional history – unlike other women participating in these conversations, such as neighbours – Fatima and Nura barely entered the conversation. Once, when I explicitly asked Fatima for her opinion on the issues being debated about her family history, she apologised for not speaking Montenegrin well enough[17] and smilingly indicated that it is 'their business'. Apart from the not entirely plausible language argument, since most of the discussion was in Albanian, this silence is interesting when one considers that the land the family lives on belongs to the family of Isa's and Sait's wives. In other words, the expropriation of the Paljević by the Yugoslav state forced them to live on what they refer to as 'foreign land'.

Although missing from patrilineal genealogical representations and often silent, women do in fact appear in genealogical narratives.[18] However, as the Sarapa case exemplifies, they do so in particular ways that are directly linked to the interrelation of identity transformation and the border.

Unlike the 'instability' of the Paljević narrative mentioned earlier, regarding the issue of Paljo's confessional belonging prior to his border crossing, the following narrative variation about what happened following the border crossing is centrally structured by female agency. 'Paljo died as a young man. His Muslim wife then disregarded the agreement that the male children will keep the Christian faith.' In this widespread explanation of why the Paljević are Muslims today, which is emphasised primarily by the Karadaglić and Vukičević,[19] female agency is made responsible for the ultimate 'rupture' of the patrilineal genealogy and the non-transmission of religious belonging through the paternal line. Hence, the narrative about this post-mortem matrilineal intervention clearly renders female agency as transgressive and unjust, and discharges Paljo[20] from bearing responsibility for the loss of religious identity. Women do appear in Isa's and Sait's genealogical narrative, although not as autonomous agents, and they are referred to as the main factor when legitimising another patrilineality-unsettling transformation: the change of national affiliation. Thus they would say: 'Our grandfather, father and uncles all married Albanian women and declared as Albanians. We cannot be something else.'

Both these cases exemplify how female agency is only deployed when seeking to sustain patrilineal belonging and relatedness in the face of identity ruptures. Even here, though, female agency has to be imagined in a specific way. Women are not only narratively utilised – by being blamed – for legitimating elementary disruptions of patrilineal order, but also are made to appear as fixed in contrast to mobile border-crossing male subjects. They appear as fixed in a twofold sense: fixed both in the space beyond the border and fixed 'outside' the patrilineal realm of belonging. Hence, one can argue that since women embody the 'outside' in multiple ways, they can easily be made responsible for any identity ruptures in religious and ethno-national loyalties that are inconsistent with patrilineal ideology. In this sense, women therefore act as unintentional agents of diversity.

Conclusion

The kind of inclusive genealogy exemplified by the Sarapa/Paljević case is far from exceptional. Such genealogies are quite common in the northern border region between Montenegro and Albania.[21] The fact that here one can easily find ethnically and religiously mixed genealogical narratives and practices of relatedness that transcend ethno-national and religious affiliation can be seen as an expression of an important regional pattern marked by pronounced inclusivity and historic acceptance of diversity. In this context, ethno-religious conflict would potentially imply forging war not only against friends and neighbours – as was the tragic case in former Yugoslavia – but also against one's next of kin.[22] This, however, is particularly unlikely in a society where kinship remains the basis of identification, social cohesion and everyday life, and implies deep historical knowledge[23] and a central reference point for belonging.

What are the implications of the encounter between European Union (EU) multicultural policies and this historic and highly integrative local acceptance of diversity along the Albanian–Montenegrin border region? Both Montenegro and Albania have entered the process of EU accession with its emphasis on multiculturalism and minority rights. Apart from bringing national legislation into line with the European Convention on Human Rights (ECHR) and the ratification of the Framework Convention for the Protection of National Minorities (FCNM), the two countries' overall progress towards membership of the EU and their implementation of the FCNM in particular are regularly monitored. My research in the region so far, however, indicates that the European Framework primarily emphasises the framing of diversity in terms of ethno-national and religious minority rights, while other aspects such as citizenship, language, social status, migration background and gender and sexual orientation are rarely addressed.

Also not taken into account are the kinds of historic inclusivity and openness to diversity that I have considered here, which are potentially subverted and destabilised by the essentialising 'national minority grid' imposed in the course of European integration. Seen from the perspective of the Albanian–Montenegrin borderland, the European future is likely to be but another specific transformation of regional border dynamics. Even as the border opens up, the inclusivity, legacies of mobility and the relationship to the state of the border-crossers are likely to remain the central means of defining oneself and relating to others in the Albanian–Montenegrin borderland.

Notes

1 I would like to thank Hastings Donnan, Madeleine Hurd, Carolin Leutloff-Grandits, Steven Vertovec, Ioannis Manos, Bruno Riccio, Fotini Tsibiriodou and Eftihia Voutira for their inspiring comments and Rosie Gant for her feedback and language editing.

2 These figures are intended to illustrate the *form* these genealogies take rather than the detailed content or names they contain.

3 As with Rivers's aim of using the genealogical method to obtain 'objective' 'scientific' knowledge (Bamford and Leach 2009).

4 Rather than representing 'timeless structures', patrilineages/tribes (Albanian *fis*; Montenegrin *bratsvo* and *pleme*) are forms of social organisation that consolidated due to the Ottoman presence (e.g. Kaser 1992: 14; Morrison 2009: 17), and which have kept changing in response to the circumstances around them.

5 In the Montenegrin context symbolic kinship based on witnessing, baptising or marriage (*kumstvo*), or 'exchanging' blood (*braca po krvi*), are prominent forms of relatedness between families beyond ethnicity and religion.

6 Local customary law – recorded for example as the north Albanian Kanuni i Lek Dugadjinit – continues to be an important reference point. Both in the Albanian and Montenegrin part of the Shkodra region there are assemblies which perform mediation in case of conflicts and prevent or mediate in existing blood feuds.

7 Following Benhabib's approach to the 'narrative constitution of the self' (2002: 15–16), which explores the individual agency associated with engaging with and transforming (collective) narratives, and Sieder's (2008) analytic disentangling of narratives as sequences of decisions, I consider genealogical narratives as a form of agency.

8 http://www.sarapi.org.

9 The Montenegrin term *bratstvo* comprises all sub-branches of a patrilineage sharing a myth of a common ancestor, as in the case of the Sarapa. The term *pleme* (tribe), however, implies a common territory, which can include several *bratstva* (such as the *pleme* Ljubotinj in the case of the Sarapa).

10 Lord Ivan Crnojević ruled Zeta between 1465 and 1490.

11 In this chapter I do not go into the peculiarities of the Serbian–Montenegrin denominational (and official language) dynamics in the context of present-day Montenegro. It should be noted, however, that this antagonism, which climaxed following Montenegro's independence in 2006, has a profound impact on local identity politics.

12 The equivalent emic expression is *rodjak* (or the diminutive *rodjo*).

13 The extermination of converts by Prince Danilo, which is the central theme of Njegoš's epic poem, lacks historical validity (Djilas 1966). Conversion to Islam was contested, but remains an integral part of Montenegro's history.

14 http://www.rastko.rs/knjizevnost/umetnicka/njegos/mountain_wreath.html#meeting.

15 See below for reflections on the gender dimensions of this process.

16 The introduction of the Bajraktar title can also be seen as an example of the aforementioned co-optive governance strategy by the Ottomans of actively incorporating segments of the occupied population into their ruling and military structures. In a similar way in the context of the Albanian highlands, the Ottomans granted the title of the Bajraktar to tribal leaders (Kaser 1992: 18).

17 At home the (bilingual) Paljević brothers and their Albanian-speaking wives only speak Albanian.

18 In spite of their exclusion from patrilineal genealogical imagery, female figures in the Sarapa/Paljević genealogical narrative appear as knots of relatedness within the patrilineal ideology. In this manner, for instance, the Paljević regarded my co-traveller Rustem as a relative, since he is the grandson of their grandfather's sister.

19 According to Isa and Sait, there was already an agreement prior to the early death of Paljo that the male children would become Muslims, while the daughters would keep the Christian–Orthodox faith.

20 Paljo's conversion, which is a part of this narrative variation, does not seem to represent a 'problem' since it is legitimized by the necessity of identity change due to the blood feud and since it was agreed that his male offspring would keep the Christian faith.

21 My fieldwork data includes other similar cases of genealogical inclusivity, such as the Alibasić, Otović and Iliković.

22 Another crucial factor is Montenegro's minority regime. Without going into detail about the complexities of minority politics in Montenegro, one can note the 'traditionally good relationship between Montenegro's Albanians and the ruling authorities' and the fact that the former see Montenegro as their state (Morrison 2009: 224).

23 This marks a major difference to the Bosnian case.

References

Bakić-Hayden, Milica (1995) 'Nesting orientalisms: the case of former Yugoslavia', *Slavic Review*, 54(4): 917–931.

Bamford, Sandra and James Leach (2009) 'Pedigrees of knowledge: anthropology and the genealogical method', in S. Bamford and J. Leach (eds), *Kinship and Beyond: The Genealogical Method Reconsidered*. Oxford: Berghahn, pp. 1–24.

Bartov, Omer and Eric D. Weitz (eds) (2013) *Shatterzone of Empires: Coexistence and Violence in the German, Habsburg, Russian, and Ottoman Borderlands*. Bloomington: Indiana University Press.

Benhabib, Seyla (2002) *The Claims of Culture: Equality and Diversity in the Global Era*. Princeton, NJ: Princeton University Press.

Blumi, Isa (2003) 'Contesting the edges of the Ottoman Empire: rethinking ethnic and sectarian boundaries in the Malësore 1878–1912', *International Journal for Middle East Studies*, 35: 237–256.

Bougarel Xavier, Elissa Helms and Ger Duijzings (eds) (2007) *The New Bosnian Mosaic: Identities, Memories and Moral Claims in a Post-War Society*. London: Ashgate.

Bushati, Hamdi (1998) *Shkodra dhe Motet: Traditë, Ngjarje, Njerëz* (Velimi I) [Shkodra and its History: Traditions, Events and People (Volume 1)]. Shkodra: Idromeno.

Bushati, Hamdi (1999a) *Shkodra dhe Motet: Traditë, Ngjarje, Njerëz* (Velimi II) [Shkodra and its History: Traditions, Events and People (Volume 2)]. Shkodra: Idromeno.

Bushati, Hamdi (1999b) *Shkodra dhe Motet. Pemë gjenealogjike familjesh Shkodrane.* [Shkodra and its History. Shkodran Family Trees.]. Shkodra: Idromeno.

Carsten, Janet (2000) 'Introduction: cultures of relatedness', in Janet Carsten, *Cultures of Relatedness: New Approaches to the Study of Kinship.* Cambridge: Cambridge University Press, pp. 1–37.

Djilas, Milovan (1958) *Land Without Justice.* New York: Harcourt, Brace.

Djilas, Milovan (1966) *Njegos. Poet, Prince, Bishop.* New York: Harcourt, Brace & World.

Duijzings, Ger (2003) 'Ethnic unmixing under the aegis of the West: a transnational approach to the breakup of Yugoslavia', *BRIIFS*, 5(2): 1–16.

Fischer, Heinz (1996) *Lehrbuch der genealogischen Methode.* Berlin: Dietrich Reimer.

Gingrich, Andre (1998) 'Frontier myths of Orientalism: the Muslim world in public and popular cultures of Central Europe', in Bojan Baskar and Borut Brumen (eds), *Mediterranean Ethnological Summer School, Piran/Pirano Slovenia 1996*, MESS vol. II. Ljubljana, pp. 99–129.

Gingrich, Andre and Richard G. Fox (2002) 'Introduction', in Andre Gingrich and Richard G. Fox (eds), *Anthropology, by Comparison.* London: Routledge, pp. 1–24.

Green, S.F. (2009) *Lines, Traces and Tidemarks: Reflections on Forms of Borderli-ness*, COST Action IS0803 Working Paper 1. www.eastbordnet.org/working_papers/open/ documents/Green_Lines_Traces_and_Tidemarks_090414.pdf. Accessed 9 August 2016.

Heiss, Johann and Martin Slama (2010) 'Genealogical avenues, long-distance flows and social hierarchy: Hadhrami migrants in the Indonesian diaspora', *Anthropology of the Middle East*, 5(1): 34–52.

Jezernik, Bozidar (2010) 'Imagining "the Turk"', in Bozidar Jezernik (ed.), *Imagining 'the Turk.* Newcastle upon Tyne: Cambridge Scholars Publishing, pp. 1–17.

Kaser, Karl (1992) *Hirten, Kämpfer, Stammeshelden: Ursprünge und Gegenwart des Balkanischen Patriarchats.* Münster: LIT.

Kymlicka, W. (2002) 'Multiculturalism and minority rights: West and East', *Journal on Ethnopolitics and Minority Issues in Europe*, 4: 1–27.

Morrison, Kenneth (2009) *Montenegro: A Modern History.* London: I.B. Tauris.

Reinkowski, Maurus (2003) 'Double struggle, no income: Ottoman borderlands in northern Albania', *International Journal of Turkish Studies*, 9: 239–253.

Sieder, Reinhard (2008) 'Erzählungen analysieren – Analysen erzählen. Narrativ-biographisches Interview, Textanalyse und Falldarstellung', in Karl R. Wernhart and Werner Zips (eds), *Ethnohistorie. Rekonstruktion und Kulturkritik. Eine Einführung.* Promedia. Vienna: Promedia, pp. 145–172.

Sugar, P. F. (1996[1977]) *Southeastern Europe under Ottoman Rule, 1354–1804.* Seattle: University of Washington Press.

Tošić, Jelena (2015a) 'Reimagining the Balkans: diversity beyond and "straight through" the ethno-national', in Steven Vertovec (ed.), *Routledge International Handbook of Diversity Studies.* London: Routledge, pp. 151–158.

Tošić, Jelena (2015b) 'City of the "calm": vernacular mobility and genealogies of urbanity in SEE', in Jelena Tošić and Sabine Strasser, *Localizing Moralities: Power and*

Temporality in SEE (Special Section) *Southeastern Europe and Black Sea Studies* 3: 391–408.

Ulqini, Kahreman (2003) *Struktura e Shoqërisë Tradicionale Shqiptare*. Tirana: Idromeno.

Verdery, Katherine (1994) 'Beyond the nation in Eastern Europe', *Social Text*, 38: 1–19.

Vertovec, Steven (2007) 'Super-diversity and its implications', *Ethnic and Racial Studies*, 30(6): 1024–1054.

Vertovec, Steven (2009) 'Conceiving and researching diversity', Gottingen: Max-Planck-Institute Working Paper 09-01.

Yuval-Davis, Nira (2011) *The Politics of Belonging: Intersectional Contestations*. London: Sage.

＊⟶＊ **5** ＊⟶＊

Living on borrowed time: borders, ticking clocks and timelessness among temporary labour migrants in Israel

Robin A. Harper and Hani Zubida

'It's like clockwork', the saying goes, meaning that things are orderly, linear, depend-able, and based on a universally shared, knowable concept of time. Standardisation facilitates communication, facilitates order and spurs development (Anderson 1991; Crosby 1997). Shared temporal references are a fundamental concept of social life (Sorokin 1943; Zerubavel 1982). Time is an orientation opportunity, allowing individuals to carve a place in that shared social space (Berger and Luckmann 1967). Sorokin (1943: 173) eloquently explains:

> (t)he possession of means and ways to 'time' the behavior of the members of any group in such a way that each member apprehends 'the appointed time' in the same way as do other members has been possibly the most urgent need of social life at any time and at any place. Without this, social life itself is impossible.

Durkheim (1965: 17) underscores this point, observing that 'If men ... did not have the same conception of time ... all contact between their minds would be impossible, and with that, all life together.'

Cross-border migration offers an interesting challenge to these naturalised views of shared time structures. Due to transnationalism, nostalgia and cultural difference, migrants exist both according to local temporal norms and home-country timescapes. In this simultaneity, time is not linear but layered, with competing, sometimes contradictory strains, imaging home while living in the new rhythms of the receiving state. This is a normal result of transnationalism and common to all immigrants (Cwerner 2001; Griffiths et al. 2013). Unlike all immigrants, however, Temporary Labour Migrants (TLM) hold time-delimited visas. For these migrants, time is bracketed and ticking. Because there is a real and knowable limit, it raises the question of how TLM think of their time as migrants. Is it the same for them as it is for other immigrants or for natives?

We posit that for TLM, time forms a separate, exclusive, parallel experience that is similar – but not the same – for all immigrants, and is sometimes different from the experience of natives. The similarities derive from shared human experience; the differences emerge from disparate legal, cultural and social experience. Migration is not just about traversing a political border but also about living in a different space with different norms. As a result, the migration process infuses all parts of a person's life, even those parts that are seemingly distinct from the migration process. Obviously, all people have some constraints placed on their time, whether self-imposed, job-related or familial. TLM experience certain unique time constraints, which are state-imposed. The state may impose time constraints on migrants for access to society, restricting entry, exit and practices in daily life. The state may place similar constraints only on subjects who have circumscribed rights, such as prisoners and those in quarantine. However, unlike prisoners and those in quarantine, only migrants request (or escape from) this time subjugation at will. But even if time is different for TLM, which factors affect perceptions of time: time-delimited visas? Local time culture? Different seasons? Experiencing nostalgia and homesickness? Being far from events in the home country? Adam (2008: 7) takes up these questions and calls for a rethinking of time in terms of multi-dimensional timescapes in which 'identities are forged, sustained, discarded and reworked ... in relation to significant others ... understanding the significance in people's lives.' In this view, time is not linear but relational and entwined so that the past, present and future are interrelated and dependent on individual and collective contexts (Adam 1998). This certainly may pose problems if temporary migrants become permanent residents and their alternate timescapes do not match their new reality.

In this chapter, we consider how TLM in Israel experience time. We use the concept 'borders' expansively to demarcate not just political borders, but social borders, time borders and even life-cycle borders. (Political borders and clock time are social constructions, like other social borders.) We explore how time generates social and/or political borders and conversely, how crossing state borders generates new concepts of time. We show that when time borders are embedded in the TLM experience, time becomes non-universal and non-linear. Our findings about how TLM experience time emerge from interviews and subsequent conversations we conducted in Israel in 2010–12 with 38 migrants (legally and illegally present, refugee/asylum seekers) from 11 countries about their thoughts, experiences and opinions about life in Israel.[1]

We suggest that 'migrant time' is a bordering process that is unique to migrants. We show how two alternative timescapes, peculiar to TLM – 'rupture time' and 'freedom time' – shape migrants' understanding of time. Further, we show how these timescapes provide an opportunity for and an impediment to immigrant incorporation.

Migration and time in Israel

Like many countries, Israel is home to a large number of TLM who have become *de facto* permanent residents. There are between 250,000 and 350,000 migrants

– approximately two-thirds of whom have fallen out of legal status. They have been joined by an additional 60,000 refugees/asylum-seekers fleeing civil war and extreme poverty in Sudan and Eritrea. Migrants come from across Asia, Africa, Latin America and eastern Europe and comprise as much as 5 per cent of the total population and 11 per cent of the labour force in Israel (Nathan 2011).

Foreign labour complementing the Israeli workforce has been a constant since the founding of the state. Until the 1980s, Palestinian day labourers formed the bulk of that. Following the 1988 Palestinian civil uprising (intifada), Israel closed the borders to Palestinians and began importing foreigners to supplant Palestinian labourers. Israeli employers realised the profitability of migrant labourers and demanded more visas for agricultural and construction workers rather than making capital investments to modernise conditions or make jobs more appealing to Israelis (Bartram 2004). Over time, employers demanded expansion of the policy to include entry of migrants to care for the elderly and to provide household assistance (i.e. caregiving). Some argue that the policy expansion was also intended to weaken the Palestinian hand in negotiations (Raijman and Kemp 2007). Table 5.1 summarises the number of legal migrant workers in Israel in 2010.

The policy to bring in workers is essentially an indenturing programme: Israel issues permits to specific recruitment agencies for a given number of migrants per year to work in agriculture, construction, hospitality, ethnic cookery/catering, nursing/caregiving and welding. In all but caregiving, there are fixed annual quotas (Harper and Zubida 2010). Israeli policy is designed for voluntary, rotating, temporary contract migrants. When contracts expire or are cancelled or workers fall out of status, there are few ways to adjust one's status. So Israel uses deportation as the main mechanism for compulsory repatriation. Many workers actually choose to become illegal workers if they are dissatisfied with their working conditions or if their contracts are about to expire. Ironically, and in contrast to the experience in most other states, workers without employment contracts ('illegal workers') have more freedom over their own time than their legal counterparts, as they are outside the time limits imposed by work permits and may take or leave jobs at will. However, clearly, they trade employment freedom for more precarious residency status (Kemp 2007; Willen 2007).

As would be expected, over time, TLM have raised families in Israel. Although they live on the periphery of Israeli society, children of some migrants – the Israeli Interior Ministry estimates there are about 1,200 children of migrant workers in Israel and an additional 2,000 of refugees/asylum-seekers – self-identify as Israelis and are being socialised as Israelis through the school system (Zubida et al. 2013). Many are stateless, as there are few means to adjust their status and to claim Israeli citizenship or to claim the citizenship of their parents' countries of origin. Some 600 are awaiting adjudication of their cases, while about 620 have been provided a means to permanent residency (Sa'ar 2006; Goren 2014). Although the Israeli government envisioned a temporary labour fix and a policy of time-delimited rota-

Table 5.1 Legal migrant workers in Israel, 2010

Country of origin	Total (000's)
Total	108.6
Asia	82.8
India	7.5
Turkey	2.4
Nepal	6.4
China	8.0
Sri Lanka	4.5
Philippines	25.9
Thailand	25.0
Other	3.1
Africa total	0.4
Europe total*	24.3
Bulgaria	2.1
FSU	11.1
Germany	0.2
United Kingdom	0.2
Romania	9.8
Other	0.9
America Oceania total	1.1
USA	0.4
Others	0.6

Source: Israeli Central Bureau of Statistics, 2013.
Note: *Including FSU European Republics.

tion of workers, many migrants (and now their descendants as well) are increasingly becoming a permanent segment of Israeli demographics. For the workers who imagined short stays and quick returns home, time morphed the locus of their lives.

Examining time

Modern Western standard temporal references are linked to the virtually universal use of the Gregorian calendar, the Christian era, international standard time and clock time (Zerubavel 1982). These structures pose a host of uncontested, shared, accepted temporal practices. The year begins in January and ends in December. Throughout most of the world, the official date of reference is the birth of Christ as the before/after time demarcation point. Zero hour is Greenwich Mean Time (GMT) and all understandings of clock time are plus or minus GMT. Standard time marks out days into seven equal units in each week. There are twelve months in every year. Months may be 30, 31 or 28 days long. Adjustments are made every four years, adding an additional day to February. Seasons are anchored to dates rather than climate, temperature or harvests. This naturalised temporalisation is sequenced and relatively invariant (Elchardus 1988). Any attempts to deviate from these constructs are disruptive, full of conflict and likely to fail (Zerubavel 1977, 1982). Because of socialisation and general acceptance, these systems of time appear universal and organic. As Edelman (1996: 129) cautions when thinking about seemingly universal units: '[c]ategories are especially powerful as shapers of political beliefs … when they appear to be natural, self-evident, or simple description rather than devised.' Due to the widespread acceptance and convenience of shared time, there is no contemporary, serious discussion about altering the construction of the calendar, clock and seasons; all remain currently uncontested.

Since time is treated as a common commodity, it has the appearance of *meaning* the same thing for all people. Rigid categorisation restricts the visibility of important processes. Attempts to log events in relation to the clock and map uses of space often overlook both simultaneity and the meanings attached to space and time (Urry 1991; Rose 1993; Moss 2010). That is not to say that all aspects of life are temporal; they are not. However, they are nonetheless constrained by our own organic, psychological, cultural and other internal and external environments (Elchardus and Smits 2006). In thinking about this functionality of the ordering of time, Parsons (1951: 301) noted that people acted 'so that different times are set apart for different activities, with different people'. That is, we simplify our understandings of the openness and complexity of time. By 'defuturizing the future' (Luhmann 1967), we can imagine a fixed sequence of stages that tells someone what should come next. This expectation for the individual is projected on to the society as a whole. Although many have posited that, as society becomes more globalised and complex, there will be an individualisation of the life cycle (Giddens 1990), empirical evidence reveals that variation is more limited (Elchardus and Smits 2006). However, in all of these cases, we can connect the multiple streams of time that run simultaneously: the countdown to the return, the time away, the time in the country, remembering, imagining and forecasting, and so on. As Adam (1994: 13) observes:

> We can grasp time in its complexity only if we seek the relations between time, temporality, tempo and timing, between clock time, chronology, social time and time-consciousness, between motion, process, change, continuity and the temporal modalities of past, present and future, between time as resource, as ordering principle and as becoming of the possible, or between any combination of these.

The meaning of time and migration

Studying the relationship between time and migration is not novel. Green (2006) identifies three common types of examinations of time in migration studies: linear, convergent and divergent. The *linear* model posits an implicit before and after comparison (e.g. sending country to receiving country). This model assumes that time interacts with space and affects experience. The *convergent* model compares how different groups arriving at the same time in the same place experience migration. Here, the study of time interacts with issues of urban reception, local policy or ethnicity. Differing reception patterns, class, skills, ethnicity, language and ability to interact with the local population each yield different modes of incorporation and identity. In the *divergent* model, time explains divergent outcomes among same-origin immigrant groups that arrive at different times or settle in different places (Foner 1979; Gabaccia 2000). The divergent analyses, for example, question why there are different outcomes for immigrants arriving 100 years ago and today.

Time of arrival and generationality have been a key concern in recent migration studies (Rumbaut 1994; Kasinitz et al. 2004; King et al. 2006; Portes and Rumbaut 2006). These studies explore the effects of individual development, time of arrival and family composition at and during migration. Similarly, there is growing academic interest in exploring the impact of migration on adults who came as children, teenagers, adults or even second and third (or even subsequent) generations (Buriel 1993; Berry 2001; Nakash et al. 2012; Zubida et al 2013; Shoshani et al. 2014). Also, an increasing number of articles examine ageing immigrants who, whether by desire or by chance, find themselves in the receiving state long after they intended to leave (Gelfand 1989; Mui 1996; Jones-Correa 1998; Treas and Batalova 2009; Yahirun 2012). New research considers migrants who returned to their country of origin after a protracted sojourn abroad and focuses on their reintegration. The role of the life cycle itself in migration trajectories remains, however, understudied. Here, the key questions are: How does immigration affect life-stage perspective? And, conversely, how does life-stage perspective affect the immigrant experience?

This intersection of time and migrant status generates dual gender-time-based borders that separate past, present and future. By crossing a political border, time is bracketed and this affects such time-dependent activities as pregnancy, nursing and the menopause. King et al. (2006: 249) observe the generalisation of the universal migrant time experience, writing:

> that descriptions, analyses and explanations for the migration of 'people', by aggregating the very different characteristics, motivations, agencies and relations of men and women, end up by failing to accurately portray the migration behavior of either sex.

Yet the King et al. analysis ignores the unique time constraints for reproduction; biological clocks do not run in concert with visas. Tenure abroad may be at the expense of bearing children with one's spouse or partner; children may not be nursed by their mothers or may never know their fathers. In other words, time-delimited visas and time-based contracts erect time-based borders that shape family relationships.

All of these approaches suggest that there is a relationship between time and how migration plays out. We will call this stretch of time that individuals spend as im/migrants *migration time*. Griffiths et al. (2013) do a masterful job of summarising the various understandings in the literature of migration time as the multiple, layered time experienced by migrants. We conceptualise migration time more simply as the chronological period that stretches between emigration and having no end (immigration) or emigration and a definite end (return migration or new emigration). Migration time includes all of the stages in between these beginnings and endings. Migration time will not be the same for all im/migrants. Since there is no 'monolithic migrant', there can be no monolithic migration time. This approach allows us to think about time and migration as a special experience, distinct from the normal life cycle in the home country; it is a time apart. We use this concept like the centre of a wheel into which and from which all spokes of migration time-related issues radiate. In this way we can begin to ask how migration status might affect understandings of time, and the implications this has for immigrant incorporation.

Migrants encompass a spectrum of immigration statuses, each with its own time borders. Immigrants normally maintain some transnational connections to the home country, but intend a fresh start in the receiving state. Refugees are thrust into a new culture, often with the understanding that there is no return to times gone by and places abandoned. Time must begin again. Asylum-seekers remain in limbo, unsure if they may stay or if they must return. Since determinations of asylum may take years to adjudicate, these migrants exist in a kind of timelessness, pursuing a future that may never transpire. TLM occupy a bracketed time period in which the state bureaucracy determines entry, exit and duration of tenure. Time abroad is a known delimited tenure as a means to (a better) life at home. For those 'temporary labour migrants' who cross the border without valid visas, work without proper authorisation or overstay visas, time is self-defined and open-ended. Migrants play chicken with the host state, always tempting/stretching time: How much longer? What will happen tomorrow? Imprisonment? Deportation? How long since the migrant had the peace of mind of secure tenure? These are the questions that construct the time frame of unauthorised migrants.

Cwerner's (2001) seminal work on migration time describes how migrants have parallel time modes in which they must adjust to local understandings of time, live a life far from the ones they love (and thus on an alternate life timeline), generate communities which exist apart from the dominant society and also from the home country, and finally carve out their own path. Part of the migration process is unlearning their own understandings of time in order to make sense of the new society. Migrants must adjust to the pace of life, to weather and climate and to the local calendar for holidays and business hours. However, Cwerner (2001: 15) cautions that the sociology of migrant time must not perceive all migration activities as functionally different from the lives of natives. Cwerner (2001) posits that migration is but one reference point in one's life, not one that shapes and colours other experiences and relationships.

We argue that Cwerner (2001) ignores the fundamental reality of TLM: they are invited guests and their tenures are limited. During the time when TLM are present, they are subjects. Their existence in the host country is predicated on the state granting them a certain amount of time in-country. The host state conceives of TLM as existing within a mutually profitable parallel timeline. The state codifies this relationship in a time-delimited visa that stipulates migrants' movements, their ability to enter, exit, return or extend their stay. Although non-citizens may make agreements to remain for a certain length of time, the state has the final word and migrants' desires are often immaterial. These migrant-specific modes shape concepts of time that impact life trajectories. Migrants' main agency is to follow the time constraints stipulated in their contracts or break the contracts and the law. Since migrants are subjects, migration time is dependent on the receiving state's whim: a migrant may lose status and face immediate deportation at any time. (This is what Griffiths et al. (2013) call 'frenzied time' and what we refer to elsewhere as 'arbitrariness' (Harper and Zubida 2010.) Since many TLM take on debt to pay visa fees and acquire start-up funds, migrants are often willing to work incessantly to repay loans quickly and then to make the maximum money possible within the bracketed visa time. The migrant must complete his goals before the visa expires. As soon as he crosses the border, he must act *as if* any given day might be his last day. This visa clock also imposes constraints on the reproductive clock, inhibiting or precluding procreation if far from a partner. It stops the clock on direct intimate physical contact and opens opportunities for reimagined relations through writing, telephoning and, more recently, social media. Visa time limits generate identifiable geopolitical time-based borders. Our findings reveal two distinct timescapes experienced by TLM: 'rupture time' and 'freedom time'.

Rupture time

TLM experience migration time from emigration to the end of the tenure, normally the visa-allotted period. Personal status laws and the visa process dictate their experience as migrants. The host state decides how many people may come, for how long and what they can do, normally irrespective of migrants' needs. Rupture time suggests that migrants are living on migrant time only to be removed abruptly from that status. For TLM, rupture can be normal and expected or normal and unexpected. It can be normal and expected because TLM are likely ultimately to leave. Departure may be desired or unwanted or even traumatic for migrants and their family, but it is an expected part of their experience as TLM. But rupture time can also be normal and *unexpected*, since migrants can be removed before their allotted time as TLM has elapsed or if they have overstepped their visa-determined time. In both cases, TLM are required to leave after a set period. There is an end to their tenure; and that end is what we refer to here as 'rupture time'. We explore now how these ruptures affect their stay.

Migrants and citizens differ in their rights to territory. Migrants depend on the host state to grant permission to enter, exit and conduct their daily lives. Citizens, by contrast, maintain unlimited access to their own national territory, entry, exit and residency rights. In short, citizens have unlimited time and migrants do not. Citizens can even confer this access to unlimited time to their descendants as property rights (Shachar 2009). Migrants' lives are largely defined by applying and waiting for time: time to get a visa, time to enter a country, time to work, time to leave. A Filipina caregiver explained how she waits and waits for a determination about her child's case. She came to Israel to work and sent her child to the Philippines but was so depressed that she brought her daughter back to Israel, knowing she had no status. When the government offered a regularisation of status to some children of TLM, she applied immediately. She had already waited several years for her case to be determined.

> I don't know how I feel, really ... [*laughs*] because always they are changing the new, the date. 'Oh it's tomorrow', and then ... We never know.

Since there are almost no legal mechanisms to adjust status, deportation is Israeli policy for those who do not leave in a timely way. The individual is powerless to negotiate status: the state informs and the migrant submits. This lack of agency in determining the length of tenure is the 'normal condition' for TLM who must apply for time, be granted time and are subject to the time limits imposed by the host state. When visas end, the result can be resignation, as an Indian caregiver explained: 'My time will be up and I will go home.' Or it can be an attempt to stretch the departure date and become a visa overstayer.

For others, the actual time issued by the state is unimportant, as working in Israel is a stepping stone to go where they really want to be. A Filipina caregiver explained that she wanted to go to Canada and it was bureaucratically impossible from the Philippines because there were too many applicants. She was under the impression that if she applied from Israel, it would be easier.

> But in here, if I can already enter in Israel, Israel is an open country. Then you have good, good relation with Canada so I can already cross country.

Time is also perceived as a bridge to the future in Israel. Migrants recognise that the law provides almost no options for permanence. Still, some long for the legal right to remain. They believe that spending time and working in Israel should confer a right to remain (*ius tempus*). Another Filipina caregiver explained:

> I think, Israel, like other countries should, when, should apply the law just like in Canada, if you stay there for two years, you will be an immigrant, in Singapore if you stay in one year you will be an immigrant ... in Filipino stay there for fifteen years or twenty years maybe I think maybe I think, I think they deserve to be an immigrant. They already spent most of their time here, and one way or another they already help the families in Israel because they do their labour here!

For those with a normal departure date who are unwilling to leave, becoming a visa overstayer is always an option, albeit a risky and stressful one. One

Filipina caregiver explained how overstaying the visa was complicated and unpleasant.

> It is good to be here in Israel because it is easy to earn money. There is one thing not good, you know, because we are now illegal. So, we are like they are treating us like animals. Before when I was pregnant with my first baby, three months pregnant, my husband took, took (the immigration police) took him. They sent him to the Philippines. I stay here alone. After four years, they bring him back here. I cannot stay here like this.

Migrants recognise their subjecthood, even when they overstay and attempt to stretch their tenure. As a follow-up, we conducted an interview with one of our interview partners from a deportation facility. The respondent, a Filipina caregiver, had overstayed her visa by a decade and was a prominent activist for TLM rights. Despite her long-standing social connections in Israel, she was deported to the Philippines one day after being arrested. She rationalised the state action regardless of the significant harm this will do to her personally.

> I don't have any bad feelings about Israel or the immigration police. They are just doing their jobs. I know that [being in Israel without a visa] is a criminal offence, for being here and being an immigrant. I think there is a reason for everything … They are right to send me back. They want me to go back. I should go back.

Here, rupture is immediate and expected. The TLM knows that this is the state policy, and even though she sought to extend her stay indefinitely, once captured she is resigned to accept the limits on time.

Most research on rupture (as a prelude to return) examines the event as an abstract concept: people are (unexpectedly) removed from their daily lives. Here, using a real-time SMS exchange between a migrant (caregiver and visa overstayer for more than a decade) and our research assistant, we chronicle the very moment when the immigration police demanded entry to her home (shared with other long-term visa overstayers) to take her into custody for deportation.[2]

> 11:33 *Migrant*: we are in [*gives address*] door are stil nocking the door by force me … Someone is on the way right now. tell me if something happens … Pls tel to Hani that the pulis (police) attacking ur rigth now they are not stopping knocking d door.
> 11:38 *RA*: Dont open the door!
> 11:42 *RA*: Are you ok? …
> 11:44 *Migrant*: Yes but they are stil attacking us rigth now they are in the fronth of our door. THANKs IF anything happen i wil tel u if they are distroying the door.
> 11:45 *RA*: Help is on the way. everything will be ok! i'm here for you. be strong they will be there soon.
> 11:50 *Migrant*: We are pinponited by are flatmate name [*redacted*] we r a little bit nervous we are in the room now they are stil in d door.pls tel Hani n tolk to [*longtime migrant*] …
> 11:58 *Migrant*: We conot make a noise they are outside or in d fronth of our door.

its almost 2hrs ... [*more back and forth about immigration police banging on the door.*]

12:19 *RA*: They wont break the door. dont open the door until i would say its ok

12:26 *Migrant*: Ok they are there the helper just tel me pls went we opene the dooe please thanks alot may the bless u. They are stil ther i think ...

12:33 *Migrant*: We are in d room praying n waiting ...

13:13 *RA*: We need you to go out of the window to another appartment or building, can you do that?

[*From this moment, no further contact could be established. The RA came to the office and asked Hani what to do. The RA then contacted a number of prominent Filipinas to get advice and share Migrant's story.*]

RA writes later:

> Tried to call Migrant again and a man answer the phone and said: '[*RA*]?' I hanged up ... After 3 days I tried to call Migrant again. She answered me and told me that she was released but that they caught [*another migrant*] and [*that migrant*] decided not to fight and to go back to the Philippines.

This text conversation reveals how time can become a border. The state decision to deport is the erection of a policy-imposed metaphorical border. The offer of time – the visa – is the way into the state and the decision to revoke it is the erection of a border that the migrant (at least legally) cannot traverse. All of this transpires without any input from the migrant – just as abruptly as he gets the decision to approve his visa, he will face the decision to deport him. This is a time-generated border over which he has no control. In both return and deportation, the border closes migration time.

Freedom time

'Freedom time' operates at the opposite end of the spectrum: time opens a border to new identity options and the border (and its crossings) offer new time options. We use the term 'freedom time' to refer to opportunities that come with traversing the geopolitical border. To contextualise, we often think about the disadvantages of labour migration. For example, labour migrants often work under harsh conditions. Their civil rights may not be respected in the host country. They frequently have little protection from unscrupulous employers and employers' families. In Israel, there are special issues. Even when the state offers protection for workers, the numbers of labour inspectors and their ability to follow up on all claims is extremely limited (interview with Department of Labor representative Iris Maayan, 2011). Migrant employment in Israel is tied to visas and work permits. Employees are bound to one specific employer. If the migrant loses his/her registered employment post, after 90 days he/she must secure and register a new position or lose the residency visa and be incarcerated and deported. However, TLM can offer some opportunities. To see this, we need to focus on the sending countries and the context from which these migrants came. Normally, economic conditions are limited in the sending country. (We know that labour migrants seek economic advantage in the receiving state.) Most labour migrants emigrate from states with precarious access to food, medical care and jobs. Furthermore, these sending states may curtail civil rights for their citizens, including freedom of expression and/or assembly. The home countries may be rife with state-sponsored and everyday street violence and corruption. Our research partners recounted experiences comparing life in their home countries with life in Israel. Although they sometimes decried the experiences they had had with their employers in Israel, they also noted that there were time-based advantages to being in Israel. For example, one interviewee from Ghana explained that he had four children in Israel and two others in his home country. He worried about the physical safety of his children in the home country, but not about his children in Israel. The Israel-based children had reacquired parts of the day that had been denied to his children in his home country by violence. In the home country, it was unsafe for children to be out after dark. In Israel, it is normal for children to be outside the house during the evenings and even at night. Children in Israel enjoy freedom of movement and assembly and parts of the day that simply did not exist for his children in Ghana. As a parent, he did not worry about them being on the street after dark, as he had done when in Ghana. By being in Israel, these TLM had regained lost parts of the clock and were freed from this time border. Labour migration provided a 'freedom' that was denied them in the home country.

> My children are out late at night … You know how the Israeli kids are, out at 2, 3 in the night. You can't do that at home. You can't be out then. It's too dangerous … People shooting on the street. It's just too dangerous … I don't worry about them at all here in Israel at night. Not at all … not at all.

In this view, time to a TLM is not only a general concept related to the state-granted visa, but also a change and improvement in daily life. Although there are constraints in the long term, there is an increase in their freedom time in daily life.

Ironically, this form of migrant freedom time is juxtaposed in an inverse way with a native 'constraint time'. That is, while migrants describe improved living standards and increased freedom in Israel, their native counterparts often describe an equal offsetting loss of freedom as a result of the arrival of the migrants. Natives complain vociferously about foreigners, being shut in their homes, afraid to negotiate the streets, especially at night or when they are alone. This generates two opposing and competing timescapes: for migrants, this new timescape opens the clock borders and allows freedom of movement; for the local population, their own fear, hostility and xenophobia narrow their time and restrict their geographical, spatial borders, curtailing their movement and the time they feel they can spend outside, in public. The clash over access to freedom time can lead to resentment, public unrest and local demands to deport the migrants under the call for public safety (Sheen 2011; Hovel 2014). This sentiment within the local population is accompanied by a sense of closure, an erection of borders both geophysical and temporal, and a sense of a ghetto community emerges. Areas that are 'declared' migrant-dominated are deemed as unsafe or unwelcoming for the native population. With the arrival of migrants, locals perceive their neighbourhoods with foreboding, as dangerous and no longer navigable in the evenings. Darkness is associated with closure. This perception of change disproportionately affects women. Community groups and the media report gender-related sexual harassment (assault, rape, etc.) through the prism of migrant male offenders and local women victims (see Kubovich 2012, 2013). This new apprehension turns the hours after dark into a taboo time for women (see Derfner 2012; Jeffay 2012) and results in demonstrations by locals (see Figure 5.1) and in violence towards foreigners. Locals try to reborder the areas where they had been dominant in an attempt to regain the time and spaces perceived to have been taken from them in the new bordering process associated with the arrival of the migrants.

TLM freedom time has other positive gendered borders as well. For many female TLM, time abroad can be a transformative experience. For some, their position in the family or community was subservient and limited by a culturally dictated, patriarchal hierarchy. When abroad, women can become decision makers, drawing up their own schedules (within the limitations of their employment contract or, like everyone, their working conditions). They gain agency in the use of times of the day

5.1 A protest by residents of southern Tel Aviv against the Israeli High Court of Justice's ruling to override the law allowing incarceration of migrants for up to three years. (The sign reads: 'Supreme Court Judges, we [the Israeli residents of southern Tel Aviv] are detained without trial for more than five years!!!)'

and personal time to come and go as they please. These modes of decision making and control of time may be closed to women in their home country. (We note that this may also be true for lower family-status males like third and fourth sons or children from second or subsequent wives.) A Nepalese caregiver explained how she and her colleagues generated opportunities that would never have existed in her home country.

> If we were home, we would never go out. Here, we go to work but then we go to our friends' houses. We stay overnight. We even have an apartment for all of us to share to make parties and just to eat food and rest on the weekends. We could never do that at home. We decide our time.

Still others take this new time away to form relationships that would not have been possible before. For some, that means building friendships with people from other ethnicities/nationalities or classes than their own. Some break from tradition and marry outside their ethnic, national, religious or racial group. Some use the opportunity to experiment with their sexual orientation, something that would have been almost impossible in their home country. Some marry an Israeli, whether to secure status or for love. This phenomenon has a significant impact on the idea of Israel as a homeland for the Jews. Some Israelis worry that such intermarriage could eventually make Israel less Jewish, and threaten the Jewishness of Israel and its reason for being. It also has implications for the state's ability to manage migrants' time in Israel, effectively weakening the state's control over who can be in the state at any time. Once a migrant (who is legally a foreigner) marries an Israeli citizen, the migrant's legal status shifts and is now covered by laws of family integrity. The clock starts again and the former migrant (after much bureaucratic status adjustment) has a claim to remain in the country. If the couple has a child, that child is eligible for Israeli citizenship. This changes state control over migrant time. It also enables the migrant to bring other family members from their home country and thus alter the entire liminal aspect of the state control. A long-time Filipina migrant explained how marriage to an Israeli changed her life trajectory and offered stability to her son (after much bureaucratic wrangling.) She further noted that after settling in Israel, she was able to help her sisters to come as well.

> When I came to Israel I never thought that I would stay here 20 years – I thought I would get married in the Philippines. Look at me today I am married to an Israeli … After I made it, I invited my sisters here. [My son] was born here and he has a citizenship, a few months ago he got it. Only now when he is 10 years old! The decision came from the Israeli court system, they would not give the child a passport so [my husband] decided to take the best lawyer money can buy and they went to court … And they made the government give [my son] a passport.

For many migrants, coming to a new country means discovering time and physical freedom. Although their work and attempts to make money to send home may take up most of their waking time, it appears that they are also freed from certain kinds of fear and are able to rescue lost time from the clock. The lack of violence on the streets creates a time freedom that in their home country seemed impossible. Moreover, migration can enable female migrants to establish agency and restructure the power relationship in their favour. And, finally, through this newly found freedom time, migrants form families with rights to remain in Israel indefinitely, further reducing the ability of the state to determine their timescapes.

Conclusion

Throughout this chapter we have presented labour migrants' experiences with time and borders. Building on the extant literature, we showed how various time experiences create time borders for TLM. These concepts of time relate to the migrants' condition of being abroad – immigrants, emigrants and subjects of the receiving state. Temporary labour migrants are different from immigrants. Immigrants are expected to adjust and become permanent residents or citizens. In contrast, the tenure of TLM is delimited by the state and state institutions. TLM must consequently conduct their lives knowing that time is borrowed and limited. Whether a migrant returns to the sending country or remains in the receiving state, timescapes and understandings of time change, and in some cases diverge and/or converge with the timescapes of the local inhabitants and significantly affect them. As a result of their (im)migrant status, migrants traverse multiple borders – political, social, biological and cultural – all of which are related to time. Each of these border crossings affects their migrant experience.

We have introduced new conceptions of migration time based on our work with migrants in Israel: 'migration time', 'freedom time' and 'rupture time'. The first, 'migration time', sets aside migration as a special experience that all migrants have, different from everyday life. 'Freedom time' is, we believe, the first instance in the literature that an examination of time and migration is perceived to be an opening of a border, an expansion of time, for migrants. However, while this timescape is a liberating experience for some TLM, when juxtaposed with the locals' timescapes it constrains the geophysical environment. This is a significant aspect of the meaning of time and affects the potential for immigrant incorporation.

By contrast, rupture time is experienced by almost all migrants, whether permanent or temporary, and marks the power of the state at the time-border to demand submission from the migrants and acceptance of state bureaucratic decisions. This is especially pertinent for TLM as the limits and extent of their time is demarcated by the state at the very moment of entry. The fear of deportation is a fear of a real state-imposed time and space border. For those with tenuous residency rights, like TLM, especially in a state like Israel where there is little ability to adjust migration status to permanent status, return is a normal part of the migrant experience. Knowing that the visa and new way of life will end is nonetheless disruptive and potentially traumatic. Migrants are subjected to the arbitrary imposition of a border and the anticipated fear of that imposition. In Israel, this reality surfaces during times of social unrest because of the conflicts with the local community.

These fundamentally different and in some cases contradictory conceptions of time and timescapes have significant implications for immigrant incorporation, immigrant exclusion and TLM policies. These intersections create possibilities, new limits and new geophysical timescapes. How does a government ease transition or develop a plan for transition, even if these are made legally possible? What does it mean for democracy and normal democratic behaviour of local civic and political engagement if 'strangers' have been sharing space but not time for decades? If adjustment of status is not an option – as it is not in many ethnic states – what does it mean for migrants when their time has run out? What happens when migrants use alternate timescapes to contest their own liminal existence? Migrants may inhabit or imagine or live alternative/parallel timescapes, but they also live in real communities with other migrants and natives alike. Reimagining time will be a critical issue for immigrant incorporation of TLM who, in some cases, have become *de facto* permanent residents.

Acknowledgements

First and foremost we would like to thank our interview partners in Israel. Without their willingness to share their border-crossing stories, we could not understand this issue in this way. We would also like to thank Israeli professional experts: Iris Maayan, Advocate at the Commissioner for the Rights of Foreign Workers in the Ministry of Industry, Labor and Employment and Hanna Zohar, Founder and Director of Kav LaOved – their cooperation and insights were highly significant to the final product. We are also indebted to Sarah Green, Lena Malm, Moshe Semyonov, Katharina Tyran and Aviva Zeltzer-Zubida. Their comments on previous versions helped us better understand borders, time and migration.

Notes

1 We recruited interviewees through open announcements at community-based organisations and by distributing advertisements in churches and the central bus station (places known to have many migrants). The interviews followed approved protocols with human subjects. Interviews lasted one hour and were transcribed, coded and analysed using standard procedures for qualitative research. All interviewees gave their consent for their interview material to be used in published material.
2 The text is presented as it was written using SMS spellings, misspellings and typos. We have purposely left the dialogue unedited.

References

Adam, Barbara (1994) *Time and Social Theory*. Cambridge, Polity.

Adam, Barbara (1998) *Timescapes of Modernity: The Environment and Invisible Hazards*. London: Routledge.

Adam, Barbara (2008) 'The timescapes challenge: engagement with the invisible temporal', in R. Edwards (ed.), *Researching Lives Through Time: Time, Generation and Life Stories*, Timescapes Working Paper Series No. 1. Leeds: University of Leeds, pp. 7–12.

Anderson, Benedict (1991) *Imagined Communities: Reflections on the Origins and Spread of Nationalism*. London: Verso.

Bartram, David (2004) 'Labor migration policy and the governance of the construction industry in Israel and Japan', *Politics and Society*, 32(2): 131–170.

Berger, L. Peter and Thomas Luckmann (1967) *The Social Construction of Reality*. Garden City, NY: Anchor.

Berry, John (2001) 'A psychology of immigration', *Journal of Social Issues*, 57(3): 615–631.

Buriel, Raymond (1993) 'Acculturation, respect for cultural-differences, and biculturalism among 3 generations of Mexican-American and Euro American school-children', *Journal of Genetic Psychology*, 154(4): 531–543.

Crosby, W. Alfred (1997) *The Measure of Reality: Quantification and Western Society, 1250–1600*. Cambridge: Cambridge University Press.

Cwerner, B. Saulo (2001) 'The times of migration', *Journal of Ethnic and Migration Studies*, 27(1): 7–36.

Derfner, Larry (2012) 'The tragedy and threat of African refugees in Israel', +972 *magazine*, 20 May. http://972mag.com/the-tragedy-and-threat-of-african-refugees-in-israel/46282. Accessed 2 August 2016.

Durkheim, Émile (1965) *The Elementary Forms of the Religious Life*. New York: The Free Press.

Edelman, Murray (1996) *From Art to Politics: How Artistic Creations Shape Political Conceptions*. Chicago, IL: University of Chicago Press.

Elchardus, Mark (1988) 'The rediscovery of Chronos: the new role of time in sociological theory', *International Sociology*, 3(1): 35–59.

Elchardus, Mark and Wendy Smits (2006) 'The persistence of the standardized life cycle', *Time and Society*, 15(2/3): 303–326.

Foner, Nancy (1979) 'West Indians in New York City and London: a comparative analysis', *International Migration Review*, 13: 284–297.

Gabaccia, R. Donna (2000) *Italy's Many Diasporas (Global Diasporas)*. London: Routledge.

Gelfand, Donald (1989) 'Immigration, aging, and intergenerational relationships', *The Gerontologist*, 29(3): 366–372.

Giddens, Anthony (1990) *The Consequences of Modernity*. Stanford, CA: Stanford University Press.

Goren, Yuval (2014) 'Will not be deported: 221 migrant workers children will receive permanency', nrg, 11 February. www.nrg.co.il/online/1/ART2/552/037.html. Accessed 2 August 2016.

Green, L. Nancy (2006) 'Time and the study of assimilation', *Rethinking History: The Journal of Theory and Practice*, 10(2): 239–258.

Griffiths, Melanie, Ali Rogers and Bridget Anderson (2013) *Migration, Time and Temporalities: Review and Prospect*. COMPAS Research Resources Paper, March. www. compas.ox.ac.uk/2013/migration-time-and-temporalities-review-and-prospect/. Accessed 2 August 2016.

Harper, Robin and Hani Zubida (2010) 'Making room at the table: incorporation of foreign workers in Israel', *Policy and Society*, 29(4): 371–383.

Hovel, Revital (2014) 'Court hands Sudanese national 18 years for attempting to rape girl', *Ha'aretz*, 20 February. www.haaretz.com/israel-news/.premium-1.576983. Accessed 17 August 2016.

Jeffay, Nathan (2012) 'Israeli anger over "African" crime wave', *Forward*, 27 May. http://forward.com/articles/156804/israeli-anger-over-african-crime-wave/?p= all Accessed 2 August 2016.

Jones-Correa, Michael (1998) 'Different paths: immigration, gender, and political participation', *International Migration Review*, 32(2): 326–349.

Kasinitz, Philip, John H. Mollenkopf and Mary C. Waters (eds) (2004) *Becoming New Yorkers: Ethnographies of the New Second Generation*. New York: Russell Sage Foundation.

Kemp, Adriana (2007) 'Managing migration, reprioritizing national citizenship: undocumented migrant workers' children and policy reforms in Israel', *Theoretical Inquiries in Law*, 8(2): 663–692.

King, Russell, Mark Thomson, Tony Fielding and Tony Warnes (2006) 'Time, generations and gender in migration and settlement', in Penninx Rinus Maria Berger and Karen Kraal (eds), *The Dynamics of International Migration and Settlement in Europe*. Amsterdam: Amsterdam University Press, pp. 233–268.

Kubovich, Yaniv (2012) 'Dozens of Israelis protest against African migrants in south Tel Aviv', *Ha'aretz*, 31 December. www.haaretz.com/news/national/dozens-of-israelis-protest-against-african-migrants-in-south-tel-aviv.premium-1.491093. Accessed 2 August 2016.

Kubovich, Yaniv (2013) 'Woman's decapitated body found in suitcase in south Tel Aviv', *Ha'aretz*, 3 August. www.haaretz.com/news/national/1.539543. Accessed 2 August 2016.

Luhmann, Niklas (1967) 'The future cannot begin: temporal structures in modern society', *Social Research*, 43(1): 130–152.

Moss, Dorothy (2010) 'Memory, space and time: researching children's lives', *Childhood*, 17(4): 530–544.

Mui, C. Ada (1996) 'Depression among elderly Chinese immigrants: an exploratory study', *Social Work*, 41(6): 633–645.

Nakash, Ora, Maayan Nagar, Anat Shoshani, Hani Zubida and Robin A. Harper (2012) 'The effect of acculturation and discrimination on mental health symptoms and risk behaviors among adolescent migrants in Israel', *Cultural Diversity and Ethnic Minority Psychology*, 18(3): 228–238.

Nathan, Gilad (2011) *The Various Solutions for the Hardships of Truly Ill Elderly in Need of Nursing Care to Hire a Care Giver*. Jerusalem: Knesset Research and Data Center, 21 February, in Hebrew.

Parsons, Talcott (1951) *The Social System*. London: Routledge & Kegan Paul.

Portes, Alejandro and Rubén G. Rumbaut (2006) *Immigrant America: A Portrait*. Berkeley: University of California Press.

Raijman, Rebeca and Adriana Kemp (2007) 'Labor migration, managing the ethno-national conflict, and client politics in Israel', in Sarah S. Willen (ed.), *Transnational Migration to Israel in Global Comparative Context*. Plymouth, MA: Lexington Books, pp. 31–50.

Rose, G. (1993) *Feminism and Geography: The Limits of Geographical Knowledge*. Cambridge: Polity.

Rumbaut, Rubén G. (1994) 'The crucible within: ethnic identity, self-esteem, and segmented assimilation among children of immigrants', *International Migration Review*, 28(4): 748–794.

Sa'ar, Relly (2006) 'Prime Minister vowed to help foreign workers' kids, but the State wants to deport them', *Ha'aretz*, 7 May. www.haaretz.com/ pm-vowed-to-help-foreign-work ers-kids-but-the-state-wants-to-deport-them-1.187017. Accessed 17 August 2016.

Shachar, Ayelet (2009) *The Birthright Lottery: Citizenship and Global Inequality*. Cambridge, MA: Harvard University Press.

Sheen, David (2011) 'South Tel Aviv residents march to demand deportation of foreigners', *Ha'artez*, 8 April. www.haaretz.com/israel-news/south-tel-aviv-residents-march-to-demand-deportation-of-foreigners-1.354760. Accessed 17 August 2016.

Shoshani, Anat, Nakash Ora, Hani Zubida and Robin A. Harper (2014) 'Mental health and engagement in risk behaviors among migrant adolescents in Israel: the protective functions of secure attachment, self-esteem, and perceived peer support', *Journal of Immigrant & Refugee Studies*, 12(3): 233–249.

Sorokin, A. Pitirim (1943) *Sociocultural Causality, Space, Time*. Durham, NC: Duke University Press.

Treas, Judith and Jeanne Batalova (2009) 'Immigrants and aging', *International Handbook of Population Aging*, 1: 365–394.

Urry, J. (1991) 'Time and Space in Giddens' Social Theory', in C. Bryant and D. Jary (eds), *Giddens' Theory of Structuration: A Critical Appreciation*. London: Routledge, pp. 160–175.

Willen, Sarah (ed.) (2007) *Transnational Migration to Israel in Global Comparative Context*. Plymouth, MA: Lexington Books.

Yahirun, J. Jenjira (2012) 'Take me "home": return migration among Germany's older immigrants', *International Migration*, 52(4): 231–254.

Zerubavel, Eviatar (1977) 'The French republican calendar: a case study in the sociology of time', *American Sociological Review*, 42: 868–877.

Zerubavel, Eviatar (1982) 'The standardization of time: a sociohistorical perspective', *American Journal of Sociology*, 88(1): 1–23.

Zubida, Hani, Liron Lavi, Robin A. Harper, Ora Nakash and Anat Shoshani (2013) 'Home and away – hybrid perspective on identity formation in 1.5 and second generation adolescent immigrants in Israel', *Glocalism*, 1. www.glocalismjournal.net/ImagePub. aspx?id=144476. Accessed 2 August 2016.

6

New pasts, presents and futures: time and space in family migrant networks between Kosovo and western Europe

Carolin Leutloff-Grandits

For many families in Kosovo, migration is an integral part of life. This is true even if they do not themselves migrate but, rather, seem 'stuck' in a village such as the one in south Kosovo where I conducted fieldwork between 2011 and 2013.[1] In fact, in this village, and throughout almost all of Kosovo, there is what one might term a 'culture' of migration. Every person has close family members who are living or have lived abroad, often for decades. This 'culture of migration' has changed through the years, in response to external and policy transformations. These have been drastic, including starkly modified European border and migration regimes as well as Kosovo's own changing societal and political situation, particularly after the end of war in Kosovo in 1999. All of these changes have affected not only experiences of border crossing but also household and family relations within the village.

Male labour migration has formed the basis of the household economy throughout rural Kosovo since at least the 1950s. While before 1960 migrants from Kosovo had travelled primarily to Turkey and Belgrade, in the 1960s they began to migrate to western Europe as so-called *Gastarbeiter* or guest workers. There, they functioned as an 'outpost' of the village household, supplying the family at home with aid in the form of remittances (Reineck 1991; von Aarburg and Gretler 2008).

With the rise of ethnic tensions between Serbs and Albanians in Kosovo in the 1980s, and especially with the intensification of this conflict after 1989, economic spurs to migration were reinforced by political concerns. The escalation of the conflict in Kosovo resulted in the relocation of women and children to Western countries. The collapse of socialism in most eastern European countries and the end of the Cold War, which changed the power geometry in the world, also affected the movements of people in Kosovo. As of 1992, trans-border mobility was restricted to those seeking asylum or family reunion. Accordingly, the migration of women and children resulted in the partial dissolution of the complex, patrilocal households in which a married couple lived with their married son(s), or several married brothers. These complex households had been widespread, especially among Albanian families in rural Kosovo (Hockenoes 2006). When the war ended and the United

Nations (UN) assumed administration of the area in 1999, the opportunity to migrate became even more restricted and was now largely limited to those seeking entry to Europe for family completion or to marry.

In this chapter, I explore how migrants and their family members in Kosovo experienced the crossing of borders between Kosovo and western Europe and the effect this crossing had on family relations and visions for the future. As my material will show, polity borders are not only spatial demarcations that delimit sovereignty and create divisions between citizens and non-citizens but function also as temporal boundaries, linked to different social orders and their varying modes of imagining time and space. I will examine how border crossings are linked to (and change) conceptions of family time and the family member's individual life course. Are migrants able to synchronise their experiences with those at home, creating a joint family perspective on two sides of the border? Or can border crossings be seen as 'travel in time and space', altering locations and creating different pasts and futures for those who travel abroad and for those who stay at home?

In order to answer these questions, I focus on migration to Germany and Austria from a village in south Kosovo during three different periods: before the 1990s, during the 1990s, and after the end of the 1998–99 war in Kosovo. My sources are biographical interviews and participant observation of village family life, gathered in the course of long-term social anthropological research carried out in south Kosovo's rural region of Opoja and in the migrants' destination countries. By interviewing several household and family members living in the Kosovo village and abroad, I was able to take a translocal approach. This allowed me to explore the impact migration had on the village's families and their relatives abroad, and what border crossing came to mean to them. In the following, I have concentrated mainly on the perspective of five male villagers whose fathers migrated in the 1960s and 1970s, and who themselves migrated in the 1990s.

First, I will provide a theoretical discussion of border crossings, their impact on notions of time and space, and what this means to the maintenance of family relations across polity borders. I will then discuss what borders meant in family relations before and during the 1990s; this is followed by an analysis of family relations and the different meanings of the border after the war. Finally, I conclude by exploring the meaning of cross-border marriages.

Theoretical frames

When one celebrates a birthday, it becomes clear that one does not conceive of time as a linear connection between the past and future. Rather, it is a multifaceted and multi-dimensional phenomenon involving individual (biographical) time, family (generational) time and historical (social and political) time. While a birthday marks the individual's biological age, it may not say much about the different roles a person assumes during their life. Family time, by contrast, says something about one's role within one's family of origin and family of procreation, while historical time affects both individual and family time through their connection to overall social, economic and cultural changes (Hareven 1982). Individual time, family time and historical time are thus closely linked, for most individual transitions are related to family transitions, and both mirror historical time.

Moreover, concepts of time differ. Modern societies build above all on a linear conception of time; each event is unique and fits into an unalterable linear order. Although links between past and future exist, 'their relationship is neither implicit nor readily predictable' (Halpern and Wagner 1984: 230, 232). The present is seen as imperfect, but progress and growth will, supposedly, create a better future (although the same factors may also obstruct improvement). This linear concept of time, when combined with the idea of progress, also leads to a spatial–temporal 'ranking' of different societies. Some may be seen as more advanced, while others are lagging behind. This makes the polity border, which divides societies by terri-tory, a timeline, as well.

The family, by contrast, dwells within cyclical concepts of time. Here, the past and future are strongly linked, events are predictable and sequential, and they reconstitute the social structure (Halpern and Wagner 1984: 233). The family is often recurrently sanctioned by life-stage rituals such as birth, marriage and death. These form (or are, at least, expected to form) more or less stable coordinates within the family and the community.

Individual time, seen as a life course, is, again, often constructed as linear. Birth, marriage and death are (more or less) unique events from the individual's perspec-tive. Nonetheless, the individual's life course is linked to family time. Even idealised (personal) futures often contain anticipated life-course stages (e.g. marriage and procreation) that may be seen as cyclical elements involving replication of the past (Halpern and Wagner 1984: 233). Furthermore, individuals are seen as having certain obligations towards both their family of origin and family of procreation. For these reasons, people often try to synchronise their life course with family time. They take the family into consideration in conceiving of their future, which may lead to overlapping or conflicting goals during the course of their lives. When they take up a new role in their life, they try to harmonise it with the roles of other family members. This has an impact on generational relations. Individual time is, finally, also linked to historical time, as the timing of life transitions is affected by historical change.

As soon as people cross polity borders, they enter new contexts of time and space. One can assume that migration demarcates a turning point in life, a moment in which migrants take up a new role. However, people respond to new societal and historical conditions within the framework of the social networks in which they are embedded, even when the framework is stretched across geographical locations and borders. In fact, transnational studies have confirmed that migrants who physically cross polity borders often maintain multi-stranded relations with

acquaintances at home. They create a deterritorialised, transnational or translocal space which cuts across nationally demarcated borders, spaces which unite
migrants and those at home. Despite being physically on different sides of polity
borders, and over great geographical distance, migrants often retain an active part in
their local village space. This locality is thus re-created 'translocally' (Massey 1991).
However, migrants may transgress a state border 'trans-temporally' as well. They
not only construct a transborder locality but also a time-space with which to fill it.

Family ties across borders, earlier life experiences and imagining and remembering traces of alternative time-spaces all allow migrants to contest the hegemonic
spatial temporal order imposed on each side of polity borders and their border
regimes. These need not be purely conservative, of course: migrants may also contest their home's family time, creating new visions for their families.

The families at home may also create new mental maps (and clocks). After all,
they are connected to both the alternative time-spaces of migrants and to international media. Appadurai (2005) introduced the concept of social imagination,
which dissolves a person's fixed position in a given physical place. Such imagining
may be created by media and other forms of communication. The new time-spaces
that then emerge can be shared by migrants, by those intending to migrate, and
those who intend to stay at home. Like the time-spaces of migrants, they are able to
challenge polity borders; they can interact with, confirm or contest polity borders
at multiple individual, social and cultural levels.

The family provides a special unit of analysis when studying the interaction of
different time-spaces engendered by the act of border crossing. For migrants as well
as those at home, the family may be an anchor, used to synchronise individual experiences on either side of the border. But the family may also be a source of conflict.
The family itself must be reproduced through social imagination, actions and practices, reaching, in the migrants' case, across vast geographical distances. This active
'family making' deserves special attention, with focus on different strategies, such
as emotional exchanges, financial support or the creation of 'marriage-scapes' as
means of linking individuals across polity borders. Border crossing may, thus, also
challenge, promote and modify the spatial-temporal order of the family.

1960–90: experiencing and transgressing borders within a family time-space

Large numbers of Kosovo Albanians began migrating to western Europe in the
early 1960s, when socialist Yugoslavia concluded labour recruitment treaties with
Germany, Austria and Switzerland. Numerous men from Kosovo migrated for
economic reasons; there was little employment in Kosovo because of a recent surge
in population and the fact that rural areas lagged behind in the implementation
of socialist modernisation (Schmitt 2008). Economic migration continued after
western Europe officially ended labour recruitment in 1973, following the global
oil crisis and resultant economic recession. Socialist Yugoslavia's special position

as a non-aligned country allowed people from Kosovo – then Yugoslav citizens – to travel to western European countries with ease. Assisted by relatives already in place, Kosovo-Albanians (and many other migrants from socialist Yugoslavia) would migrate and search for a job, often successfully, as their cheap labour was still in demand in many economic sectors. This also applied to many migrants from the south of Kosovo, who went to Austria, Germany and Switzerland from the 1960s on. As a 50-year-old migrant I interviewed said in retrospect: 'At that time there were no borders, but there was enough work.'[2]

The migrants remained an integral part of their home village and family, at least in a functional sense. Their continued membership in multiple, patrilinear organised households, which had been widespread in this region before the 1990s, transgressed spatial borders and blurred the geographical boundaries of the village. Before the 1990s, the bulk of labour migrants were men with families at home in the village. Their fathers had often arranged their marriage with a woman from the region, either before or during migration. But the men had left their wife and children at home, in the joint households headed by their father, brother or uncle (see Pichler 2009 on Albanian migrants from Macedonia, Reineck 1991). The migrant men sent a considerable portion of their salaries home to their fathers, who disposed of it; the patriarchal, authoritarian order of village, family and community life remained uncontested. In fact, the migrants reaffirmed their membership in the patrilocal household and the local community. These arrangements even contributed to the 'freezing' of patrilocal household structures and values (Reineck 1991).

The time-space shared by migrants and their family members at home was further reinforced by the former's cyclical visits. Working hard abroad, migrants visited their families at least annually. This changed the yearly rhythm in the villages, for the migrants' visits were the climax of the year. Since migrants mostly visited during the summer months, family festivals such as weddings and circumcisions, which centred on the village and stressed the cyclical nature of family time, were increasingly scheduled for summer. Cyclical family time-space was also maintained by the plans of many migrants to return 'home' someday, to the place they had left, the place to which they belonged and for which they longed (von Aarburg and Gretler 2008). Saving money was central to their life abroad – an abstemious present of postponed consumption, the money invested in a better future at home.

For migrants, life abroad was also experienced as disrupted time. They lived apart from their family and had to care for themselves. They had to manage the transition from small face-to-face village communities to the anonymity and complexity of life in large towns. A large majority worked in blue-collar jobs, with low status and, often, difficult conditions. Many lived in barracks, shared with acquaintances. Many directed their life towards the family at home. They consumed only very moderately, in order to save money to send back; what little spare time they had was usually spent with other migrants rather than with people from the destination society. In at least one respect, they lived under inverted gender norms. Gendered usages prevalent in their village communities were changed: for instance, the men often had to clean, wash and cook for themselves. Thus, although the men directed their lives towards the (still very patriarchally organised) village, their life worlds differed in several important respects from those whom they had left at home.

When the men visited their homes in Kosovo, they often did not talk much about their experiences. This was in accordance with a view of the future in which their children would not join them abroad. The future of the family was at home, in Kosovo. The money they sent was used for the necessities of everyday life, for building houses and educating children. Their financial contributions and the consumer goods they brought home from abroad, such as washing machines and other household equipment – uncommon in the villages in Kosovo at that time – were meant to improve living conditions at home. Their children were to be spared the sacrifices they themselves had made for the sake of the family (see also Reineck 1991).

However, in these holidays at home, there were often difficulties in synchronising the perspectives of those who had stayed at home and those who had long been abroad. The lack of common everyday experiences made it difficult to communicate and to create common dreams and ideas of the future. Migrants, for example, had not seen their children grow up; holidays were often too short to create unstrained emotional relations between fathers and children and between spouses. Although strongly attached to their homes as the places to which they belonged, migrants had difficulty transforming this emotion into actual relations, into 'ways of being' (Levitt and Glick Schiller 2004). This further impeded the sharing of life perspectives, creating disparate time-spaces. 'I went into another world', as a 60-year-old migrant, who had worked in Austria from the early 1970s, put it. The time-space gap between migrants and those at home also appeared in the narrative interviews of villagers who had been children before the 1990s, when their fathers had been abroad. Agim, born in the mid-1970s, explained to me that his father, who had moved to Germany in the early 1970s, had remained a stranger to him during his childhood. He had come home once a year for two to three weeks at a time, but was then busy meeting other relatives, working the farm, and so on. When they finally came closer to each other towards the end of the visit, the father had had to leave again, and the relationship cooled. Ylber, born in the early 1970s, also remembered that his father had been abroad during his childhood. Ylber did not complain about this, as he had had very close relations to his grandmother, with whom he shared a bed. By contrast, he perceived his father as German, with different cultural habits, scarcely belonging to his family.

Nonetheless, the products their fathers brought home made a great impression and influenced the ways the future was imagined by their children and by village youth, reinforcing the respect felt for migrants. As Ylber put it, he thought that the migrants, including his father, came 'from planet Mars' or 'a land of honey and milk'. He reminisced:

In every third house there was someone abroad. And we went to this house and asked when they would come home. We wanted to see them. When they came for a visit, we would come to visit them in the evenings. We received biscuits. The one who came from Berlin was like an astronaut for us. A pilot. We thought that there was Berlin somewhere outside, within an empty space. Then he came home and brought the first television. And I asked myself how is this possible, how is it possible that humankind is creating something like that?

Ylber joined most of the young villagers in dreaming of a future in which they could own and consume Western products, ranging from sweets or 'original' Marlboro cigarettes to televisions. Some even thought about migrating to Western countries. However, their fathers mostly disappointed them, as they did not want their children to move abroad. Alban, whose father was in Austria, had always wanted a Swiss army knife:

> Every time my father returned from Austria, I asked him if he had bought a knife for me, but he always said that the knife-seller had died. To this day, I feel the need to buy such a knife as soon as I enter a flea market in Germany. I have a whole collection of them at home. It is like I need to overcome my longing for it while I was a child.

That their fathers often ignored their wishes did not stop the children from dreaming; it only worsened their personal relations. They dreamt of going to western Europe in order to achieve material prosperity and a better life for themselves. In fact, despite labour migrants' attempts to direct their life towards their homes, despite their sending back remittances and paying many cyclical visits, the common time-spaces shared by migrants and many villagers were increasingly challenged. Older migrants saw their future back home, while many young villagers dreamed of a better future in western European countries.

Asylum and family reunion migration as challenges to family time

In 1989, Kosovo's autonomy was annulled. Simultaneously, Albanians were pushed out of public institutions, discriminated against and suppressed. In 1991, when socialist Yugoslavia dissolved into bloody wars in Slovenia, Croatia and Bosnia–Herzegovina, Albanian men feared being drafted into the Serbian-dominated army, as well as prosecution and violence. They urgently needed to get out of the country. Political motives for outmigration were added to economic ones. At the same time it was increasingly difficult to cross the border between Kosovo and the European Union (EU), as European border regimes tightened after 1992 and the Yugoslav passport lost its function (Fassmann and Münz 1996; Bauböck and Perchinig 2006). Suddenly, the border became a solid membrane for Kosovo Albanians as well. Migration into western European countries was restricted to those applying for family reunion or cross-border marriages, or those who were able to cross the border without documents, whereupon most applied for asylum.

During this crisis, numerous 'guest workers' fetched their dependents. They applied for family reunion with their sons and, to a lesser extent, their daughters and wives. This was an emergency measure, done only because their dependents needed a safe place. Many sons reacted with ambivalence. Some unreservedly welcomed the opportunity to go abroad, for they had dreamt of the 'Golden West' and the life they could build there. But others had wanted to complete their education in Kosovo and to build a life at home, a future dream brutally interrupted by political factors.

The fact that sons (and, sometimes, other family members) were now united with fathers with whom they had not had a chance to develop a close relationship also caused friction. Ylber recalled going abroad in 1991, a few days after his seventeenth birthday. He took a train together with his father, who had been living in Austria since 1973 and who was returning from his yearly visit home. He remembered that he had been a smoker, but could not confess this to his father, as this would have been disrespectful. Smoking secretly in the train, he realised that he was running very short of cigarettes. After they arrived in Linz, he got up very early in the morning in order to buy cigarettes somewhere. He described the experience:

> I tried to remember my way and when arriving in a supermarket, I only said 'cigarettes', as I did not speak a word of German. Someone then gave me a packet of Marlboros. I wanted to pay, but I did not understand anything. He said something, but I do not know what, I only realized that he gave me the cigarettes and went away. It was a packet of Marlboros. To smoke Marlboro was a dream for me. Everyone wanted the best.

In the many cases in which only the sons joined their fathers, the men had to manage a household without women. The father, who worked full-time, had very little time to care for his sons and often little understanding of their needs and sorrows. This often led to conflicts, as it did with Agim, who was 14 when in 1991 he joined his father in Berlin, somewhere he had always envisioned his own future. However, in the shared male household, problems between Agim and his father became overwhelming and two years later, after a series of conflicts, Agim moved out and found shelter in a shared flat owned by the youth welfare council. He remained there until he finished school and began work, when his salary made it possible for him to rent his own flat. In retrospect, Agim maintained that his father had not supported his outmigration, not even in the 1990s when most other migrants had sent for their families in order to save them from the ethnic conflict in Kosovo. With this, the father had undermined the unity of the family.

Other young migrants could not count on applying for family reunion and thus being able to go abroad, either because their father had already come home, or because he had never migrated in the first place. In such cases, youths faced crossing borders as undocumented or illegal migrants, a very difficult endeavour. As one migrant said: 'The way to Germany was very long, very expensive and very risky.' But even then, border crossing often remained a family affair, at least in part. Undocumented migrants were often supported by relatives who organised their trip and paid the human traffickers who were to bring them over the border. Alban, for example, crossed the Hungarian and then the Austrian and German borders as an undocumented migrant in 1994. He had had the help of his wife's relatives, who paid the traffickers a few thousand deutschmarks. His father-in-law then took him in until he applied for asylum and was placed in a refugee barracks.

Like Alban, most migrants who could not legalise themselves via family reunion applied for asylum as soon as they reached their destination. The application was followed by a long administrative process in which migrants often had to wait for years for a decision on their right to stay. For many, this period was an insecure, empty waiting time. Asylum seekers had no right to work, no right to continue their education and no right to leave the country, let alone a right to visit their relatives at home. Instead of finding a safe haven, a better future, so often associated with migration into the 'Glorious West', migration created a 'no-time' for some of the migrants, a life without a foothold.

The asylum seekers' enforced and prolonged absence from home put great pressure on kinship relations. A 45-year-old woman told me how the man she had married in 1991 migrated abroad soon after their wedding. He applied for asylum and so could not return; husband and wife had no personal contact for years. The household in Kosovo did not have a phone, and the letters he wrote were addressed to his parents, as this was a sign of respect.

Family relations were also strained because asylum applicants did not have the right to summon family members, which meant they could not rescue their spouse and children from the tensions in Kosovo. Even after they had been granted a residence permit, some lacked the economic security that was the precondition for acquiring permission for family members to join them. As a result, many families were reunited only after many years, if ever.

In some cases, attempts to reunite the family were prevented not by legal barriers but by relatives at home in Kosovo. Some parents, for example, opposed the outmigration of their son's wife and children, arguing that they did not want to be left alone and needed their daughter-in-law to care for them. Genc, now 50, left Kosovo for Austria in 1991 using his Yugo-passport. Soon after, the Yugo-passport was declared invalid and Genc stayed on illegally. He worked hard and saved money to pay for traffickers to bring his wife and children to him. However, his father intervened because Genc's brother was soon to marry and Genc was expected to pay for the wedding, something he could not have done had he spent the money on traffickers. Anyway, his father argued, his parents needed their daughter-in-law at home to clean and cook, as well as to prepare for the wedding.

In other cases, family reunion remained incomplete. Even at best, reunion could add to the burdens the migrants experienced in the destination countries. Suddenly they had to support a whole family and find schooling and a home for their children.

Dritan, for example, who had left Kosovo in 1986 at the age of 24, brought his wife and his two sons (aged 13 and 15) in 1995. He said the time of family reunion had been a happy time, as they were finally together again, but also a very difficult period. He was pressured to earn much more money than he had earned before, as his family's living costs were considerably higher in Austria than they had been in Kosovo. In Kosovo, his family owned a house, whereas in Austria he had to pay rent. He was forced to work as much as possible, and had almost no time for his family. For his sons, Dritan said, this period was still more difficult. They had to go to school without speaking German; their parents could not give them support, as the father was too busy working and the mother was helpless herself. Furthermore, he had left his daughter, 10 years old at that time, with her grandparents at home. On the one hand, he had not wanted to deprive his own parents of her company; on the other, he would have had to find and finance a larger flat. In order to apply for a family reunion, the migrant had to show that his flat was 'sufficient' to house all arriving family members. In this case, as in many others during the 1990s, migration was a highly ambivalent process; reunion with some family members often meant that other family members were left behind.

People worried about those who remained behind in dangerous, economically depressed Kosovo. Many migrants remained strongly home-oriented. They tried to put money aside to send home to their families, parents and (male) siblings. In the 1990s, this was done irrespective of whether the migrants managed to bring their spouses and children or not. The ethnic conflict and the flight from Kosovo were experienced as a time to show solidarity with those at home; individual aspirations were subordinated to meeting the needs of the crisis. This homogenised the experiences of migrants. Many prioritised solidarity on a family level; the escalating ethnic conflict also strengthened national unity and promoted political activism. Living far from home, without being able to make direct contact, enhanced many migrants' patriotic feelings. Many believed in the Albanian cause and nation. They helped finance parallel Albanian schools and hospitals in Kosovo, as well as the military expenses of the newly founded Kosovo Liberation Army. Such activities allowed migrants to create a common national time-space that transcended polity borders. They believed in the future of Kosovo, in a highly patriotic, not very pragmatic sense. Those who did not save money to send to relatives at home or who disregarded their familial bonds were considered 'lost' to the community (Dahinden 2005).

After 2000: the difficulties of creating new futures here and there

The military engagement of the North Atlantic Treaty Organization (NATO) in Kosovo in spring 1999 ended Serbian dominance there. The social conditions in Kosovo were profoundly changed. Under the protection of the United Nations (UN), Albanians could now enter the administration (again). The need to build state structures created many new jobs for Kosovo Albanians and encouraged some migrants to return earlier than planned. Albanians – at home as well as abroad – were initially very enthusiastic about Kosovo's future. However, this enthusiasm soon waned. Migrants who had been immobilised abroad pending a decision on their asylum application returned for the first time after many years to a situation that was much worse than they had imagined. Alban, who had been abroad for six years, told me that he had been very impatient to return home but was completely disappointed after his arrival. He found his parents' house in very bad shape. Everyone was older; everything looked poor and run-down. After having been welcomed by his relatives, he withdrew to his room and cried.

Although migrants and villagers joined in massive efforts to build houses and businesses, the region's internal problems persisted. For years after the war, the production sector continued to be underdeveloped, unemployment and corruption remained high, and state social services were extremely meagre. Meanwhile, social stratification inside Kosovo increased, as some families gained economically from the post-war transformation, while others suffered poverty and insecurity due to the area's very high unemployment rates – especially in economically marginalised regions such as southern Kosovo. Many Albanians from rural Kosovo, at home as well as those visiting from abroad, believed that Kosovo was not moving forward as hoped for; it had come to a standstill. Alban's brother Dritan, who had been a refugee in Germany for seven years and who had returned voluntarily in 2001, said: 'I tried to live in Kosovo, but it is impossible. The system does not let us live there. There is no work, no money, no life, and no freedom. For this I have not returned.' In 2003, soon after he returned, he gave nearly ten thousand euro to human traffickers in order to move his whole family abroad. However, once there, his family's asylum applications were turned down, because Kosovo was now considered a safe place for Albanians. Others who managed to cross the border with the help of traffickers remained abroad as undocumented migrants, sometimes for years, a condition of crippling insecurity. The border regime had become even harsher for Kosovo Albanians after the war.

The declaration of Kosovo's independence, announced by the Albanian government in February 2008 and since recognised by more than one hundred countries, did not change this. Kosovo is still the only country whose residents need a visa to enter almost all European countries (visa-free travel is only possible to Albania, Montenegro and Macedonia); it is, consequently, more marginalised than ever. This means that Kosovo's time-space status has dipped below even that of its erstwhile 'rival' Serbia, for whose residents EU visa requirements were lifted at the end of 2009. I often heard villagers and migrants discuss this time-space ranking: Kosovo, they said, was at least twenty years behind western European countries and its future was very uncertain. The Kosovo border to western Europe, now more than ever difficult to cross legally, was seen, also, as a timeline, dividing 'modern' countries with promising futures from Kosovo, which was perceived as falling far behind.

Even worse, it was a place that would *never* reach the future to which its residents aspired. As Ylber said to me (as 'a German'): 'Do you know, it will take very long. This part here has been created by God, and it will never be like the Germans want it to be.'

Many middle-aged and elderly migrants joined villagers in thinking that Kosovo had been a better place before the late 1980s. Ylber, for instance, told me that socialism had offered more opportunities than did the current regime: pupils like him had received university scholarships, and those with good education had been able to find good jobs. In post-war Kosovo, scholarships were few and meagre and 'you need to be a thief in order to receive a job', as one university-educated villager put it.

With the passing of time, migrants gradually changed their relations towards their home and destination country. Those who had secured permanent residency rights said that they could not relinquish the opportunity offered after having waited for so long and endured so much. Those who had not yet brought their children to join them but who could do so now did so – this time without their parents protesting. Others envisioned staying abroad for their children's sake, for they had adapted to the new language and environment much more readily than their parents. Migrants hoped for a better future, if not for themselves, then for their children, in a country which offered more social security and greater life prospects than did Kosovo. Alban, for example, said that he remains a Kosovo Albanian in his heart, but that he wants to stay in Germany because of its welfare state, which he regards as 'European' and which gives him and his family the social security they increasingly lack in Kosovo. Should Kosovo's state ever improve, Alban said, he would return, but he has no faith in this. Alban's wife said that their only daughter, who is 5, might never want to return, in which case they would remain with her as the most important person in their lives.

This attitude involves tacit reorientation, from a future in the home village towards a future in the country of immigration. It also entails a transition from belonging in a complex family based on values of patrilocality and seniority to being abroad in a nuclear family centred on children. This was a new spatial positioning. It changed social and temporal coordinates, putting those at home at the lower end of the scale, prioritising those abroad. The new ranking also found expression economically. As Alban, who had migrated in the 1990s and who had held refugee status for many years, put it: 'I do not save as much as I did earlier, but I do not mind. I need money for my daughter. She says, "I want this and this." She wants to go to McDonald's and she needs clothes and she wants toys.' He is thus living more in the here and now and less in a future 'at home' in Kosovo.

However, when migrants decided to opt for family reunion in the destination country, and thus a possible future abroad, many realised that they had lost irretrievable time while waiting (for residency permits, labour permits, etc.), years they could never recover. Further, many suffered from low economic and social status. Alban and Agim, for instance, were both more or less long-term unemployed; they lived off social transfer payments and kept busy by doing smaller jobs on the side. The combination of social transfer payments and temporary jobs was a relatively dependable, even respectable income, but offered no chance for social advancement. This was very frustrating. Agim felt that he had, in part, suffered discrimination from the German authorities and citizens, which made him angry; while Alban felt marginalised and was pessimistic about his future prospects.

Ylber was better off, as he had a permanent job at the railway company. He also did weekend jobs to increase his income. He complained, however, that his life was a bit boring. The days looked all the same, without much time for anything but work and family obligations. At weekends, he and his family would shop and visit relatives, but they were all very much looking forward to their home visit to Kosovo, where they could relax and have a good time in the circle of relatives and friends. In Germany, Ylber experienced the time-space of his destination country as being governed by a temporality that was secure and materially rewarding but cold, dull and boring. Times 'at home', in Kosovo, by contrast, were adventurous, exciting and emotionally warm, although also full of insecurities and inadequacies.

Despite practical considerations which made a future abroad attractive, many migrants still invested in housing 'at home' in Kosovo. Indeed, post-war Kosovo was characterised by a house-building boom. The new houses were often built in Western styles, in order to symbolise the migrant family's modernity and progress. At the same time, building a house confirmed a cyclical notion of time. Houses express migrants' sense of belonging and membership in the local community, as well as incarnating the migrant's dream of returning 'home'. Building a house symbolised their presence despite their absence. The house linked the village to their personal migration experience, in a spatial–temporal sense. Migrants stressed the fact that they built their house(s) for their son(s), so that sons would remain connected to the village and to their fathers' relatives and thus to a place that was associated with home. The house constituted a spatial–temporal bridge for the migrants' sons.

The building of houses 'at home' also redefined family relations, and questioned household configurations and notions of solidarity with those 'at home'. As in other parts of rural Kosovo, customary law decreed that each brother should receive a more or less equal share of his parents' landed property and housing. However, if a complex household with two or more brothers was divided before a migrant brother started building his house, the migrant's house was often larger and nicer than the houses of his brothers. Unsurprisingly, household divisions in combination with outmigration could adversely affect fraternal relations. Those at home felt both envious and puzzled as to why the migrant brother was now, after household division, diverting money that had formerly gone to them into house-building. The migrants themselves were critical of this type of behaviour. As Ylber put it,

> It was much, much better when I and my generation were young. There were better times for this country. You could hardly imagine building a house for yourself and

abandoning your brother, for example. This happens often here now. Today, this is normal ... I think a lot about Kosovo and I ask myself what has gotten better since the time I left.

The division of the household often left the brothers at home insecure and vulnerable, for they could no longer count on regular remittances. At the same time, it increased the need to send an additional person from the at-home household abroad, despite the legal difficulties that stood in the way of this, especially after the war. At that point, family reunion and marriage constituted the few options left for those seeking to migrate legally. Many villagers sought to marry their sons (and, to a lesser extent, daughters) to someone living abroad.

Sometimes, complex households remained undivided after the war. Migrants, accordingly, still belonged to the joint household of their parents and/or brother(s), even if they obviously maintained nuclear households in their destination countries, and also exerted sole control over the money they earned. In many cases, however, such migrants continued to support their relatives, at least their close relatives, in one way or another. In some cases, migrant brothers financed the building of a house with several floors for all household members at home. Others even financed the building of identical houses for all their brothers, which were often placed next to each other, in a chain. Such identical houses were seen as a visible expression of the unity of brothers, the column of a strong and successful (patrilocal) family. But in the new millennium, even supportive practices of this sort were open to critique.

This happened to Genc, who had left Kosovo during the 1990s and who had had his wife and sons (then 14 and 16 years old) join him in 2005. Although Genc's father had died at that time, Genc and his younger brother did not divide their common household in the village. Instead, some years later, Genc invested in renovating the common household's home, inhabited, at that time, exclusively by his younger brother, his wife and two sons. The brother was long-term unemployed, and the children in school. Genc viewed this positively. He explained that his home village is the place where his heart is warm again and in which he needs to invest. At the same time, he criticised aspects of the situation; he feels, to some degree, like a visitor in his own home. Furthermore, he complained that his chances of supporting his brother were limited, as he had to finance his family abroad.

More generally, migrants used investment in houses to re-create ties they had disrupted through outmigration and the relocation of family members. They tried to create a common family space, which could serve as a refuge from the challenges and the disappointments they experienced abroad. It was also to provide for the continuation of the (male) family line. However, this was not easy. It was increasingly unclear how migrants were to interact with brothers who had stayed at home and who had their own families. It was not possible to join their brothers in a common vision of the future, not even after investing in that future by building a joint family house or even two (or more) identical houses at home.

In this situation, several migrants linked their vision of the future to children who had either been born abroad or, in many cases, been brought there, often when in their teens. The future of the children suddenly became the decisive factor for the fortune of their parents. The parents' own vision of the future had faded; they now hoped to fulfil themselves in the life project of their children (see also Schiffauer 1991). Their children were the ones who would become economically successful in the destination countries; the children were also given the task of maintaining a bridge to parental homes in Kosovo.

Migrants tried to support their children's efforts in both directions. During their annual visits home, they took their children with them. Spending a lot of money on family gatherings and festivities during these weeks, they were happy whenever they felt that their children were also developing a sense of Kosovo as their home.

Upside down: repositioning the village and creating new family bonds

Relations between villagers and migrants were also challenged by the technical achievements of the information technology era. These transformed life in the village, not least by shifting the clear-cut spatial–temporal hierarchies between places like Kosovo, and 'the West'. In the years preceding the war, most Kosovo villages had few, if any, telephone connections. By the end of the war, nearly every household had one or several mobile phones, a television, and – especially important – a computer with internet access. The latter enabled village youth to connect to global youth culture without themselves moving physically, unimpeded by polity borders. It helped generate and form images of the good life and of the future to which they aspired. Village youth used Facebook to create their own internal chat-forums, circumventing the village's established age and gender barriers. Young people, especially young women and girls, began wearing 'Western' outfits, the tight jeans and shirts which could be bought in the flourishing sector of Western-style shops in nearby towns, or which had been brought as presents by visiting migrants. Villagers could now keep in daily contact with those abroad by using Skype, Facebook or Messenger (see Levitt 1998; Peleikis 2003; Appadurai 2004; Leutloff-Grandits and Pichler 2014).

Middle-aged migrants living abroad met these changes with astonishment and criticism. Instead of celebrating the fact that villages were 'catching up' with what could be termed 'global modernity', they expressed a rather conservative view of these changes. They said that village girls showed too much skin and were too familiar with men and that this was a sign of degraded morals. As Ylber put it: 'Today you will not catch a boyfriend as soon as you do not use make-up and have Messenger. But you cannot move the clock back.' Others complained that the pace of change in Kosovo was faster than it was abroad, and that the changes were not always for the better. According to Alban: 'It was healthier in former times. People cared for each other. They cared for the elderly and the ill. Today, no one cares for them.'

But villagers could also be critical of migrants. Some villagers claimed that (at least some) migrants behaved in an uncultured and primitive fashion. I was asked several times why 'we' (as 'Westerners') seemed unable to improve and 'cultivate' their relatives abroad, for they did not seem to change for the better. For example, I was told that when entering Kosovo by car, migrants would immediately start throwing their waste out of the car windows – something they did not do abroad. While in Kosovo, they would allow themselves to ignore legal prescriptions like speed limits, norms they accepted abroad, and would indulge in problematic, disrespectful behaviour, especially concerning gender norms. They did this, ironically, while commenting adversely on the weak rule of law in Kosovo and criticising the 'uncultivated behaviour' of the locals themselves. Other villagers, conversely, found migrants too 'Westernised', particularly when it came to moral standards. Their outfits were seen as a marker of degraded morality. While it was more or less accepted that young women in the village might wear miniskirts (even if many did not), a visiting migrant teenager in a miniskirt easily provoked negative comments: the skirt was interpreted as a sign that she was dating boys, or would like to, and thus had low moral standards. Young migrant men with earrings and fashionable hairstyles were likewise condemned as womanisers, and hence unreliable marriage partners for young village women.

Nonetheless, the images and ideals of Western lifestyles fed young villagers' desire to travel abroad to a better more modern life, as well as the material security which many Kosovo families lacked. Young men and especially young women felt trapped in their village and in Kosovo as a whole. They missed relative gender equality, opportunities for education and/or for employment. Kosovo was seen as restricted, backward, lagging behind. The future was abroad.

Accordingly, both village boys and girls were attracted to the idea of marrying a migrant, even if there was substantial criticism of how some migrants behaved. Most sought to marry someone who had migrated when a child or teenager, or who had been born abroad but still had 'roots' in Kosovo. This type of trans-border marriage became one of the few ways open to those who wished to build a future that linked their own village to a 'better world'. Their parents, who were eager to help their children find a good partner, supported this. They used their connections to relatives abroad (via Skype and/or face-to-face contacts during migrants' home visits) to search for a suitable son- or daughter-in-law.

In many cases, their enquiries were met with sympathy, as many middle-aged migrants wanted to marry their own children to partners from home. In other cases, the young people got to know each other during summer visits, when Kosovo villages turn into sites of happy socialising and celebration, as the streets fill with new cars with foreign number plates. The numerous weddings, often between villager and migrant, lavishly held during the summer in the circle of hundreds of relatives and other guests, became a major site for migrants and villagers to socialise and seek out attractive partners. In this way, interfamilial and intergenerational bonds could be re-established across polity borders without involving material flows from migrants to villagers.[3] Cross-border marriages opened up a 'marriage-scape', which created (a hoped-for utopia of) joint, villager–migrant temporal space. Here, polity borders furnished incentives for new forms of solidarity, exchange and communication. The certainty that migrants would come home once a year to enjoy themselves and relax also affected the village's temporality. Every summer, for a few weeks, the village was suddenly upgraded to modernity. In so far as Kosovo then became the destination for masses of returning migrants, the hegemonic hierarchical spatial order of Europe was challenged. Kosovo was, for a few weeks at least, no longer marginal.

Conclusion

As has been shown, translocal Kosovo Albanian family relations have changed rapidly during the last few decades due to changing border regimes and migration patterns. The different views, positions and linkages that are created between villagers and migrants include different concepts of space and time, past and future. These are brought into play and even nurtured by the experience of polity-border crossing, which structures both the view of 'home' and of the migrants' destination countries. These views, positions and linkages reflect the interaction between historical perceptions of time and individual as well as family concepts of time, which are embedded not only in visions of a linear past and future, but also in cyclical repetitions. Border crossing may thus challenge and reconfigure the balance between different temporal conceptions, be they on the level of the individual's life course, the future of the family, or the general socio-political situation. This redirection of ideas of time and space means that border crossing may also contest the hegemonic timespaces which polity borders supposedly enforce. The crossing of polity-borders puts family relations under very special constraints but also creates very special opportunities when they are over east–west borders (with their strict time hierarchies).

Until the 1990s, male migrants tried to sustain a cyclical notion of time, which reconnected them to the family and the village community and committed them to a reconstitution of the social order while investing in their future at home. However, they often also experienced a 'ruptured time' abroad, distancing them from family members at home. This was even more the case when their sons directed their gaze towards the West and saw their future increasingly as being abroad. During the 1990s, many migrants sent for their sons as a response to the intensified ethnic conflict and tightened EU borders. This resulted in a situation often contrary to their former plans and vision.

After the war, in the new millennium, when Kosovo did not go through its hoped-for transformation and border crossing from Kosovo to western Europe became even more difficult, those migrants who had managed to obtain a residency permit in a EU country planned for their own and their children's future residence abroad. More than ever, the polity border symbolises the line between modernity and backwardness. However, many migrants remain oriented homewards, seeking to integrate their children into cyclical family time, in order to create a future vision that they can share with the family. They want their children to establish emotional ties to Kosovo and to choose a villager as a marriage partner, a desire reciprocated by many young village men and women, who increasingly imagine their future abroad.

By retying family bonds, especially through cross-border marriages, solidarity can be re-created, and hierarchical differences and fractures transcended or even reversed. In the summer months, when trans-border marriages are celebrated in the circle of kin, the village functions as the temporal centre that gathers together translocal kin networks, and is sometimes even seen as a site of accelerated modernisation. The border is thus not only a line of separation, but also a mechanism for bringing relatives on both sides together, in the creation of multi-faceted relations and ties.

While the acts of migrants and villagers are influenced by their position on this side or that side of the polity border, they use these borders for their own constructions of past, present and future. They can take these borders 'seriously', using them to divide the culturally normal from cultural 'Otherness'. Or they can circumvent and disempower polity borders by creating shared migrant-villager time-spaces. The fact that people do not relate to the border only as individuals but within a network of kin and acquaintance creates overlapping networks of border-crossing time-spaces that both shape and promote, but may also weaken, cross-border ties.

Notes

1   This chapter is based on the FWF-financed research project 'The Kosovo family revisited' (Project Number P 22659-G18). Blerina Leka, to whom I am very grateful, assisted fieldwork. I also want to thank Hastings Donnan and Madeleine Hurd for their very valuable comments and for editing this chapter.
2   All interview citations are from fieldwork and have been anonymised for reasons of privacy.
3   Not all children of migrants in the 1990s like to return on 'home visits' or feel happy and at ease 'at home'; and not all married or wanted to marry a partner from Kosovo. Nor were all marriages with regional partners free from conflicts.

References

Appadurai, Arjun (2004) 'The capacity to aspire: culture and the terms of recognition', in V. Rao and M. Walton (eds), *Culture and Public Action: A Cross Disciplinary Dialog in Development Policy*. Stanford CA: Stanford University Press, pp. 59–84.
Appadurai, Arjun (2005) *Modernity at Large: Cultural Dimensions of Globalization*. 2nd edn. Minneapolis: University of Minnesota Press.

Bauböck, Rainer and Bernhard Perchinig (2006) 'Migrations- und Integrationspolitik in Österreich', in H. Dachs et al., *Politik in Österreich*. Vienna: Manz, pp. 726–742.

Dahinden, Janine (2005) *Prishtina – Schlieren. Albanische Migrationsnetzwerke im transnationalen Raum*. Zurich: Seismo.

Fassmann, Heinz and Münz, Rainer (1996) 'Österreich – Einwanderungsland wider Willen', in Heinz Fassmann and Rainer Münz (eds), *Migration in Europa: historische Entwicklung, aktuelle Trends, und politische Reaktionen*. Frankfurt: Campus, pp. 209–228.

Halpern, Joel M. and Richard A. Wagner (1984) 'Time and social structure: a Yugoslav case Study', *Journal of Family History* 9(3): 229–244.

Hareven, Tamara K. (1982) *Family Time and Industrial Time*. Cambridge: Cambridge University Press.

Hockenoes, Paul (2006) 'Cutting the lifeline: migration, family and the future of Kosovo', European Stability Initiative, Berlin–Istanbul, 18 September. http://www.esiweb.org/pdf/esi_document_id_80.pdf. Accessed 2 August 2016.

Leutloff-Grandits, Carolin and Robert Pichler (2014) 'Areas blurred: Albanian migration and the establishment of translocal spaces', in Harald Heppner and Christian Promitzer (eds), *Southeast European Studies in a Globalizing World*, Münster: LIT.

Levitt, Peggy (1998) 'Social remittances: migration driven local-level forms of cultural diffusion', *International Migration Review*, 32(4): 926–948.

Levitt, Peggy and Nina Glick Schiller (2004) 'Conceptualizing simultaneity: a transnational social field perspective on society', *International Migration Review*, 38(145): 595–629.

Massey, Doreen (1991) 'A global sense of place', *Marxism Today*, June, 24–29.

Peleikis, Anja (2003) 'Lebanese in motion: gender and the making of a translocal village', Bielefeld: transcript.

Pichler, Robert (2009) 'Migration, architecture and the imagination of home(land) an Albanian–Macedonian case study', in: Ulf Brunnbauer (ed.), *Transnational Societies, Transterritorial Politics: Migrations in the (Post)-Yugoslav Area*. Munich: Oldenbourg, pp. 213–236.

Reineck, Janet (1991) 'The Past as Refuge: Gender, Migration, and Ideology among the Kosova Albanians.' University of California, Berkeley, Ph.D. thesis.

Schiffauer, Werner (1991) *Die Migranten aus Subay. Türken in Deutschland: Eine Ethnographie*. Stuttgart: Klett-Cotta.

Schmitt, Oliver Jens (2008) *Kosovo: Eine kurze Geschichte einer zentral balkanischen Landschaft*. Vienna: Böhlau.

Von Aarburg, Hans-Peter and Sarah Barbara Gretler (2008) *Kosova-Schweiz: Die albanische Arbeit- und Asylmigration zwischen Kosovo und der Schweiz (1984–2000)*. Münster: Lit.

7

Silenced border crossings and gendered material flows in southern Albania

Nataša Gregorič Bon

My friend Maria and I were sitting on the front porch of the house of the village teacher, Naso, admiring his garden in the spring sun.[1] Naso was in the kitchen, preparing a welcome drink (*qeras/kerasmo*[2]). Within a few minutes he was in the doorway, holding two glasses of peach juice, which he carefully set on the table in front of us. He smiled and said:

> When a man is at home alone he brings the drinks in his hands and not on a tray as his wife would do. This is because he respects his wife. According to the village ways most of the work is done by the woman while her husband is sitting in the coffee-shop (*cafeteria*), debating with his friends.

Naso paused for a moment, looked into the distance and recited a line from the poem *My village* (*Fshati im*) by well-known Albanian poet Andon Zako Çajupi (1990):

> Lying in the shade, men
> playing, busy chatting,
> misfortune cannot strike them,
> for they're living off their women.[3]

With a smile on his face he turned to us and added: 'Drink, drink! The juice is delicious; my wife brought it from outside (*nga jashtë/apo okso*).'[4]

The juice Maria and I were drinking that afternoon was ordinary peach juice to us, but for Naso it stirred up meanings that were synonymous with well-being, modernity and Greece. Despite the fact that the Albanian market offers numerous goods imported from various parts of Europe and Asia, Naso and his fellow villagers boast about the goods their migrant relatives send from the countries of their emigration. This has a historical context to it, since during the years of the communist regime (1945–90) the importation of 'foreign' goods was restricted and crossing the state border strictly forbidden. Many people in Albania, especially those born before the 1990s, consequently value highly goods from beyond Albania, referring to them as 'things from outside' (*gjëra nga jashte/ pragmata apo okso*). Thus Naso boasted about the juice he served us, despite the fact that as a 'co-ethnic Greek' he could cross the border officially even before the liberalisation of the visa regime in Albania in 2010. The juice, along with other 'things' (*gjëra/pragma*) sent from Greece by his migrant wife Frosina,[5] embody the different regimes of value (Greek vs. Albanian), as well as the geo-political power of the location from which they originate. The goods that female migrants send to their husbands who stay behind not only reify the meaning of the Albanian–Greek border but also materialise the presence of absent females who live abroad.

The chapter focuses on material flows, which are sporadically sent across the border or given to husbands by female migrants. In contrast to remittances, mate-rial flows reflect temporality, materialise interactions between migrants and those who stay behind, and provide a window onto the social, cultural and economic characteristics of the destination countries. I am interested here in the role and meaning of these flows in migration processes and border crossings. The material flows transgress polity borders and social boundaries, reconstruct existing relation-ships, reaffirm marriage and create material wealth. They stand in as a material pres-ence for absent female migrants, since they materialise the relationships between female migrants and their stay-at-home husbands. They also bring 'migrant worlds' into closer view (Basu and Coleman 2008).

I argue that material flows not only eradicate the spatial distance between Athens and Dhërmi/Drimades but also temporally collapse past, present and future. Following Mazzucato (2010), who conceptualises migrant remittances as part of the reciprocity of social relations, the chapter contends that material flows are entailed in reciprocal exchanges and function as insurance policies, because for female migrants and their husbands they guarantee the future.

Many scholars of migration in Albania concur that male migrants are the first to migrate, with their wives and children joining them afterwards, once their lives in the destination country stabilise (King et al. 2006; King and Vullnetari 2009). This pattern is especially true of northern Albania. However, as Vullnetari (2009) has shown, it is often female migrants who are actively involved in the migration process. They often represent 'the most important pillar for supporting the family migration strategy', for it is they who decide who in the family is going to migrate and who is not (2009).[6] Following this lead, and in contrast to the majority of schol-arly work on migration in Albania and in Europe generally, which largely focuses on remittances in the male domain, this chapter argues that in Dhërmi/Drimades remittances are partly owned and sent by female migrants.

Due to the greater demand for housekeeping services and elderly care-oriented labour, which are often considered to be 'women's work', European migration has become increasingly feminised. In Dhërmi/Drimades, however, female migration is viewed through the dominant patriarchal lens in the village, which effectively 'silences' women's crossing of the Greek–Albanian border in order to maintain the image that men are still the breadwinners.

Although remittances are returned and managed by female migrants, they paradoxically re-establish the patriarchal ties in the 'home' location. The opening vignette illustrates the power relations that pertain to gender roles within which women are perceived as (re)producing while men enjoy the 'products' of their work. In this perspective, remittances are ambiguous: on the one hand, they provide female migrants with feelings of security and independence, while on the other they re-empower their husbands who stay behind.

My data, gathered during long-term research in Dhërmi/Drimades, document the active role of female migrants who live in Greece (mainly Athens) and send remittances to their husbands who have remained in the village or returned there after retirement. Except in one case, the perspectives on the role and meaning of female migration that I consider were gathered from the women's husbands. In this chapter, remittances are thus described through the gaze of the men who receive and make sense of them. These flows are concretely visible in the gradual construction, rebuilding or refurbishing of village houses, and through receipt of goods such as food, drink and clothes that are regularly sent from Greece.

Following Glick Schiller (2006: 4–5), the chapter shows how transnationalism defines a *particular* locality by taking into account the wider power relations that seep into it. These power relations are a significant focus of studies of remittances that explore how the sending of things, of money and the overall reciprocal exchange of ideas and care constitute, reaffirm and renew the relationship between migrants and the families left behind (Glick Schiller and Fouron 2001). This brings us to a more complex understanding of the meanings of citizenship and family relations.

Baldassar (2007) argues that remittances and other transnational connections such as 'staying in touch' not only maintain communication between migrants and their relatives but also maintain emotional connections among them. In this way remittances and transnational care influence the meaning of the family. More recent scholarship (Drotbohm 2009) looks at transnational care through the prism of changing power relations and how the meaning of the family is redefined in the process. Drawing on these findings, the chapter considers whether remittances and other material goods returned to Dhërmi/Drimades by female migrants do in fact change existing power relations and whether, instead, they merely reconstitute 'habitual' gender relations.

I begin by introducing the Albanian–Greek border and the 'borderwork' conducted there in order to follow the course of the material flows and the rhythms through which the temporality of the polity border is constituted. I then present the theoretical framework for analysing the material flows before arguing, in the third section, that the reciprocal exchange of 'things' and care binds the migrants and those at home into a shared cyclical time-space. In conclusion, I consider the relationship between linear and cyclical time-space, the first being characteristic of borderwork and the second of material flows, though both are grounded in the rhythms that relocate the polity border. 'Border' here is thus shown to be less a line that is fixed and given, than a set of lines that can disappear, reappear, shift and take on different shapes (see Green 2011, 2012).

'Borderwork'

The Himarë/Himara municipality stretches along the southern Albanian coast and lies 60 km away from the Albanian–Greek border to the south. The *Malet e Vetëtimë* ('Thunderbolt Mountains') enclose the area on its northern and north-eastern sides. The area opens up on its south-western side with the mountain of Çika and descends towards the Ionian coast, with the Greek islands of Othonas and Corfu in the distance. The dual name Himarë/Himara identifies the Albanian–Greek border as a 'location of unfinished business and ambivalent attitudes' towards the ethnic, political, historical, cultural and economic differences among the inhabitants (Green 2012: 115). Unlike those living in the areas of the recognised national Greek minority (Saranda, Gjirokastra and Delvina), the bilingual inhabitants of Himarë/Himara are not considered a part of this minority. According to national Greek politics and mainstream Greek public opinion, they are classified as *omogheneis* or 'co-ethnic Greeks' living in Albania. This status gives them the right to receive Special Cards for Aliens of Greek Descent (*Eidiko Deltio Tautotitas Omogeneis*), and even before the liberalisation of the visa regime in 2010 allowed them unrestricted passage across the Albanian–Greek and other European Schengen borders. In spite of the fact that in practice most of the villagers do not travel beyond Greece, they frequently emphasise their ability to travel 'freely' to the countries of western Europe. They often use this privilege to differentiate themselves from other citizens of Albania, whose border crossings are still controlled, despite the liberalisation of the visa regime.

Before the beginning of the communist era, marriage in Dhërmi/Drimades tended to be endogamous.[7] Many endogamous marriages were arranged by the parents of the young couples. According to my conversations with the local people, there were two main reasons for this: one was to keep the land within the village, and the other to maintain and protect their Christian faith, which they felt might be eroded with interfaith marriages in a predominantly Muslim Albania. Under communism the endogamous pattern almost completely vanished but was revived when communism collapsed.

Due to land erosion and the lack of land suitable for cultivation, as well as other wider economic, social and political pressures, people from Himarë/Himara have for many centuries moved back and forth to southern Albania, Epirus, Corfu and Othonas in Greece, and to Venice and Naples in Italy. During my fieldwork between 2004 and 2005, many of those in this area born between 1926 and 1945 told stories about how their ancestors moved across the mountains and over the sea (see Gregorič Bon 2008: 161–181). The stories describing journeys across the Thunderbolt Mountains spoke of women undertaking the journey to the fertile valley of Labëria in north-eastern Albania, where the inhabitants were usually described as uncivilised and backward. By contrast, stories of overseas trading relations emphasised male voyages to the Venetian Republic, Naples and Corfu, which were seen as economically and socially prosperous and developed.

These stories are forceful encapsulations of the remembered paths taken by the storytellers' ancestors. Through these accounts, the storytellers reconstruct their own past as well as re-create their present and relate it to the places across the sea and the border with Greece. Understanding this is important for understanding the people and places of this area. Like these stories, the historiography of this area also shows (see Gregorič Bon 2008: 99–159) that the people of contemporary southern Albania, Epirus and Corfu traded amongst themselves in the period before communism and constituted common space between them. These movements brought about a multiplicity of connections between people and places, in contrast to the Ottoman administration and ensuing political divisions (the formation of nation-states) which encouraged differentiation and inequality. Nonetheless, the significant differences of that period were less to do with the present-day Albanian polity borders founded in 1913, and more to do with the religious differences between Muslims and Orthodox Christians that were introduced with the Ottoman Empire.

The movement of people and things for economic and/or social reasons continued in this period and the polity border was experienced and narrated by these people as the 'road' (*to dromo*) which 'closed' after 1945 with the establishment of the communist dictatorship. For almost fifty years the Albanian borders were strictly controlled (De Waal 2005: 5–7; Green 2012: 111), which not only prohibited the cross-border movement of people and goods, but also prevented any information about the country from leaking out (Green 2012: 111). Despite the fact that Albania's border marked stark differences between Albania and other countries, these differences rarely mattered in people's daily lives. However, this changed with the collapse of the communist regime in 1990, when the 'road' was (at least for the Greek-speaking Orthodox Christians) 'reopened' and massive migration of Albanians followed (Vullnetari 2007: 32–35).

Scholars of migration estimate that after 1990 more than a quarter of Albania's total population migrated, mainly to Greece and Italy (Bajraba 2000; King and Vullnetari 2009; Vullnetari 2009: 2). Massive migration shattered the meaning of the Albanian–Greek border and introduced differences that were no longer definable on the basis of nation-states, but on the basis of global economy and politics with their capacity to define power and hierarchal structures of places. Within this hierarchical restructuring, some places, states, people and things are considered as belonging to the 'West', and therefore as 'civilised', 'modern' and 'European', while others are labelled as part of the 'Balkans', and hence 'uncivilised' and 'not-yet-modernised'.

The collapse of communism also influenced migration patterns in the Himarë/ Himara area, where the majority of residents migrated to Greece. In recent years, due to the decollectivisation of agriculture and the restitution of land to former owners, emigrants to Greece began to return to the village. They are reconstructing old houses and building new ones, as well as building tourist facilities along the village coast.

The data gathered by my population census of Dhërmi/Drimades between 2004 and 2005 show that in 15 out of 60 marriages (where at least one or both spouses originate from the village) the wife lives and works in Greece while the man remains behind. In the majority of these cases both spouses used to live in Greece where they migrated after communism. Due to their status as co-ethnic Greeks, they have a right to health and social security in Greece. Following retirement, many men decide to return to Dhërmi/Drimades while their wives, who are still working, remain in Greece. The main reason for their return is the real estate they own in Albania, the lower cost of living and the social position they can attain in their home village.[8] While these 'translocal marriages' (i.e. where both spouses come from the same village or region but one is working abroad while the other returns to Albania) constitute only 25 per cent of village marriages, the stories of the couples concerned illustrate the migrant worlds of Dhërmi/Drimades.

Material flows

So far I have suggested that for the inhabitants of Himarë/Himara the rhythms of mobility and enclosure have over time generated multiple meanings of border. Before 1945, the Albanian–Greek border was perceived as the 'road' along which people, things and ideas travelled. After 1945, due to the political direction of the communist leader Enver Hoxha, these movements became subject to a strict prohibition on border crossing. The border or the 'road' was closed for more than four decades, and although the people living on each side were very aware of this political divide, social, economic, monetary and political differences between them did not figure much in their daily lives. But in 1991, after the fall of the communist regime, the polity border again became an important part of their lives and itineraries and represented the material power engendering a 'regime of mobility'[9] (Wang 2004: 352).

There has been a lack of scholarly work on gendered border crossings and/ or gendered emplacement and displacement in Europe, a gap which this chapter addresses by following the flow of things and money across the border that creates ambiguity in gender roles and shifts the border. These border relocations and material flows produce a gendering of time-space, in which the reciprocity of material flows gives rise to two contrasting gendered temporalities: linear time and cyclical time, which are associated with men and women, respectively.

Migrant remittances and material flows to the migrants' country of origin represent an important part of global and transnational flows, for they are often the main source of income of particular households and economies in many developing countries (Wong 2006: 355). According to the World Bank, remittances are essential to Albanian households in surmounting their economic difficulties (De Soto et al. 2002: xiv). Between 2004 and 2005, remittances amounted to US$1,100 million and generated 14 per cent of Albanian gross domestic product (GDP) (Vullnetari and King 2011: 55). In 2009, due to the economic crisis across Europe and the United States, the scale of remittances decreased to 9 per cent of GDP in Albania (2011: 55). Still, in the same period, they were three times greater than the value of foreign exports and covered a relatively large part of the trading deficit (2011: 55).

In Dhërmi/Drimades the material flows are part of reciprocal exchange and constitute affective transnationalism where personal and emotional relations between spouses who are 'separated' by polity borders are forged in a distinct way. They secure the material exchange, renew and maintain social relations and establish the material presence of absent migrants (Cliggett 2003). Through material flows migrants maintain and affirm their sense of belonging to their place of origin. As touched on earlier, the material flows bring the mobility of migrants and material culture together (Basu and Coleman 2008). Movements and migration are 'grounded in objects' (Basu and Coleman 2008: 232) such as food and goods, as well as in language and practices. They are also grounded in relationships that mediate and create contexts of movement as well as pauses, or give rise to temporary or permanent settlements. 'Certain forms of materiality can also provide powerful ways of indexing the status and/or agency of the migrant' (Basu and Coleman 2008: 232). As we shall see, the material flows sent by female migrants not only reify the women's absent presence in Dhërmi/Drimades, but also compensate for this absence; and they both materialise female agency and index their husbands' status.

In the following section I examine husbands' narratives about their absent wives to show how the continuity of material flows transcends the spatio-temporal differences between Greece and Albania, improving the economic and social position of female migrants' husbands and ensuring the (common) future of the married couple.

Present in their absence

Frosina

On that sunny afternoon when Maria and I were talking with Naso, his wife's absence was experienced not only through his way of offering the drink or through the drink itself (juice from Greece), but also through his narrative. In our many discussions, Naso rarely mentioned his wife Frosina, who was still living and working in Athens. This conspicuous silence can be attributed to a society still dominated by masculine mores where, as in Çajupi's poem, the majority of work is effectively done by women but the 'fruits' of that labour are mostly enjoyed by the husbands without giving due recognition to the contribution of their wives.

A few years after the fall of communism, Naso and Frosina – whose marriage was arranged by their parents – migrated to Athens with their children. As they both originate from one of the villages of the Himarë/Himara area and are entitled to the Special Cards for Aliens of Greek Descent, they did not have trouble finding a job there. But despite their Albanian university degrees, Naso and his wife sought jobs as manual workers. Naso, who had been a history and philology teacher, worked in the construction industry, while Frosina, who had been a geography teacher, worked as a cleaning lady. In 2003, when Naso lost his job, he returned to Dhërmi/ Drimades, where he and Frosina built a house on the land that Frosina had inherited from her father. Their sons, who remained in Greece like their mother, sporadically send money to Naso to pay for the new house. Throughout most of the year Frosina stays in Greece and visits Dhërmi/Drimades only two or three times a year, for Christmas, Easter and the summer holidays.

Naso often talked to me about building his house, work on which began in 2002. Yet only when explicitly asked did he mention Frosina's involvement in the construction and furnishing of their house, despite her regular financial contributions.[10] Although, as we saw earlier, 25 per cent of marriages in the village are translocal, the absence of migrant wives is rarely mentioned or openly discussed. Naso often said that he 'felt' his wife's presence in his everyday life, due to regular phone calls and the receipt of things she sent him. But in other respects her contributions went unremarked, like those of other migrant village women. Housekeeping, usually the domain of women, is now carried out by the men, sometimes with help from relatives or with hired help, while the material flows that contribute to house-making and are usually the domain of men are delivered by the migrant women. However, this reversal of gender roles is silenced. Since 'house-making' is a culturally gendered activity, the social credit for 'making' a house is attributed to the man and only rarely to his wife.

In 2002, Naso and Frosina spent their savings from working in Greece to build the foundations and basic structure of the house. A year later Naso retired and returned to the village where he hired labourers to build the first floor and three small rooms. Naso himself painted and furnished one of the rooms where he installed a small kitchen, a bed and a table that Frosina had bought in Athens. When Frosina returned to the village for her winter holidays they hired workers who tiled the bathroom and put in a washbasin. They paid them partly from Frosina's savings and partly from Naso's pension. After the holidays, Frosina returned to Athens where she lived in a one-room rented apartment. When relatives return to the village, Frosina always sends with them money for the house and food for Naso (stuffed peppers, meat, cheese, vegetable pies, tinned food, biscuits, beer, coffee and juice). Sometimes she even sends small items of furniture. The couple were planning to furnish one of the larger rooms in their new house when

Frosina retired, using the remaining furniture from her apartment in Athens. Naso explained that they are very attached to this furniture, which was bought gradually with savings when they were both living in Greece. It represents the life they had together in Athens, and their success and well-being which they had established gradually.[11] As Basu and Coleman (2008: 317) might say, the very materiality of the furniture evokes and embodies their shared migratory experiences in Greece, while in the meantime Frosina's regular food parcels represent the materiality of her migration.

The 'presence' of absent female migrants is entailed not only in things such as goods and food but also through their mobile phone calls and their constant care for their husbands. As Dhërmi/Drimades is in the vicinity of Corfu, it is within reach of Greek mobile phone networks, enabling Naso and Frosina to talk inexpensively at least once a day. Like Naso, several villagers with relatives in Greece own two phones, one connected to the Albanian network and the other to the Greek one. Because Greece and Albania are in different time zones, the mobile phones connected to the Greek network are set to Greek time, which is one hour ahead of Albania.

During these phone calls, Frosina would ask Naso if he was eating properly and how the house was progressing. Such questions made them feel connected. When I asked Naso if he missed his wife, he explained that he did not, because they talked every day on the phone and regularly sent 'things' to each other: 'Yesterday my cousin, who lives in Athens too, brought me stuffed pepper that she sent through him and some money to pay the workers that made the ceilings in one of the rooms.' In contrast to many other migrant situations, such as Kosovo (Leutloff-Grandits, personal communication), home-made food in Dhërmi/Drimades travels in both directions.

Even though these material flows are instrumental rather than emotional, they are a medium through which the couple stays in touch and maintains connections. The rhythm of material flows is reciprocal and Naso in turn sends Frosina olive oil, olives, oranges and mandarins via their relatives. Such reciprocity is typical between geographically distant couples and a common means to sustain a 'connection', which Drotbohm (2009: 144) suggests is a less emotional and more technical way of keeping in touch than is maintaining 'relations', which has an implication of obligation and responsibility towards those who stay behind.

Despite the fact that 'things', such as furniture, food and other goods, cross the border officially, and that the migrants find themselves paying import tax on furniture, there is an all-pervasive sense in their minds that these border crossings, because of their continuity and reciprocity, somehow defy or transcend the polity border between Albania and Greece. This case study also demonstrates how gendered material flows can impact the meaning of the family in which conventional relationships may be reversed. Men return or stay behind and take care of the household, while women become the main breadwinners and live abroad.

Sofia

Sofia's husband Ilia, who was born in Dhërmi/Drimades in 1935, told me a rather different story to that told by Naso. Like many other teenagers at the time, Ilia did not see a future in working in the village cooperative and enrolled in the agronomy school in Durres, the coastal city in central Albania. After completing secondary school, he got a job in Tirana as an agronomist and married Sofia. Sofia was also born in Dhërmi/Drimades and moved to the capital after her marriage, which, like Frosina's, was arranged by her parents. She got a job in the bakery. After the fall of the communist regime in 1990, Ilia and Sofia decided to migrate to Greece with their children. First they moved to Ioannina where they settled with relatives, who had migrated there some time earlier. After two years they moved to Athens, where they rented an apartment. Eight years later, when one of their sons married, they moved to his apartment which they bought with their savings. Ilia worked in various manual jobs as a painter or labourer, while Sofia worked as a cleaner in the mornings and in the evenings cared for her grandchildren. In 2000 their children, who by then were 20, 22 and 26, decided to migrate to Washington, DC in the United States, where Ilia's brother was living. He found jobs for them. Ilia was 65 and retired and decided to return to Dhërmi/Drimades. Sofia decided to move with her children to the United States to continue to care for her grandchildren while their parents were at work. When asked about his wife's decision to migrate to the United States, Ilia explained that many villagers live alone while their wives are abroad so such an arrangement is not unusual. Childcare remains a gendered task in south-eastern Europe, and many women choose to remain in their place of migration if their grandchilden have been born there.

By claiming the status of political refugees, Sofia and her children were able to live and work in the United States but unable to return to Albania. Today Sofia lives in Florida together with the family of one of her sons. Occasionally she sends her savings and other goods such as medicine, clothes and electrical appliances to Ilia.

Like Naso, Ilia rarely talked about Sofia. He mentioned her only when he referred to one of the things she sent from the United States. Besides material objects, Sofia also sent money (US$400–1,000) twice per year. She usually transferred it through the Western Union money transfer. Ilia invested this money in the construction of a new house. At first, Sofia sent letters and photographs almost every month showing their life in the United States, but later wrote only two or three times a year. Ilia and Sofia normally keep in contact through overseas phone calls and talk to each other at least once a week.

When Ilia returned to the village in 2000, he temporarily moved to an old family house inherited by his younger brother. That same year he began building a house on land inherited from his father. With his savings, the pension which he received from the Greek government as a recognised co-ethnic Greek, and with the help of remittances from his wife, Ilia built two storeys of the house and moved in a year later. He consulted Sofia about matters regarding the house architecture and interior design. They spoke frequently about this over the phone, as house-making is their investment in their future. They also discussed their son and grandsons now living with Sofia, and Sofia would caringly inquire about Ilia's eating habits, his health and general well-being. As with Frosina and Naso, the flows between Sofia and her husband are reciprocal and when relatives or friends visit Florida, Ilia asks them to take olive oil, olives, *raki* (brandy) and honey to Sofia and their children.

Ilia soon realised that the house needed constant work and that he was incapable of doing it on his own. He thus decided to invite a young family from northern Albania, recommended to him by one of his friends. Six months later the family moved to the first floor of the house while he settled on the second floor. The family helps him cook and maintain the house. Though a patriarchal tone is still maintained, marital relations between Ilia and Sofia have changed slightly. Due to the lack of physical contact between them, as well as between Ilia and his children, he considers the family whom he employed to care for him to be his second family.[12]

Ilia once remarked to me that it seems unlikely that Sofia will ever return, a topic they never discuss on the phone. Although divorce is increasingly common in Albania, it is mainly among young couples, and older couples still view divorce with disapproval and disgrace. Sofia's return is only an exit strategy in case things turn upside down 'overnight'.

Lambrini

In contrast to the narratives described above, Lambrini told me herself about her own migratory career. In 1995 she returned to Dhërmi/Drimades from Athens where she had lived and worked for two years. Unlike Frosina and Sofia, Lambrini had lived in the village for most of her life and worked as the manager of the shop that was part of the village cooperative during communism. Her marriage had also been arranged by the couples' parents. Her husband Kosta was a teacher in a neighbouring village and a few years later was appointed as principal of the primary school in Dhërmi/Drimades. After the fall of the regime the cooperative shop was closed down and the government decided to sell it. Lambrini and Kosta had only 500 Leks of savings which was not enough to buy the shop that was valued at 20,000 Leks. Because Lambrini had envisioned her future in this shop, which was, as she noted, part of her life, she decided to find a job in Greece and move there for a couple of years, until she could save enough money to buy it. Kosta could not join her because he still had a job in the village. Lambrini asked her brother, who had been living in Greece since 1991, to find her a well-paid job in Athens. In the early spring of 1993 she left the village and her family and moved to Athens for two years, where she got a job as a caregiver to an elderly lady, living in her house and saving most of her earnings. Lambrini noted how much she missed her husband and children. She could not talk to them every day, as there were no mobile phones at the time. While Lambrini was working in Athens, she returned only at Christmas, and her 19-year-old daughter took care of her father and siblings. She remitted one-quarter of her monthly salary via a relative and saved the rest to purchase the shop. Kosta invested Lambrini's remittances in renovating the house, which had been built in the 1970s. When Lambrini returned to the village she bought the shop, which she later refurbished and reopened as a grocery shop. Her plan had been to extend the range of goods on sale and to include agricultural equipment and clothes, which would make the shop more like the one she had managed for the cooperative. Even though Lambrini realised her ambition and is officially the manager of the shop, the villagers refer to it as 'Kosta's shop' or as 'at Kosta's'.

Some years after she returned to the village her children also decided to emigrate. Her son, who had studied theology but not completed the course, later returned to Albania where he married and settled in his parents' house. Her daughters found jobs and started their families in Greece. Whenever they need support, Lambrini visits Athens and stays with them for a couple of weeks. This again illustrates the translocal caring relations that involve border crossing but still unite and reaffirm existing family relations.

Cyclical rhythms

The material flows initiated by female migrants from Dhërmi/Drimades are reciprocal, for in exchange for the money, furniture, food and care that they contribute, they receive food (such as olives, olive oil, *raki*) and reassurance from their husbands. Due to the different regimes of value on each side of the border, the things that cross are not seen as imbalanced by those involved.[13] The seasonal and reciprocal sending and receiving of things generate rhythms that give rise to cyclical notions of time which transcend the materiality of the polity border. The border is thus de-reified by this repeated exchange which collapses the distance between female migrants in Greece and their husbands in Albania and generates a common time-space between them.

This shared time-space works as an insurance policy, reassuring the female migrants that there is a home to return to if and when the time comes. By sending things home to their husbands, Frosina, Sofia and Lambrini invest in a secure future. Material flows are thus part of their mutual relations, rights and obligations, for they create and reaffirm the marriage bond and its entailments. The labour and effort that the three women invest in their material flows similarly ensure that they are never alienated from these flows. Put differently, the furniture and money that the female migrants invest in 'house-making' represent their inalienable wealth that in turn generates male prosperity and social capital. The material flows are like extensions of the female migrants, functioning as a kind of proxy presence in their absence. Their husbands cannot directly manage the labour and effort that their migrant wives invest in the production of material wealth but they can enjoy their care and manage the material wealth (such as money, furniture and food) sent to them.

The rhythms of material flows arguably silence the ruptures that result from border crossing and the labour of female migrants, and they replicate the existing power relations between husband and wife. Men perceive their wives' crossings of polity borders as non-transformative and even replicative, especially of gender roles. Despite the fact that it is the female migrants who produce the wealth, largely supporting their households, it is the husbands who manage this wealth and maintain more or less intact the patriarchal power relations as a result. The rhythm of material flows thus transgresses both the continuity implicit in remitting wealth earned by women and the discontinuity embodied by their border crossings.

Gendered dimension of time-space

Compared to female migrants from northern Albania, the migrants from Dhërmi/ Drimades enjoy greater liberty in managing the material wealth earned as migrants. Thus we saw, for example, that Lambrini was able to invest her savings from Greece in the village shop in her natal village. And though Naso, Ilia and Kosta perceive their wives' remittances as part of their marital male prerogative, their wives can still freely manage them and decide when, how and what they will remit. Material flows in Dhërmi/Drimades are ambiguous in so far as husbands conceptualise them as the husband's right and the wife's obligation, while at the same time wives retain the power to manage them themselves as active agents in the migration process.

The stories of Frosina, Sofia and Lambrini disclose their active economic and social role, which in their husbands' narratives and wider village discourse are often muted and implicit. Thus Naso, Ilia and Kosta rarely explicitly referred to the material flows sent from Greece by their wives, an invisibility perpetuated in wider village discourse when, for example, villagers refer to 'Kosta's shop' even when it is Lambrini who manages it.

Most of what Frosina and Sofia remit from Greece is invested in houses that are locally regarded as belonging to their husbands. Ilia and Kosta, and even Naso, who is building the house on the land which his wife inherited from her father, all describe house construction in the first person. '"House-making" by Albanian migrants is not only a simple house-building process; it also ensures a constant dwelling and dynamic "proxy" presence for migrants in their community of origin' (Dalakoglou 2010: 761). Despite the fact that women play a central role in the house-making process, their role is hidden from public view because of the wider gendered village discourse.

The narratives outlined above illustrate women's multifaceted absence expressed in the narratives of their husbands: their physical absence from the daily life in the village, social absence from the village's discourse and also the absence of their voices from the present text. Except for Lambrini, the narratives of Frosina and Sofia are presented through their husbands' voices. The role of women is marginal in public life in Dhërmi/Drimades. Frosina, Sofia and Lambrini are only partially visible and related to their husbands' homes and their houses. They are always ambiguously positioned between public and private, affinal and kin-group, migrant destination and home, and this generates their relative location. In other words, even though their role as migrants and wives is important and crucial for the survival of their families, their social status and position often remain hidden in village life and discourse.

The male house construction and the female investment in the house[14] highlight the gendered dimension of time-space. While the male time-space is grounded in the linear production and construction of the house that is visible in public space, the female time-space is grounded in the cyclical reproduction of home and descendants in domestic space. The seasonal and reciprocal flow of things, ideas and people constitutes the rhythm which brings into relationship as well as separates linear and cyclical processes and/or male and female time-space.

Temporality of the border

I have suggested in this chapter that material flows not only entail remittances but also reify the 'presence' of female migrants in the village through their contribution of money, furniture, food, letters, postcards, photographs and telephone calls. These flows indirectly fulfil their obligations, enabling them to feel that they are caring wives and mothers, so that effectively their physical absence is overcome.

Povrzanović Frykman (2009: 107) argues that 'displacement of people may bring the replacement of objects'. In Dhërmi/Drimades these objects are part of the cyclical and reciprocal exchange between female migrants and their husbands. 'House-making' and care transcend the geographical, physical and emotional distance between migrant wives and stay-at-home husbands, and de-reify the polity border. The rhythm of the women's movements combines apparent opposites: the dynamics of mobility with the enclosure enforced by the border; the emplacement and displacement of people and things; and the linearity of borderwork with the cyclical time-space of material flows. From this perspective, the material flows are a mode of temporalisation that continuously relocates the border, while also materialising the presence of otherwise absent women.

We have seen that material flows reaffirm the relationship between female migrants and their husbands who stay behind. They reassure the woman's position in the social network in her place of origin. In this sense, material flows are active agents of migrant worlds (Dalakoglou 2010). They constitute the common time-space in the same manner that this common time-space constitutes the material flows. Unfinished houses, the village shop, food, furniture and other goods reveal the migrant worlds of Frosina, Sofia and Lambrini. They materialise their life in Greece and their continuous returns to Albania. These migrant worlds not only reflect their lives in emigration but they also translate one time-space (Athens, in the Eastern European Time Zone) to another (Dhërmi/Drimades, in the Central

European Time Zone) and thereby create new time-spaces (see Basu and Coleman 2008). The latter break the old rhythms, introducing new ones that conjoin linear male time with cyclical female time.

Baldassar (2007) and Drotbohm (2009) contend that remittances and the transnational care of family members have the effect of changing husband–wife relations. While agreeing with this, this chapter further suggests that in Dhërmi/ Drimades the change in marital relations becomes silenced when men manage, control and enjoy the material wealth remitted by their migrant wives. Silencing their wives' absence is thus a male 'strategy' for maintaining the patriarchal village order which appears to leave marital relations unchanged. To return to Çajupi's poem: men are lying in the shade, busy chatting, as they live off their wives' work and care that in turn generates their symbolic wealth.

Acknowledgements

I thank the people of Dhërmi/Drimades who allowed me to explore their life stories. Earlier versions of this chapter were presented at conferences at the Universities of Berlin (Humboldt) and Tampere and as guest lectures at the Universities of Helsinki and Ljubljana. I am also indebted to the editors for their insightful comments and suggestions and to the Slovenian Research Agency for financial support.

Notes

1 Maria and Naso are from Dhërmi/Drimades, a Greek- and Albanian-speaking village in the southern Albanian region of Himarë/Himara (the official Albanian/local Greek names, respectively).
2 As the people living in the villages of Himarë/Himara are bilingual, I refer throughout to both the southern Albanian and local Greek dialects.
3 *Burrat nën hie, lozin, kuvendojnë, pika që s'u bie, se nga gratë rrojnë!* (Çajupi 1990).
4 Meaning 'from Greece' or 'abroad'.
5 Frosina always brings 'things from outside' whenever she returns from Athens. These 'things' can be food such as feta cheese, coffee, cream, biscuits, sweets or items like shoes and clothes, furniture, household appliances and money (€300–500).
6 Vullnetari (2009: 13) argues that the scholarly work on Albanian migration represents females as passive actors in the migratory process. It generally assumes that patrilinearity still represents the core pattern of kinship, especially in northern Albania (Backer 1983; Young 2000). Material flows are therefore mainly associated with men who are usually considered to be the core actors who send, receive and administer the remittances, while women play only a marginal role in this process (King et al. 2006; King and Vullnetari 2009: 28). However, this trend is gradually changing as female migrants from Albania administer their incomes more frequently than in the past and assume more complex roles in supporting migration than is often supposed.
7 After marriage the woman theoretically joins her husband's household and adopts the surname of his patriline. There are a few cases of a man moving after marriage to the

house or land under the agreement of his wife's father (in 5 of 86 *ikoyenia/familje*). If a woman is from Dhërmi/Drimades and marries within the village, the villagers often refer to her by her maiden name or by the surname of her husband's family. Although she may adopt the surname of her affinal group, she is never considered as fully belonging to her affines or in-laws. All her life, even after she has had children and become a mother, her in-laws continue to refer to her as *nifi/nusja*, the bride.

8 Some of these men also return because of lack of work in Greece. They can draw their pensions through a local branch of the Greek bank in Himarë/Himara but may visit Greece for medical treatment if required.

9 According to Wang (2004: 352), passports and visas form 'a regime of mobility that has been specifically designed by the state to control the movement of people'.

10 Since the fall of the pyramid investment schemes in 1997, which ended with an economic crisis and loss of government control over the state, Frosina, like the majority of Albanians, does not trust bank transfers anymore and remits her earnings via returning relatives.

11 Many of the villagers in similar circumstances do the same and equip their house with furniture they had owned as migrants, explaining this in terms of both nostalgia and parsimony.

12 Ilia is not exceptional as there are other cases in the village where elderly men or women (usually widows) are taken care of by a family coming from another part of Albania.

13 The reasons for this pertain to the geopolitical power of 'things' and cross-border currency differentials. Until 2010, when the economic crisis in Greece reached its peak, migrants living in Greece never expected their Albanian relatives to send them clothes, furniture or money. Even in 2014, when many of the migrants have returned, they still consider Greek and other foreign goods to be of 'better quality' than those available in Albania.

14 In Greek and Albanian there is only one word used for the house and home: *spiti/shtëpi*.

References

Backer, B. (1983) 'Mother, sister, daughter, wife: the pillars of traditional Albanian patriarchal society', in M. Utas (ed.), *Women in Islamic Societies: Social Attitudes and Historical Perspectives*. London: Curzon, pp. 48–65.

Bajraba, K. (2000) 'Contemporary patterns in Albanian emigration', *South-East Europe Review*, 3: 57–64.

Baldassar, L. (2007) 'Transnational families and the provision of moral and emotional support: the relationship between truth and distance', *Identities: Global Studies in Culture and Power*, 14: 385–409.

Basu, P. and S. Coleman (2008) 'Introduction. Migrant worlds, material cultures', *Mobilities*, 3:3, 313–330.

Çajupi (1990) *Baba-Tomorri*. Tirana: Shtëpia Botuese 'Naim Frasheri'.

Cliggett, L. (2003) 'Gift remitting and alliance building in Zambian modernity: old answers to modern problems', *American Anthropologist* 105:3, 543–552.

Dalakoglou, D. (2010) 'Migrating-remitting-'building'-dwelling: house-making as 'proxy' presence in postsocialist Albania', *Journal of the Royal Anthropological Institute*, 16, 761–777.

De Soto, H., P. Gordon, I. Gedeshi and Z. Sinoimeri (2002) *Poverty in Albania: A Qualitative Assessment*. World Bank Technical Paper 520. Washington, DC: World Bank.

de Waal, C. (2005) *Albania Today: A Portrait of Post-Communist Turbulence* London: I.B. Tauris.

Drotbohm, H. (2009) 'Horizons of long-distance intimacies: reciprocity, contribution and disjuncture in Cape Verde', *History of the Family*, 14: 132–149.

Glick Schiller, N. (2006) 'Introduction: what can transnational studies offer to the analysis of localized conflicts and protests?', *Focaal – European Journal of Anthropology*, 47: 3–17.

Glick Schiller, N. and G.E. Fouron (2001) *Georges Woke up Laughing: Long-Distance Nationalism and the Search for Home*. Durham, NC: Duke University Press.

Green, S. (2011) *Traces, Tidemarks and Legacies*. 110th Annual Meeting, Montreal, QC, Canada, 16–20 November.

Green, S. (2012) 'Replacing Europe', in R. Fardon et al. (eds), *The Sage Handbook of Social Anthropology Volume 1*. London: Sage.

Gregorič Bon, N. (2008) *Prostori neskladij: Etnografija prostora in kraja v Dhërmiju/ Drimadesu, južna Albanija*. Ljubljana: Založba ZRC, ZRC SAZU.

King, R., M. Dalipaj and N. Mai (2006) 'Gendering migration and remittances: evidence from London and Northern Albania', *Population, Space and Place*, 12: 409–434.

King, R. and J. Vullnetari (2009) 'The intersections of gender and generation in Albanian migration, remittances and transnational care', *Geografiska Annaler: Series B, Human Geography*, 9: 19–38.

Mazzucato, V. (2010) 'Reverse remittances in the migration development nexus: two-way flows between Ghana and the Netherlands', *Population, Space and Place*, doi: 10.1002/psp.

Povrzanović Frykman, M. (2009) 'Material aspects of transnational social fields: an introduction', *Dve Domovini/Two Homelands (Tematski sklop/Thematic Section: Migrants' Transnational Practices. The Movement of People and Objects)*, 29: 105–114.

Vullnetari, J. (2007) *Albanian Migration and Development: State of the Art Review*. IMISCOE Working Paper No. 18. http://edoc.bibliothek.uni-halle.de/servlets/ MCRFileNodeServlet/HALCoRe_derivate_00003672/Albanianmigration.pdf. Accessed 2 August 2016.

Vullnetari, J. (2009) *Women and Migration in Albania: A View from the Village*. Oxford: Blackwell.

Vullnetari, J. and R. King (2011) *Remittances, Gender and Development: Albania's Society and Economy in Transition*. London: I.B. Tauris.

Young, A. (2000) *Women who Become Men: Albanian Sworn Virgins*. Oxford: Berg.

Wang, H. (2004) 'Regulating transnational flows of people: an institutional analysis of passports and visas as a regime of mobility', *Identities*, 11(3): 351–376.

Wong, M. (2006) 'The gendered politics of remittances in Ghanaian transnational families', *Economic Geography*, 82(4): 355–381.

8

Missing migrants: deaths at sea and unidentified bodies in Lesbos

Iosif Kovras and Simon Robins[1]

Migrant deaths at sea

In March 2013, a body was found on the shores of Eressos, the village where Sappho the poetess was born, in the west of the island of Lesbos (Dimopoulou 2013). The young woman was the daughter of a Syrian family who had fled the Syrian conflict and sought asylum in the European Union (EU) by crossing the Aegean from Turkey. The girl's mother and sister were also found dead on the same day on the shores of neighbouring villages. The two girls were born in Greece but the family had decided to return to Syria some years before. Their deaths could have been avoided had a new Greek citizenship law – relaxing criteria for the acquisition of Greek citizenship to children of immigrants born in Greece – been implemented (Christopoulos 2012).[2] The two girls could have legally entered the country as Greek citizens, instead of risking their lives to cross the militarised border illegally. These three deaths reflect the biopolitical power of the two key instruments of contemporary sovereign states, namely control over borders and citizenship.

Incidents of migrants and refugees dying in their efforts to cross the Aegean border and enter Greece and the EU have become a tragic consequence of contemporary EU border policy, as they have in many other parts of the Mediterranean. In October 2013 a shipwreck of unprecedented magnitude near the Italian island of Lampedusa left approximately 364 immigrants dead (Shenker 2013). Deadly incidents have also taken place in the Spanish coastal enclaves of Ceuta and Melilla, where migrants and refugees try to reach the EU border (Morcillo 2012). The Mediterranean Sea kills would-be migrants regardless of their legal status, not discriminating between refugees and economic migrants.

One of the key features of EU border policy is that the border is not constructed territorially, but by the sea itself as a potentially fatal barrier to entry. Sea borders remain the entry point of choice for the majority of 'irregular' immigrants to the EU (Frontex 2012), while according to data from Frontex, the EU agency for external border security, the Aegean coast remains the second most common entry point for migrants (Frontex 2013). Hence, the specific nature of the (sea) border, coupled

with the fact that border crossers usually follow illegal and non-conventional channels, increase the risk of deadly accidents. Most importantly, structural flaws in the
design of the policy of border security partly account for the growing number of
shipwrecks. For example, coastguard patrolling is embedded within a securitisation
framework designed to deter illegal migrants from entering the national sovereign
territory of the state (Leonard 2010). It is questionable as to the capacity of a deter-
rence mandate to serve simultaneously the effective rescue of migrants in danger.
We cannot address this complex issue here, but it is worth noting that due to the
growing incidence of 'push-backs' by coastguards, immigrants often destroy their
inflatable dinghies in order to pressure guards to save them, thus increasing the risk
of a deadly accident at sea (Papadopoulos et al. 2008: 184). Whilst border security
and its relationship to the epidemic of deaths at sea constitutes a highly complex
and underexplored phenomenon, this chapter focuses primarily on the management of the dead in the aftermath of a shipwreck as well as the local response to
these deaths.

In what follows, we first discuss the theoretical insights that can be drawn from
the study of the phenomenon of dead migrants at the EU border, using concepts
provided by Agamben's biopolitics. We argue that the body of the dead migrant
found within the territorial borders of the EU but denied any of the dignifying
obligations that law demands for dead citizens permits an interrogation of both
theoretical and practical understandings of the border. We then discuss the case
of Lesbos, exploring how the study of the management of dead migrants can shed
light on the political and bodily experience of border crossing. It will be shown how
the different policies of the state to the crossing of the border by a dead migrant or
a live one, as well as the difference in response to a dead citizen and a dead migrant,
introduce novel categories of inclusion and exclusion. In the final part of the chapter, we highlight the divergence between the state-led discourse of migration as a
threat and its associated securitisation, and the humanitarian response of the people
of Lesbos, which has paved the way for the emergence of a 'hybrid' local discourse.

Migrant deaths at sea: theoretical insights

The tragedy of migrants killed attempting to reach the labour markets of EU states
is a direct result of a neo-liberal globalisation that encourages liberalisation of all
markets except that for workers and people. The growing phenomenon of migrants
dying in their effort to cross the EU border poses a double paradox to the founding
tenets of the EU. Whilst the EU is based on a principle of free and open movement internally, it has increasingly been defined externally by its commitment
to exclude non-citizens from entry to its territory (Wallerstein 2002). Second,
although the EU's 'normative power' is based on the premise that human rights
are to be respected independent of any political consideration (Manners 2008),
this normative power fades when it comes to the deaths of migrants at its borders.

Their deaths, whether bodies are washed up on Europe's southern coastline or lost forever in the depths of the Mediterranean, are a direct result of the securitisation of migration (Karyotis 2012), which reflects an explicitly racial narrative that those fleeing the chaos and misery of the south to the pocket of liberality that is the EU are a security threat. The border has become more prominent in security discourse precisely because it represents the boundary between security and chaos. '[T]he border marks a fundamental biopolitical distinction between life that (literally) counts in the registry of the nation-state, and life that does not' (Boyce 2012: 71).

This discourse impacts upon migrants in a plethora of ways, most notably through the idea that the sea and its dangers to migrants are doing the job of defending the EU's borders against the migrant invasion. This resonates with European states' externalisation of elements of border and immigration control to the territory of states of migrant departure or transit, and to the militarisation of the Mediterranean. The deaths at sea, as a part of this externalisation, success-fully delocalise migrant deaths, removing them from the legal and moral purview of Europeans. The legal responsibility for deaths is shifted from the state to the migrant,[3] accompanied by a moral shifting of responsibility for the fact of migra-tion, as well as for dignifying and identifying the bodies of migrants found on EU territory.

Critical border studies has increasingly turned to both Foucault's biopolitics and Agamben's concept of *bare life*, understood as what remains when human existence is stripped of the encumbrances of social location and bereft of the qualifications of political inclusion and belonging (Agamben 1998). Politics for Agamben is an ongoing tension between inclusion and exclusion, between forms of life that the sovereign will protect and represent and those it will not: this defines the mean-ing of what it is to be human and thereby identifies an exception, the migrant as something other than human, which, for whatever reason, cannot be made sense of in terms of the nation-state. This prescription resonates with how the EU and its member states treat migrants at their borders. Increasingly in critical border studies Agamben's powerful conceptualisation is reduced to an understanding of mere 'exclusion'. Its power, however, lies precisely in the fact that bare life revolves around the zone of indistinction between 'outside and inside, exclusion and inclu-sion' that is created by sovereign power (Agamben 1998: 91). The liminality of bare life coincides with the illegal migrant's effort to negotiate both border and sovereignty, confined to a status without the 'right to have rights' (Arendt 1951: 177), even when within the borders of an entity such as the EU. Sovereign power in contemporary Europe lets migrants die at the border by framing their deaths as accidents, unrelated to the machinery of militarisation and securitisation that accompanies those deaths (Albahari 2006).

The literature has reached a consensus that borders are not value-free; rather, they reflect sovereign strategies of political inclusion and exclusion (Johnson and Jones 2011: 62). The most important innovation of the border is that it serves as a tool of inclusion (for the in-group, largely citizens), but at the same time excludes the rest of humanity. As Paasi (2011: 62) argues: 'bordering separates and brings together. Borders allow certain expressions of identity and memory to exist while blocking others.' We argue that common graves and the political lives of migrants even after their death highlight the power of contemporary borders in institutionalising power relations. The sovereign state assigns migrant bodies a status that is inconsistent with full recognition of the personhood of the migrant. We subscribe to the performative model of the border (Salter 2011) and argue that the study of the phenomenon of missing migrants can shed analytical and critical light on the study of contemporary borders. As a non-governmental organization (NGO) activist stressed:

> the question of the dead is the most appalling spectacle I have ever seen, because I visualized the death and what it means not to be able to cross the border. So, the theoretical framework about walls, securitization, acquires a new dimension when you see decomposed bodies. Even more tragic is the fact that you cannot bury them as they deserved to be buried and that no one could identify them.

The sovereign state has physical boundaries – the border – but also political and legal boundaries – membership, largely defined by citizenship (Aleinikoff 2001). The fact that the border is defined not territorially but by the capacity of the Mediterranean Sea to kill migrants trying to reach the EU, coupled with the lack of legal status their bodies have on EU soil, denied the rights and entitlements of citizenship, leads to migrants becoming 'missing'. For every migrant body washed up on Europe's beaches, there is a family awaiting news from a son or husband.

The biopolitical concern over the management of the living is not reflected in management of the dead. When 'illegally' (alive) within the EU, migrants forgo many of the rights that citizens take for granted; being subject to surveillance, controlled and limited, they are the subjects of perhaps more of the state's attention than any other class of person. When dead within the EU, they are denied even the limited attention that law obliges for a European body. A live migrant is thus a threat to be managed, while a dead one appears as an irrelevance to be ignored. The situation is not peculiar to Lesbos or to Greece, as is evident from the Italian island of Lampedusa:

> While the living that arrive to Lampedusa are instantly engulfed within the governmentally run, and international organization influenced, judicial and medical matrix, from which they can only emerge under the labels of either economic migrants, refugees or expellable persons, the dead that make it to Lampedusa ... are dealt with by local municipalities and people, and, unless identified and repatriated, are granted indefinite leave to remain. (Zagaria 2012)

We seek to understand living migrants as objects of interest to and under the control of biopolitical regimes, and conceptualise their deaths as vital to how sovereign power and the nation-state operate. Yet, once migrants are dead, they become marginal to the concerns of the biopolitical: the body of the migrant occupies an indeterminate space that is neither fully inside nor outside the social and legal order. For the body of the migrant the idea of 'inside' and 'outside' that appears at the heart of the concept of the border is largely irrelevant: the body is an object of disdain wherever it is found, consistent with Foucault's understanding of the remit of the interest of sovereign power:

> [D]eath becomes, insofar as it is the end of life, the term, the limit, or the end of power too. Death is outside the power relationship. Death is beyond the reach of power, and power has a grip on it only in general, overall, or statistical terms. ... Power no longer recognizes death. Power literally ignores death. (Foucault 2003: 248)

The EU has failed even in Foucault's 'statistical terms', not even being able to count how many migrants die. This is compounded by a refusal to ensure that states do what they can to identify migrant bodies, confirming they remain not only uncounted and unmourned but unnamed, denied the one thing that could humanise them: states have abandoned responsibility for either the life or death of the victim. 'Disappearance produces a condition of uncertainty and liminality – an undocumented individual subjected to an undocumented death – such that this death not only fails to count as a crime, but even to count as death' (Boyce 2012: 77).

The maintenance of a determined ignorance of migrant deaths at the Mediterranean border by member states and EU institutions is only occasionally threatened by an incident of such proportions that it cannot be ignored.[4] For the populations of the island communities most exposed to them, however, the deaths of migrants are traumatic precisely because they are frequent, visible and impossible to ignore. The empirical work of this study indicates that the people of Lesbos reject the securitised vision of immigrants promoted by the Greek state and the EU, and attempt both to push local institutions to take action and bypass them to act on their humanitarian impulses as best they can. One way of perceiving this contrast between state discourse and popular understandings on Lesbos is in terms of a centre-periphery model with the political and biopolitical perspectives of the centre remote from both local governance on the island, which must actually deal with migrant bodies, and from opinion shaped by regular exposure to the dead (e.g. Shils 1975). More relevant, however, may be Migdal's model of 'state-in-society', which 'depicts society as a mélange of social organisations, rather than a dichotomous structure' (Migdal 2001: 49). The range of social organisations that exist alongside the state are seen to be constantly competing to construct social norms: societies are ultimately a product of this ongoing dynamic struggle. In such a model, state discourse (paralleled by and echoing that of the EU) is merely one source of norms, challenged by NGOs and others and – for the people of Lesbos – by a daily experience that contradicts that discourse. The mélange model may be particularly relevant for weaker states, and the experience of the research reported here is that the

Greek state, even while a member of the EU, is unable – or unwilling – to enforce legal norms at its borders when they concern dead migrants. In Lesbos the result is that locally formed perspectives can challenge, in a limited way, the biopolitical discourse of the centre. The practical orientation of this work seeks to address how the periphery can influence the centre, and how state policy can be impacted by those who live at the border and who actively resist both the securitisation agenda and the racialised neglect of migrant bodies.

The body of the dead migrant, found within the territorial borders of the EU but denied any of the dignifying rights that law demands for dead citizens, permits an interrogation of both theoretical and practical understandings of the border. In this chapter, the following themes will be pursued:

- The nature of governmentality and the difference in the response of the state to the crossing of the border by a dead migrant or by a living one, as well as the difference in response to a dead citizen and a dead migrant.
- The failure of the Greek state to make significant efforts either to ensure the dignity of dead migrants in terms of appropriate burial or to identify the dead and ensure that relatives are informed.
- The divergence between the state-led discourse of migration as a threat and the resulting securitisation, and the humanitarian response of the people of Lesbos to the deaths on their beaches.

Missing: the political and bodily experience of the border

Since the mid-1900s the Aegean islands have been the scene of humanitarian disasters that have generated a constant flow of refugees. The first major wave of refugees came as a result of the forced expulsion of the Orthodox population from Asia Minor by Kemal Ataturk in 1922: destitute refugees flooded the Aegean islands (Clark 2006). During the Second World War and the Nazi occupation of Greece, Greek citizens crossed the Aegean in an effort to reach Turkish shores and join the resistance forces in the Middle East (primarily Lebanon and Egypt).[5] Although during the height of the Cold War refugee flows declined, throughout the 1980s Kurds and leftists persecuted by the military regime in Turkey crossed the Aegean border to seek asylum in Greece and other European countries.

More recently, and especially after the destabilisation of the Middle East, massive waves of refugees and immigrants from Afghanistan, Iraq, Iran, Syria and Egypt started inundating the Aegean islands, which have become a principal entry point to the EU (see Figure 8.1). Although accurate data remains unavailable, it is estimated that in the period 2007–8 the number of arrested 'illegal' immigrants entering the Aegean was 29,000 (Troumpeta 2012: 21). The construction of a wall in the region of Evros in 2012 in an effort to deter border crossers entering from Turkey, coupled with the turmoil in Syria, led to a dramatic increase in the flow of migrants to the

8.1 Map showing location of Lesbos

Aegean islands, as the main local border to enter the EU. In the first quarter of 2013, 1,623 irregular migrants were arrested in the Aegean islands, compared to only 118 in the same period the previous year (UNHCR 2013). Lesbos, the biggest island in that part of the Aegean, has become the main entry point for migrants.

One of the most disturbing and underexplored phenomena associated with the most recent surge of border crossing in the Aegean is the growing number of migrants who die when their overcrowded and often flimsy vessels sink. Mountz (2011: 118) has argued that 'nation-states are using islands to capture liminal populations, […] facilities on islands serve the purpose of isolating migrants from communities of advocacy and legal representation, and in some cases from asylum claim processes that can only be accessed by landing on sovereign territory'. We show that although islands are sometimes strategically deployed to institutionalise this exclusion, the direct experience of shocking events such as mass fatalities in shipwrecks, coupled with more personal ties to local authorities, create opportunities for advocates for migrants to address effectively some of the problems.

The political lives of migrant bodies

In her book on the 'political lives' of dead bodies, Verdery (2000) captures the symbolic capital of human remains and how these are deployed by political leaders to meet political objectives. The graves of unidentified migrants are politically significant because of the absence of political capital invested in them; in essence, it is the silence that circumscribes these graves that makes them politically potent.

Some of these silences became more evident during our fieldwork on Lesbos in 2013 when, using a snowball sampling technique, we conducted semi-structured interviews with local stakeholders, NGO workers and members of migrant communities on the island.[6] The most revealing experience was a visit to the local cemetery where the remains of most migrants who die in their effort to cross the Aegean are buried. The graveyard was shocking and disturbing, with bodies covered by earth with no proper marker or headstone.

As Figures 8.2 and 8.3 show, the only mark on the graves of migrants is a broken stone on which is written the (purported) nationality of the migrant, a number and a date of death.[7] According to a local activist, since the identity of the victim is rarely known, the nationality is based either on information from survivors of shipwrecks

8.2 Grave of victims of a 2007 shipwreck, Mytilene cemetery, Lesbos, July 2013

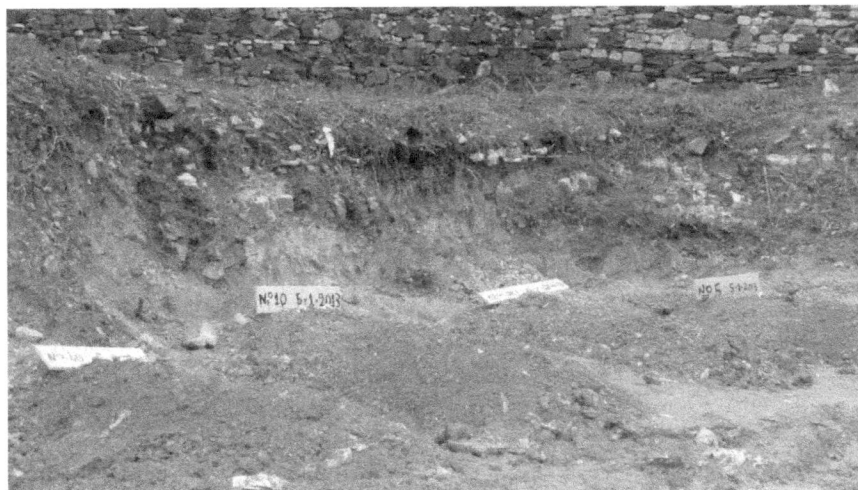

8.3 Graves of victims of a 2013 shipwreck, Mytilene cemetery, Lesbos

or on an informed guess on the part of the authorities. A local priest argued that since there is no credible way to identify the body in the absence of documentation, 'individuals become a number in the cemetery of Mytilene'. As Sant Cassia (2005) shows for Cyprus, the issue of missing persons and the scale of the phenomenon can often become a powerful political symbol. In fact, a long-standing central tenet of Greek foreign policy on Cyprus has been to put pressure on Turkey to identify the remains of the bodies of the missing, framed as a fundamental right of the relatives. Yet, at the same time, cemeteries along the external borders of Greece are full of unmarked graves containing the unidentified bodies of migrants who died in their effort to cross the Aegean. Certain bodies thus clearly do not count once they are dead bodies. Butler (2010) has distinguished between persons who are 'grievable', whose lives are seen to matter and to be worthy of grief after death, and those who are not 'grievable'. This points to a connection between those marginalised in life, such as irregular migrants, and those unmourned in death: only by giving such people a value in life can they have a value in death. As Green (2012) suggests, the process of identification of the remains depends on citizenship, which thereby introduces a novel exclusion, this time of the dead.

In an effort to understand the procedure following a shipwreck and the burial of the victims, as well as to identify the state agencies tasked with managing this problem, we turned to the local authorities. It quickly became obvious that there is a legal and bureaucratic ambiguity around the problem, creating a grey area where no authority assumed responsibility. The coastguard maintained that his duty is limited to handing over the dead body to the hospital, after which responsibility is passed to the district attorney. Assuming that the death is not caused by criminal action, the district attorney ceases to take responsibility, and the body is left in the local hospital with the forensic surgeon, whose duty ends with the examination of the corpse. To our question as to what happens next, the forensic surgeon had no answer, explaining only that speedy burial was necessary as at the time the hospital had no facilities to store bodies for more than a few days. The director of social services at the hospital subsequently told us that in general they take care of the unidentified bodies, although the hospital has no budget for burying dead 'illegal' migrants, only for the short-term treatment of living migrants. When asked how a dead body can carry a legal status ('illegal', in this case) allocated only to the living, she politely suggested we speak with the mayor, as due to lack of funds the hospital usually asks the municipality to take responsibility for the burial. In the end, it became obvious not only that there is no standardised procedure to deal with the bodies of migrants, but also that this grey area serves to ensure that local authorities take no legal or moral responsibility.

Those familiar with Greek bureaucracy might interpret this as a common tactic of 'blame avoidance'. Yet, we argue that the management of dead migrants reveals a more deep-seated structural pattern of power relations and material interests. As Green (2012: 576) puts it: 'borders always involve a form of classification and categorisation of the world'; on Lesbos this entails a distinction between living and dead border crossers. A range of specific legal statuses are ascribed to the former, such as 'legal', 'illegal' and 'asylum seeker'; and, following the detention of 'illegal' immigrants, administrative procedures are very detailed, with responsibility for them residing with the central government, since they are regarded as a threat to national security. By contrast, the management of the bodies of dead border cross-ers is circumscribed by legal and bureaucratic ambiguity. Migrant deaths are seen as a mere accidental deviation from the (securitisation) norm, and their management left in the hands of local authorities.[8] In the face of the failure of the authorities to identify bodies, even in the unlikely event that they are informed by a survivor, the families of the dead cannot afford the exorbitant cost of identification and repatria-tion of remains. Thus, while poor (living) migrants experience the greatest barriers to *entering* the EU, it is also these poorest families which face the most difficulty with *exiting* the EU when their migrant relatives are dead. As a result, their bodies are destined to stay in common graves.

The growing incidence of shipwrecks and deaths along the Aegean coast has generated new categories and divisions even among dead migrants, further insti-tutionalising power relations. As exploitation often thrives in contexts of human grief and vague legal procedures, it is hardly surprising that the identification and repatriation of the bodies has become subject to exploitation by smugglers, whose networks continue to thrive in the aftermath of a shipwreck. Smugglers are usually the first to know about a shipwreck and to inform the families of those affected, who then enlist the smugglers' help to identify and return the body (Interview 4). This was confirmed by an interview with migrants who were actively engaged in one of the burials on Lesbos. Despite its obvious importance to the families, the repatriation of the corpse is an extremely complicated and expensive procedure. As a consequence, only a handful of families have managed to get bodies back. A local journalist evocatively referred to this as the 'contraband of human souls'. Migrants currently residing in Lesbos revealed that they were aware of only two families which had managed to repatriate their dead relatives, and that they were able to do so only because one of the victims was a relative of an Afghan minister who mobi-lised the Afghan embassy in Athens to intervene with the Greek bureaucracy.[9] Of the 22 bodies from the shipwreck concerned, presumably all from Afghanistan, the Afghan embassy intervened in only two cases.

Our interviews with a group of migrants who had participated in the burial of the victims of one of the biggest shipwrecks in December 2012 confirmed the expense and difficulty of repatriation. One remarked: 'most frequently the family does not have the money to bring them [bodies] back as the money is usually spent to pay the smugglers. Only the rich get back, the poor stay here.' The cemetery of Agios Panteleimon where migrants are buried was once the cemetery of the destitute, a symbolic association not lost on those concerned.

Moreover, as long as the death of migrants is framed as an accident, their burial is seen as an act of benevolence, rather than an act of justice or a moral obligation on the part of the state. For example, the former mayor of Lesbos clearly indicated that there was no budget (allocated by the state or the EU) to cover the expenses associated with the burial of migrants. To organise a burial he had to raise funds from local sponsors or 'beg local offices organising funeral services to give us the coffins'.

The border raises a number of further obstacles to the treatment of the dead. Following a shipwreck the relatives usually attempt to visit the island to identify the body and, if possible, repatriate it. Yet families frequently experience difficulties entering Greece and are turned away or even detained for several days because they do not have the correct documents. In the meantime, the body is buried and the families left without a body to mourn. One observer told us of Abbas, 'who came to find his father; he had documentation and he came from Germany where he resided permanently. When he came to the port the border agency thought his papers were faked and denied entry. He then tried to come again, this time by airplane, but he had the same problem and we [members of the NGO] had to intervene to release him.'

The border also introduces a novel distinction between the local dead and the remains of migrants. Not only are the unidentified bodies of migrants buried in common graves without following the appropriate religious custom and rituals, but as space in Greek cemeteries decreases, there is pressure to exhume migrant bodies to create space for locals. The gravedigger informed the leader of a local civil society group that 'there is no space available; next time we have a shipwreck there will be no space'. His tone was compassionate, yet he also seemed to imply that the burial of local dead should take moral precedence over foreigners. Moreover, most dead migrants will never be identified. According to Greek death rituals, some years after the burial – usually five to seven – the remains must be exhumed and returned to the family. If no one claims the remains, they are disposed of. There is therefore no realistic possibility of identifying the remains of a migrant who died in a shipwreck more than seven years earlier. Identification is also made more problematic by the unscrupulous and unsystematic burial of migrants. A member of a local civil society group told us of a relative of a migrant who died on the neighbouring island of Chios. Although he had travelled from Australia and had spent a fortune trying to trace and identify his dead relative, the gravedigger could not remember the precise burial spot, and no systematic data was stored as to which body was buried where. Once a tractor started digging, it became clear that he was buried in a mass grave along with other victims, making identification impossible.

The reaction of the islanders to migrant deaths

The shocking experiences related to the deaths at sea and migrant bodies washing up on local beaches set the stage for the emergence on Lesbos of a small, yet vocal, civil society response in support of migrants. Green (2012: 149) has suggested that the locals show sympathy for migrant bodies primarily because they are not buried or mourned according to their religious and cultural preferences. As a local activist indicated: 'these people do not die *en masse* in urban cities like Athens or Salonika but at the borders, in the islands. So, in this local context the mobilisation of the community can provide a quicker and more effective solution to the problem.'

The traumatic experiences of dead bodies and common graves bring shame upon the people of Lesbos. The degrading situation in the detention camps on the island was another source of shame. For several years hundreds of migrants were gathered under humiliating conditions in the asylum camp of Pagani (Troumpeta 2012: 21). The camp was closed in 2009 following the mobilisation of the local community. These shocking and shameful images are part of the islanders' daily life. Following the closure of the asylum camps, migrants were detained in the island's main port of Mytilene, corralled in the open air for days at a time without access to washing facilities or food and exposed to extreme heat and cold. Such conditions, coupled with the fact that most local families are refugees from what is now Turkey, partly explain why islanders are more predisposed to see migrants in a humanitarian light. Even those locals who subscribe to the policy of securitisation, and who refer to the border crossers as 'illegal', are critical of the 'Eurocrats' who use the island as a filter to prevent the human flow from entering the core of the EU. One argued, for instance, that 'the bodies are washed up here, not in Germany'. In essence, they feel that this is a broader problem that cannot be managed by the local community and which gives it bad publicity.

These local experiences have created the space for a small but active civil society group to help immigrants, at times quite effectively.[10] The islanders have adopted a 'hybrid' position between policies of securitisation and humanitarianism towards migrants and thus conceptualise the border very differently from mainland Greeks. As the leader of the group pointed out, the locals 'see this as primarily a humanitarian problem, not a political one'. In the following section, we argue that the humanitarian lens through which locals approach the problem is not limited to the community, but also involves the local authorities. In turn, this has created opportunities for civil society to push for the accommodation of migrant demands, at times even replacing the sovereign state. To explore this further, we examine the interaction between local advocates for migrants and state agents at the border to show how this interaction influences state policy.

Borders, state capacity and opportunities

There is no single border in the abstract; borders are always context-specific, relational and performative. The state's capacity to play out the symbolic and tangible politics of the border is thus pivotal. Much literature on (critical) border studies is built on the study of powerful states, including the United States, Canada, Australia and the EU (as a supranational institution). Whilst every state's objective is to reaffirm its sovereignty, especially with regard to the border as one of the central state institutions, state effectiveness varies from country to country. In this sense, the study of the Greek state and how the border plays out on the island of Lesbos is instructive. In addition to being the scene of substantial flows of refugees and migrants over the past century, the Aegean islands have also been the centre of the Greco-Turkish dispute, one of the most significant aspects of which is the legal definition of the continental shelf and territorial sea, essentially the border (Heraclides 2010). In fact, the 'Aegean dispute' has made islands like Lesbos some of the most heavily militarised Greek territories. The presence of the army is visible in the daily lives of the islanders as there are military vehicles and hundreds of soldiers in the island's capital of Mytilene. The national border remains a powerful daily practice in that specific part of the Aegean.

Even when a state strives to perform its sovereignty, however, it can lack the capacity to do so in a robust way: in Greece this creates opportunities for local advocates for migrants. The literature offers a picture of the state as being a purposeful and unitary actor that is able to implement its policies, while in reality the case of Greece reveals a slightly different story. The arbitrary interpretation of rules and laws for most scholars is seen as an intentional strategy of 'nation-states [to] exploit legal ambiguity' (Mountz 2011: 118); yet, at times this grey area creates opportunities for local groups to influence, oppose and even contravene state decisions (Migdal 2001).

The heavy structure of the Greek bureaucracy, and the personal ties that are often seen as the root cause of corruption and clientelism at the local level in Lesbos, provide a breathing space for local advocates for migrants. A leading member of the group expressed this as follows:

> [W]e know each other from other activities, so you have a specific identity, a quality as an individual and this has multiple advantages: access to public services, understanding how the local community is functioning … and this is an important point distinguishing islands, as personal contacts create more durable relationships with local authorities which at the end of the day are more effective.

This dense network of contacts in a small island like Lesbos has provided local civil society with opportunities to engage and promote effectively the demands of migrants, which at times challenged state policies, or even substituted for the state.

An example of local society substituting for the state is the establishment of the first 'open' reception centre for migrants. By late 2012 the dramatic increase in the influx of migrants created a major problem for the local authorities which could not accommodate them in local penitentiaries. In response, a group of local activists asked the mayor for permission to reopen a children's campsite in order to accommodate them. A local doctor who worked closely with migrants and refugees vividly described this initiative:

It was an unprecedented and innovative action that contravened the mainstream model of reception centres for immigrants. That was an open public space of hospitality where migrants are not detained [and] where everyone could visit and volunteer. ... So something unprecedented occurred with regards to the strategic planning of the government on immigration: while they used to send them to ghettoes and detention camps ... it became clear that an open reception centre could be even more effective under the auspices of the local community, the collaboration of the migrants themselves and the solidarity of the people.

In fact, the same participant told us that the local authorities were actually relieved because a particularly pressing problem, the responsibility for accommodating migrants, was taken off their hands by local people. In other words, a responsibility, deemed to be emblematic of sovereign authority at the border – the management of detention camps – was successfully assumed by the local community. Most importantly, the state authorities (at local level) subtly consented to relinquishing these sovereign powers to the local people.

The direct exposure of local authorities – whose responsibility is to secure the border – to these traumatic experiences and pressing problems associated with the management of the massive influx of migrants has made them sometimes deviate from the policy of securitisation deployed by the central government and the EU. By contrast, the 'hybrid' discourse that at local level encompasses policies of both securitisation and humanitarianism has enabled local advocates to address effectively some of the most urgent problems facing newly arrived migrants.

When asked about the most important obstacle migrants face, the police security director in the port of Mytilene replied: 'it's the phenomenon per se. It's a humanitarian disaster. Many people within Greece, but especially in Europe, are not aware of the magnitude of the problem. We are tasked to deal with a humanitarian crisis.' He thought of the problem as a shameful event for the island, as 'it exposes the island and the country globally'. This did not prevent the same individual from referring to asylum seekers as 'illegal', thereby remaining loyal to the securitisation discourse. This 'hybridity' is a prevalent feature of the discourse adopted by locals and clearly deviates from the state discourse. It emerged in most interviews and informal chats on the island. For example, the mayor of Lesbos condemned the central government for its failure to appreciate the humanitarian dimension of the problem, saying that 'in Athens [the government] doesn't understand that the problem is growing'.

Representatives of the state whose responsibility it is to implement the securitisation agenda on Lesbos thus feel that they are required to deal with a problem exceeding their powers. Their daily duties bring them into contact with some of the cruellest experiences of this humanitarian disaster and lead them to question the capacity of 'securitisation' to address its complexities. As a result, it is not only ordinary people who distance themselves from the securitisation discourse, but also the local authorities, thereby creating what Wilson and Donnan have called 'ambivalent border communities' (2012: 11). It is this sense of indeterminacy, combined with the porous organisation of the Greek state, which creates opportunities for local activists to push for more effective responses to certain problems. Over the years, those who advocate on behalf of migrants have established relations of trust with the local authorities, and this has enabled them to press for specific demands, such as DNA tests on missing migrants, or support for 'illegal' migrants when organising the burial of a compatriot.

Conclusion

In this chapter we have explored some of the issues emerging from the study of those border crossers who did not make it across the frontier and who died at sea. In sharp contrast to the growing media coverage of shipwrecks in the Aegean and Mediterranean Sea, a notable silence surrounds the management of the dead bodies of border crossers following these disasters. This is a consequence of attempts to frame these deaths as 'accidents' within a broader policy of securing EU borders, a policy which remains intact. Yet, this approach fails to account not only for the growing number of 'accidents', but also most significantly for the complete silence surrounding the management of drowned migrants. Following the prevalent approach which introduces a number of legal distinctions among living border crossers – 'illegal vs. legal' or 'refugees vs. economic' migrants – once dead the very same individuals are stripped of all legal status as human beings entitled to inalienable human rights. As the chapter has shown, the border continues to be a powerful instrument of the sovereign state, denying both dead migrants and their relatives a decent burial and the identification of remains. In essence, the management of dead migrants – missing to their relatives – sheds light on the important, yet underexplored, bodily and political experiences of crossing the border.

The island of Lesbos is at the sharp end of the EU's securitisation agenda in response to the increasing flow of migrants. Islanders have seen an escalating toll of migrant bodies on their beaches which local and national authorities have chosen largely to ignore. While living migrants are subsumed in the rigours of the biopolitical response to their presence, detained and controlled by the sovereign state, those who die making the journey are ignored and neglected.

The experience of Lesbos is not an exception but echoes a growing phenomenon in international politics where more heavily militarised border enforcement has increased the level of human suffering. At the Mexico–US border, for example, concerted operations of the US government seeking to deter undocumented migrants from Mexico since the late 1990s have had dire humanitarian consequences, leading to thousands of deaths at the border (Cornelius 2001). In both Lesbos and the Arizona desert, migrant deaths have acted as a catalyst for a proactive mobilisation of local NGOs and humanitarian groups (Hagan and Rodriguez 2006; Hellman 2009). In Arizona the 'Humane Borders' group has set up a programme to create maps identifying the locations of migrant deaths, while interfaith organisations such as the 'No More Deaths' group have tried to save lives by leaving water and food for those crossing the desert (Zanowiak 2006).

The comparative experience of deaths in Lesbos and the Mexico–US border exemplifies a common theme of the corporeality of border crossing. The interaction between corporeality and spatiality drives the subjectivity of migrant bodies. While the border determines the subjectivity of a living migrant body, the dead migrant bodies produced by the border are objects of far less interest to sovereign power than the bodies of citizens. A performative understanding of the construction of the border sees the border being built by and upon the bodies of migrants.

Notes

1 The authors are listed in alphabetical order; equal contribution is implied. We are very grateful to Hastings Donnan, Effie Latsoudi, Katerina Polychroni, Anna Vallianatou and the two anonymous reviewers for their insightful feedback on earlier drafts of the chapter.

2 This reform of Greek citizenship law was originally enacted in 2010 (N. 3838/2010): 'Current provisions for Greek citizenship, the political participation of repatriated Greeks and lawfully resident immigrants and other provisions.' However, in February 2011 the Greek Council of State ruled that the article relating to the naturalisation of the children of migrants born in Greece was unconstitutional. Subsequently, the law was revised and the new provisions once again restricted the naturalisation of children of immigrants born in Greece.

3 A recent trend has been to portray the migrant as a passive victim and instead to blame traffickers, who remain essentially invisible.

4 An example is that of the deaths of more than 300 migrants off the coast of Lampedusa in October 2013 that briefly saw the issue trouble the front pages of European news media.

5 For an excellent account of this phenomenon of border crossing, based on oral history, see Makridakis 2010.

6 The vast majority of interviews were semi-structured in an effort to make it easier for the interviewees to express their views. Most were conducted in Greek, but a number of the interviews with immigrants residing in Lesbos were carried out with the support of a translator who facilitated the interviews. We are indebted to Katerina Polychroni for her invaluable support.

7 Indicative of the arbitrary and uncoordinated procedure for recording migrant burials is the fact that at different periods there have been different approaches to keeping track of migrant graves. When shipwrecks were less frequent, the information on the grave included the nationality and the number of the victim of the specific shipwreck (e.g. 'Afghan 2'), often on a marble cross taken from a recently exhumed grave of a local. More recently, with the increase in the number of shipwrecks, coupled with the greater diversity in the origins of migrants, it became more difficult to determine the nationality of the victims (see Figure 8.3).

8   As is also the case in Lampedusa in Italy (Zagaria 2012: 18).
9   Access to official data on the number of repatriated bodies was not possible, so we turned to local participants who had helped families in their efforts to trace their relatives lost at sea. This raises a broader problem of access to and credibility of data gathered by national authorities, revealing the 'grey area' that circumscribes the management of migrant bodies.
10 The primary organisation, 'The Village of All Together' (*To Χωριό του Όλοι Μαζί*), is an umbrella group of different sub-groups, all active in the reception and accommodation of migrants. Due to the growing number of shipwrecks, they have recently become active in managing the problem of the dead as well.

References

Agamben, G. (1998) *Homo Sacer: Sovereign Power and Bare Life*. Stanford, CA: Stanford University Press.

Albahari, M. (2006) *Death and the Moral State: Making Borders and Sovereignty at the Southern Edges of Europe*. Working Paper 136. University of California, San Diego: Center for Comparative Immigration Studies.

Aleinikoff, T.A. (2001) 'Policing boundaries: migration, citizenship and the state', in G. Gerstle and J.H. Mollenkopf (eds), *E Pluribus Unum? Contemporary and Historical Perspectives on Immigrant Political Incorporation*. New York: Russell Sage Foundation, pp. 1–30.

Arendt, H. (1951) *The Origins of Totalitarianism*. Orlando, FL: Harvest.

Boyce, G. (2012) 'Beyond the sovereign gaze', *Arizona Journal of Interdisciplinary Studies*, 1: 68–88.

Butler, J. (2010) *Frames of War: When is Life Grievable?* London: Verso.

Christopoulos, Dimitri (2012) *Who Is the Greek Citizen? The Status of Greek Nationality from the Creation of the Greek State until the Dawn of the 21st Century* [in Greek], Athens: Vivliorama.

Clark, Bruce (2006) *Twice a Stranger: How Mass Expulsion Forged Modern Greece and Turkey*. London: Granta.

Cornelius, Wayne A. (2001) 'Death at the border: efficacy and unintended consequences of US immigration control policy', *Population and Development Review*, 27(4: 661–685.

Dimopoulou, Angeliki (2013) Ανθρώπινα ναυάγια στη Λέσβο Τvxs Ρεπορτάζ ['Human shipwrecks in Lesbos'], tvxs. http://tvxs.gr/news/%CE%B5%CE%BB%CE%BB%CE%AC %CE%B4%CE%B1/%CE%B1%CE%BD%CE%B8%CF%81%CF%8E%CF%80%CE% B9%CE%BD%CE%B1-%CE%BD%CE%B1%CF%85%CE%AC%CE%B3%CE%B9%C E%B1-%CF%83%CF%84%CE%B7-%CE%BB%CE%AD%CF%83%CE%B2%CE%BF. Accessed 24 August 2016.

Foucault, M. (2003) '17 March 1976', in *Society Must Be Defended*. Lectures at the Collège de France, 1975–76. New York: Picador.

Frontex (2012) 'FRAN Quarterly: Quarter 4, October –December'. http://www.frontex. europa.eu/assets/Publications/Risk_Analysis/FRAN_Q4_2012.pdf. Accessed 3 August 2016.

Frontex (2013) 'FRAN Quarterly: Quarter 1, January–March'. http://www.frontex.europa.eu/assets/Publications/Risk_Analysis/FRAN_Q1_2013.pdf. Accessed 3 August 2016.

Green, Sarah (2012) 'The transnational lives of undocumented dead bodies in the Aegean', in Sevasti Troumpeta (ed.), *The Refugee and Migrant Issue: Readings and Studies of Borders*. Athens: Papazisi, pp. 133–158.

Hagan, Jacqueline and Nestor Rodriguez (2006) 'The Church vs. the State: borders, migrants and human rights', in Pierrette Hondagneu-Sotelo (ed.), *Religion and Social Justice for Immigrants*. New Brunswick, NJ: Rutgers University Press, pp. 93–103.

Hellman, Judith Adler (2009) *The World of Mexican Migrants: The Rock and the Hard Place*. New York: The New Press.

Heraclides, Alexis (2010) *The Greek–Turkish Conflict in the Aegean: Imagined Enemies*. Basingstoke: Palgrave Macmillan.

Johnson, Corey and Reece Jones (2011) 'Rethinking the border in border studies', *Political Geography*, 30: 61–62.

Karyotis, George (2012) 'Securitization of migration in Greece: process, motives, and implications', *International Political Sociology*, 6(4): 390–408.

Leonard, Sarah (2010) 'EU border security and migration into the European Union: FRONTEX and securitization through practices', *European Security*, 19(2): 231–254.

Makridakis I. (2010) 'Συρματένιοι, Ξεσυρματένιοι· Όλοι. Χιώτες πρόσφυγες και στρατιώτες στη Μέση Ανατολή: Αφηγήσεις 1941–1946' [Syrmatenioi, Xesyrmatenioi, Oloi: Chiot Testimonies of Refugees and Soldiers in the Middle East: 1941–1946]. Athens: Estia.

Manners, Ian (2008) 'The normative ethics of the European Union', *International Affairs*, 84(1): 45–60.

Migdal, Joel (2001) *State in Society: Studying How States and Societies Transform and Constitute One Another*. Cambridge: Cambridge University Press.

Morcillo, Juan (2012) 'Los 29 muertos que nadie reclama', *ABC*, 3 March, http://www.abc.es/20120203/espana/abci-inmigracion-estrecho-muertos-201202022001.html. Accessed 3 August 2016.

Mountz, Alison (2011) 'The enforcement archipelago: Detention, haunting, and asylum on islands', *Political Geography*, 30: 18–128.

Paasi, Anssi (2011) 'Borders, theory and the challenge of relational thinking', *Political Geography*, 30: 62–63.

Papadopoulos, Dimitris, Niamh Stephenson and Vasilis Tsianos (2008) *Escape Routes: Control and Subversion in the Twenty-first Century*. London: Pluto.

Salter, Mark (2011) 'Places everyone! Studying the performativity of the border', *Political Geography*, 30: 63–65.

Sant Cassia, Paul (2005) *Bodies of Evidence: Burial, Memory and the Recovery of Missing Persons in Cyprus*. Oxford: Berghahn.

Shenker, John (2013) 'Mediterranean migrant deaths: a litany of largely avoidable loss', *Guardian*, 3 October. https://www.theguardian.com/world/2013/oct/03/mediterranean-migrant-deaths-avoidable-loss. Accessed 3 August 2016.

Shils, E. (1975) *Center and Periphery*. Chicago, IL: University of Chicago Press.

Troumpeta, Sevasti (2012) 'The borders, the island and the refugees', in S. Troumpeta (ed.), *The Refugee and Migrant Issue: Readings and Studies of Borders* [in Greek]. Athens: Papazisis, pp. 13–29.

UNHCR (2013) 'Syrians in Greece: High Commission's proposals' [in Greek], 17 May. http://www.unhcr.gr/fileadmin/Greece/News/2012/Syria/pc/Syria_Position2_april_2013_2.pdf. Accessed 3 August 2016.

Verdery, Katherine (2000) *The Political Lives of Dead Bodies: Reburial and Postsocialist Change*. New York: Columbia University Press.

Wallerstein, Immanuel (2002) 'Immigrants', *Commentary* 90 Fernand Braudel Center, Binghamton University, 1 June. http://www2.binghamton.edu/fbc/commentaries/index.html. Accessed 3 August 2016.

Wilson, Thomas and Hastings Donnan (2012) 'Borders and border studies', in Thomas Wilson and Hastings Donnan (eds), *A Companion to Border Studies*. Oxford: Wiley-Blackwell, pp. 1–26.

Zagaria, Valentina (2012) 'Grave Situations: The Biopolitics and Memory of the Tombs of Unknown Migrants in the Agrigento Province', unpublished MA thesis, Department of Anthropology, London School of Economics and Political Science.

Zanowiak, Kendall (2006) 'Caring Networks of NGOs: NGO Assistance to Undocumented Migrants along the U.S.–Mexico Border.' lanic.utexas.edu/project/etext/llilas/ilassa/2007/zanowiak.pdf. Accessed 3 August 2016.

Index

Page numbers in *italics* refer to figures and tables. An 'n.' after a page reference indicates the number of a note on that page.

EU authorised representative for GPSR:
Easy Access System Europe, Mustamäe tee 50,
10621 Tallinn, Estonia
gpsr.requests@easproject.com

www.ingramcontent.com/pod-product-compliance
Lightning Source LLC
Chambersburg PA
CBHW031135270326
41929CB00011B/1630